A Prairie Home Commonplace Book

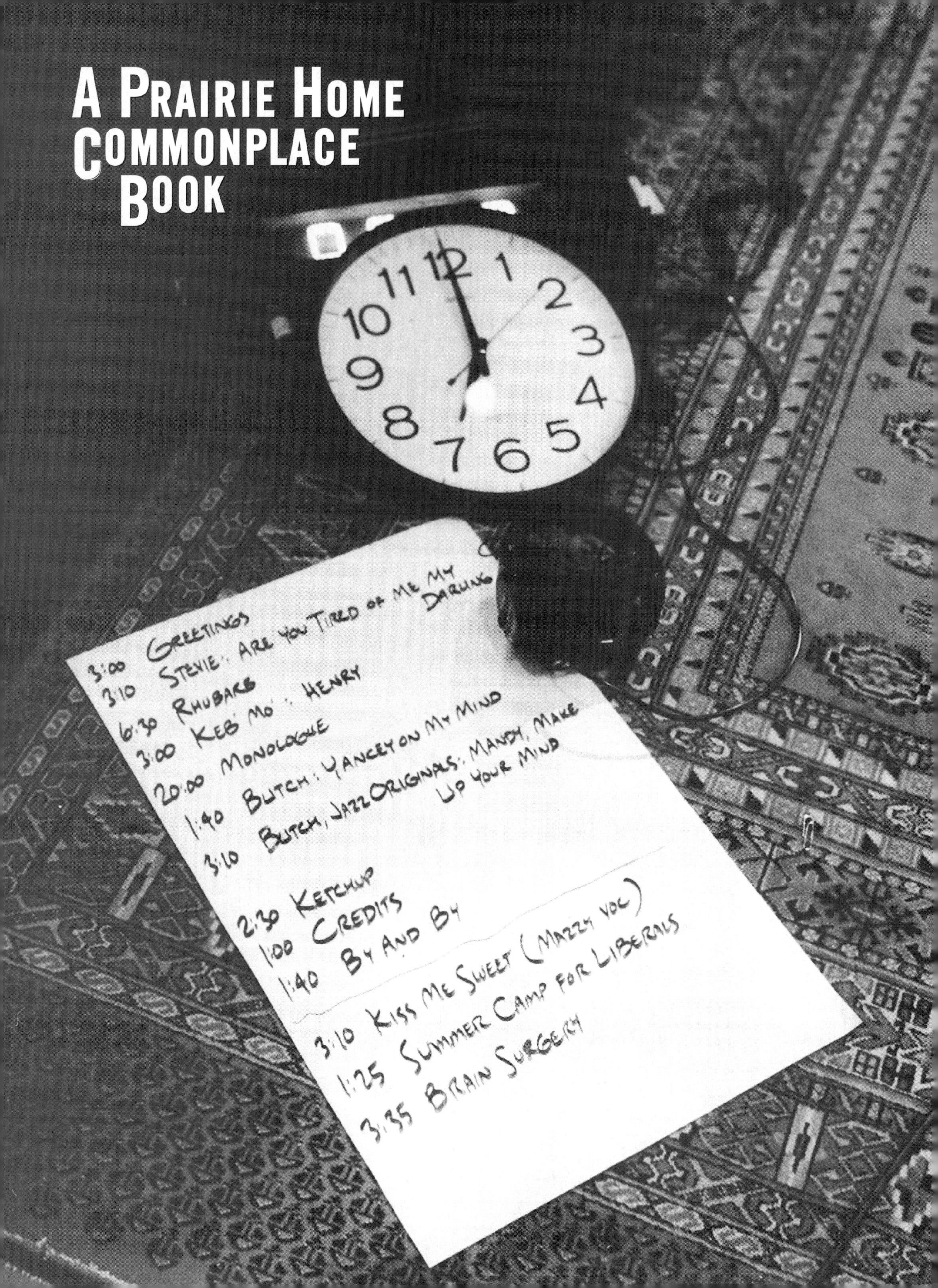

A Prairie Home Commonplace Book

25 Years on the air with Garrison Keillor

Edited By Marcia Pankake

HighBridge Company
1000 Westgate Drive
St. Paul MN 55114

HIGH
BRIDGE

Published by HighBridge Company,
1000 Westgate Drive, St. Paul MN 55114

ISBN 1-56511-345-4 hc
ISBN 1-56511-291-1 pb

Printed in the United States of America

Cover photograph by Jonette Novak;
Garrison Keillor at the Majestic Theatre,
Dallas TX, Third Annual Farewell Tour,
1989

Design by Two Spruce Design,
Scott and Kristi Anderson

HighBridge Company
1000 Westgate Drive
St. Paul MN 55114

Editor's Note

For their ready and invaluable help the editor thanks Julie Jackson,
Kate Gustafson, Scott Rivard, Kay Gornick, David O'Neill,
Rich Dworsky, Stevie Beck, Chris Tschida, Kathy Mack,
Marguerite Harvey, Tiffany Hanssen, Andrea Murray, Pam Stewart,
John Pearson, Sallie Neall, Renée Cardarelle, Margaret Pick,
Jim Cogswell, Jan Roseen, George Swan, Scott Anderson,
and especially Garrison Keillor and Jon Pankake.

All scripts, and all songs and poems unless otherwise specified, are
written by Garrison Keillor.

Copyright Acknowledgments and Permissions

Contents

Introduction

It's a long time ago now. "I got you a one-song gig on a St. Paul radio show," my agent had barked into the phone. "Probably a Norwegian fire drill; get in and get out fast." The cornfield drive from Ames and last night's coffeehouse had been smooth. I wheeled the battered Coupe de Ville across the Wabasha Street bridge and into an alley behind the World Theater. It was 5:10, Saturday afternoon. A set of metal stairs led up to a loading dock door. I tapped on the door, it opened, and someone gestured me into the darkness. We were backstage and on the other side of a backdrop, bright lights, monitor speakers, and audience hum told me that the show was going on. I stumbled after the guy who had opened the door, trying to adjust my eyes to the dim light that leaked in from the stage. "Wait here," he whispered and hustled off.

I was in front of a chalkboard under a light bulb. The order of the acts and their times were on the board; plenty of erasures told me that they were just south of winging it. Maybe my agent had been right for a change. I was to go on in ten minutes, following a song by Keillor and Karen Morrow, and just before the Modern Jazz Quartet. Off to my left a guy was doing silent, tiptoe jumping jacks. As my eyes adjusted to the gloom I saw it was Chet Atkins, who was chalked in after the MJQ. Guys in black T-shirts and headsets watched the stage intently, waiting to make microphone changes between acts.

I was on. One of the staff guys prodded me up to the stage and pointed out a microphone. Keillor was already introducing me as "the singer as anonymous as his song...welcome the Masked Folksinger." Huge applause, rather heady for a guy who usually played to fifteen people in a coffeehouse. I looked at the mike through which three million people were listening to me. The house was silent, expectant. Keillor exited. I launched into "Love Henry," a song I call a miniskirt ballad: long enough to cover the subject and short enough to be interesting.

I doffed my fedora to the polite applause and started offstage as Keillor came back on to introduce the MJQ, who had slipped into their places during my song.

Smooth show. Nice audience. I had time to make Baraboo and yet another coffeehouse that night, so I hung around backstage to watch the rest of the show. "I sure like those old songs," a voice whispered. I nodded to Chet, one old pro to another, as he eased into place ready to go on.

The show was apparently running long. During Chet's number Keillor huddled at the board with the cast, shuffling scripts as they decided to drop a commercial for dog cough drops. Erase it. Karen Morrow did voice exercises getting ready for her showstopper medley. Big finish. The house lights came up and the crew immediately began striking the set as efficiently as they had run the show. Some fans hung down front to talk to Tom Keith, and the stately, elegant peace of an old theater after a show settled like dust from the wings.

That was my gig on A Prairie Home Companion. Now, in this book, it is your turn to go up those alley stairs, knock at the big stage door, and ease backstage while the show goes on. Check out the board, read some scripts, pause in the greenroom, watch the cast and crew shape the show, visit with the guest performers, catch a monologue or skit. Now, take a deep breath in the cool darkness back by the brick wall behind the set. Got it? That's show business, friend.

THE MASKED FOLKSINGER

A

Absolutely Essential

CURRENT STAFF: Stevie Beck, Katie Burger, Tom Campbell, Mike Danforth, Alan Frechtman, Kay Gornick, Kate Gustafson, Tiffany Hanssen, Marguerite Harvey, Sam Hudson, Jeff Johnson, Jason Keillor, Andrew Leonard, Kathy Mack, Andrea Murray, David O'Neill, Russ Ringsak, Scott Rivard, Kathy Roach, Brian Sanderson, Andrew Sullivan, Chris Tschida, Mike Wangen, Dan Zimmerman

Class officers, 1999: Treasurer Kate Gustafson, President Tiffany Hanssen, Secretary Andrea Murray, and Vice President Mike Danforth. All of them good students, active in clubs and full of school spirit, and all of them looking forward to the day they graduate from the PHC staff and start earning some real money.

Advice

Wherever I may go in the world
As long as I shall live,
I'll always remember Mama
And the advice that she would give.
I think of it more with every year,
Especially on New Year's Day,
When I think of making resolutions,
I can hear my Mama say.

CHORUS:
Don't put yourself down.
Mind your p's and q's.
Pick up a penny for good luck.
Never buy cheap shoes.
A stitch in time saves nine.
Pride goeth before a fall.
If you wait until you're finally ready
You'll never do much at all.
It's so much simpler to tell the truth;
Time brings all things to light.
You make a better door than a window.
You may as well do things right.
This too shall pass.
Life is not fair.
Don't chew with your mouth open,
And always wear clean underwear. ➥

GK rehearsing PHC at the Minnesota State Fair Grandstand, August 1986. "My Aunt Elsie and Uncle Don attended that show, whom I had put into Lake Wobegon monologues as Aunt Myrna and Uncle Earl, so that day I did one about her winning second prize for her lemon meringue pie in a State Fair Grandstand Bake-Off. As the entries baked, trapeze acts performed and there was an auto thrill show. She was tickled, of course."

She said, Wait till you'll have children,
So I did and there you were,
And now you ask me for advice,
I pass along some from her.
And I'm sure that you'll ignore it
And go your own sweet way,
And someday when I'm not around,
You will hear your papa say.
CHORUS

Ants

GK: We moved to Summerville, Mom and Dad and Sis and I, when Dad got out of the ice business—1947—ice was going downhill. He went into sand for a while, and then clay, and finally into cement. It was Dad who gave me the nickname Buddy. He was embarrassed to say my real name, Claude, so he called me Buddy.

Dad: How you doin' there, old Buddy boy? Why don't you run along outside and play? We'll call you when supper's ready.

GK: Dad was always sending me outside to play, but I didn't have any friends in Summerville. Nobody liked me, and so, to have the nickname Buddy, I felt ridiculous. I'd sit in my backyard huddled under a wheelbarrow and guys leaned around in the alley and lobbed mud balls at me. (FLIGHT OF MISSILES, BWANGS.) I sat huddled under the wheelbarrow until dark and then I went in the house (DOOR OPEN, LITTLE FOOTSTEPS ON THE LINOLEUM) and—my family had forgotten to call me in for supper.

Mom: Oh. Buddy. Where were you?

GK: You ate supper without me?

Dad: Didn't know you were hungry.

GK: Of course, I was hungry. Hungry for beauty, hungry for love, but I didn't fit in in our family because they were all so talented and I was just me. School was where older people told you stuff that slipped right through your mind in two seconds, like trying to hold a gallon of water in your hands. I looked forward to summer vacation, and then summer arrived, and I huddled there under my wheelbarrow, and got bored. Nothing to do. Nowhere to go.

Mom: Go to the library.

GK: I've read all the books.

Dad: Go swimming.

GK: Can't.

Dad: Make model planes out of balsa wood. Enter them in contests and win cash prizes. Be interviewed in the newspaper.

GK: I can't imagine anything worse.

Mom: Go. Out. Seek and ye shall find. Knock and maybe they'll let you in. Come back for supper.

GK: I crawled back under my wheelbarrow, like a bug under a rock. And watched ants moving around in the grass. Thousands of them. A New York City of ants. Some carrying stuff in, some carrying stuff out. Like there were two departments. A carry-in department and a carry-out department. I wonder if they know I'm here. I wonder if they'd notice if I put my face down real close. I wonder if they'd notice if I puffed on them—pffff—yeah, they noticed. (TINY DISTRAUGHT VOICES, PITTER OF ANT FEET) They're all running around looking up.

Ant 1: Jim! Run! The sky is falling!

Ant 2: Wait! I gotta get my leaf!

GK: Jim, huh? I never thought that ants have names, but of course they must. Live in families, moms and dads and kid ants. And on Sundays, their uncles and aunts visit. I wonder what they call their aunts: maybe they call them persons. Uncle Bob and Person Evelyn. I wonder if they know how big the world is or if they think this yard is the whole world. I wonder. Here, Jim. Easy. Just gonna pick you up.

Ant 2: No, no, no, no.

GK: I won't hurt you. Just going to hold you up in the air so you can see everything—See? that's your city down there and that's the garage and—up you go—

Ant 2: Oooohhhhhhhhhh—

GK: You're flyin', Jim. How you like it? Eeeeeeeooooooowwwwwwww—

Ant 2: Uhhhhhhhhhhhh—

GK: Gonna do some loops now, Jim. Eeeeeerrrrrr—

Ant 2: Noooooooo—

GK: And here's the birdbath over here, Jim. You know how to swim, Jim?

Ant 2: No, no, no, no.

GK: Can't hear you, buddy. Do you swim? Wriggle your legs if you want to swim. You do? Okay—here you go—(ANT CRY) Oh no. Jim? What happened? You okay? I didn't mean to hurt you. What is it? Oh, no, you broke your leg. (ANT WEEPING) I'm sorry. Here, I'll put you back down in your city. They'll take care of you. (ANT SIREN) They'll take you to the hospital, Jim. That'll mend up real quick.

Funny, they don't all run down the hole when I put my face down here. They're not scared at all. Maybe they know something. Maybe they know that one of these days they will be bigger than us. Some night, while I'm asleep upstairs with the windows open and suddenly I feel a cold shadow and wake up and look and in the windows are giant insect eyes staring at me...

Ant 1: It's him, Jim. The kid who busted your leg.

Ant 2: Yeah, Person Esther. It's him.

Ant 1: Stick your good leg in there and grab him.

Ant 2: I'll get him—and we'll take him out and rip his arms off.

Ant 1: He's skinny, but I'll bet he'll taste real good if we feed him enough maggots.

GK: He snaked his long hairy leg toward me and it got closer and closer and when it almost grabbed me—

Mom: Buddy? Supper. Meat loaf!

GK: I've never stepped on an anthill since then. I find ants in the kitchen, I help them find another home. Live and let live, I say. 'Cause you never know. As unlikely as it seems most of the time, there may be such a thing as justice.

Aspirations

The celebrity of my youth was my high school English teacher, Mr. Anderson. "Wild Bob," we called him. He wore heavy black horn-rim glasses with the oblong lenses that made him look like a raccoon, or a burglar in a cartoon, and he owned three sportcoats, each with leather patches on the elbows—a first in my town, which made him an object of pity among our mothers, who thought he was poor. He was the first sophisticate I knew, the only person in town who'd been to New York and liked it. Mr. Krueger had been through New York on his way to join his post office battalion in France after D-Day and had spent two days locked in his room at the Dixie Hotel reading the only book he found there, not eating for fear of what might be in it, but Mr. Anderson had actually gone to New York of his own free will, had a whee of a time, and returned to tell about it. He had made the mistake of telling someone that he had spent $15 for a meal

in New York, and word got around—it confirmed some people's suspicions, that teachers were a feather-brained bunch who probably earned more than was good for them, and that New York was the very place that would lead a man to such excess and indulgence. Mr. Anderson pointed out that it was a meal for two, but still $15! I come from people who can't sit and eat in a restaurant without reflecting on how much less it would cost to have made the meal themselves at home. So Mr. Anderson didn't speak openly of New York after that. But he confided in me. I was, he said, "different from the others." "You're cut from different cloth," he told me. I hoped he was right; I hoped it was wool tweed. Later, I found that he said this to a lot of kids. It was lovely, though, to be confided in by this man who had been to New York. He went on—he'd been to a Broadway play—it was wonderful, he said, but the plot was a little weak—and I marveled at it: that a man I knew had been to Broadway and that he could criticize it on top of it. Amazing! He told of walking in the street full of people at two o'clock in the morning, but my favorite of his exhibits was the menu of the restaurant where he had spent all that money. It was a Chinese restaurant and the menu

was a lavish red and gold booklet...a shade of red I'd never seen, and gold almost like real gold, and a red tassel and gold scrollwork around the borders and a picture of a Chinese lady and gentleman sitting together under umbrellas held by two men in PJs— and inside the names of foods I'd never had, and Chinese writing—the mysterious East! An East that was part of my country, the

GK, Anoka High School, Class of 1960.

U.S. of A., and yet connected to the whole world. I could've looked at that menu every day if he'd let me. I was a true scholar of that menu. To me it was a token of another people, and by studying its every detail, I could learn about life there. And clearly it was a life of undreamed of splendor and extravagance, and clearly a man would be right to spend $15 on supper even if it was his last $15, *especially* if it was—just as in fairy tales a poor peasant gives his last pennies to strangers and then is rewarded with a bag of gold for not having been cautious—this was New York.

It is what we're not. We're savers. We eat in the kitchen. It's Saturday night. Supper is leftovers—a fleet of little plastic dishes, warmed-over casseroles, a few tomatoes here, some zucchini there, all carefully saved in the icebox to be eaten down to the last bit. Even a half cup of chicken gravy saved, reheated, put on toast. Everything on the plate must be eaten—at this table you don't take a flyer on a dish and decide you don't like it after all—it's yours, you eat it, there are children hungry in Asia, and this is supposed to make us careful eaters. This afternoon, Mother washed and waxed the kitchen floor, and when the wax dried, before anyone stepped on it, she carefully spread newspapers across the floor to save the shine, which now we cannot see, which makes no sense to me. You could leave the floor dirty and cover it with newspapers and get the same effect. But it makes perfect sense to her.

From the looks of his menu, I'd say they don't do this in New York. Magnificent city with shiny floors and people walk right across them with their shoes on—no papers!—and order big meals, exotic dishes, and eat a few bites and go to a Broadway show, but not like my people who if they spend money on anything they by God make every effort to like it or die trying but when I go someday to a Broadway show, I'll say "Ehhh! Extravagance!" Yes, I am different from the others, cut from different cloth, born to be extravagant and to wear a flashy white suit and years later still trying, but the truth is that my favorite attraction is still the Staten Island ferry, out and back for a quarter, that's where I go first—I'm still their boy—and even now, at this most extravagant moment, on stage on West 43rd Street, between Broadway and The Avenue of the Americas—The Avenue of The Americas! Me! From Lake Wobegon!—standing in

reflected splendor. At this moment my mother walks onstage with an armload of socks, and I see it's not a stage, it's my bedroom; there's my dresser; this isn't a microphone, it's the handle of a Hoover upright vacuum cleaner; and these lovely faces before me are flowers, the blue violets on the wallpaper, and she says, "What are you doing?" I say, Practicing. Practicing a speech. "For what?" For school. "But I sent you up here two hours ago to clean your room! You haven't touched a thing that I can see. It looks like it was hit by a cyclone." Yeah, well, I was just about to do something about that. "Well, you make sure you do. This is disgraceful. I don't see how you can live like this." I will. I really will. "You keep saying you will but you never do. How are you ever going to make something of yourself if you can't learn how to buckle down and do a simple job and get it done." I will. I really will. I promise. "And for heaven's sake put that vacuum cleaner away. You keep leaning on it like that, you're going to break it." Yes, ma'am.

Atkins

Chet Atkins called up PHC in the spring of 1983, said he'd been listening to the show, and said, "When are you going to have me up there to play on it?" And so up he came a few weeks later with his wife, Leona, and his trusty sideman, Paul Yandell, to pick a few tunes for union scale and go out to dinner afterward and tell stories about Nashville. His coming was, of course, a huge boost to the show—the audience swallowed its gum when he was introduced, newspaper reporters called the next week, St. Paulites who'd never noticed the show suddenly did—and it said a lot about Chet that he'd pick up the phone and call up himself and come up to Minnesota on a lark. Chet is probably the most famous guitarist in the world, the name that every other guitarist on the planet knows. (In Outer Mongolia, there probably are a certain number of yak herders trying to learn "Windy and Warm" and "I'll See You in My Dreams" out of the *Chet Atkins' Guitar Instruction Book* while listening to the tape cassette over and over and over.) He's a member of the Country Music Hall of Fame, has won about a dozen Grammies, was a powerhouse producer at RCA who propelled a lot of big careers, and yet he always was a musician walking around with a guitar in his hands, and that's who he is around the show. And of course he started out ➙

Leo Kottke and Chet Atkins rehearsing, June 12, 1987.

GK playing Autoharp, 1976. "Loved to play it. Almost got the hang of tuning it. Well tuned, the Autoharp is an orchestra in your hands, and semi-tuned, it is a contraption with wires, a sort of cheese grater."

in radio, in Knoxville and Cincinnati, and at Springfield MO, and then on the Grand Ole Opry. He and GK did "The Sweet Corn Tour" together in the summer of 1988, a concert at Carnegie Hall, and an *Austin City Limits* with Johnny Gimble and the Hopeful Gospel Quartet.

Auctions

It's getting into the season for auctions in Lake Wobegon. Time of year for people to clear out their belongings and move on. Two are scheduled tomorrow. All Mr. Knutson's property will be sold at 1:30 (2 mi S of HS, west 1/2 mi, south 1/2 mi, lunch by the WCTU). He just completed his harvest and is quitting farming and going to Willmar. And the estate of Miss Elsie Meinhart will be auctioned off at 3. She completed her harvest too and is going to heaven.

Mr. Knutson's won't take long because those Norwegian bachelor farmers don't have much: a dresser, a table, two chairs, an iron cot, and two truckloads full of what auctioneers like to call "antiques." Usually that means it's broken.

Miss Meinhart, R.I.P., was a collector, though, and she spent her life attending auctions. Her house was so full, she had to go to the hospital to die. Now it'll all be hauled out on the lawn and sold again. Horse collars and crocks and door knobs and singletrees and glassware and miscellaneous. Most of it miscellaneous.

Auctions are a religious occasion. Of course, everything is a religious occasion, if you believe in God. And this is one. Consider our homes, how cozy and tight and everything in its place and the longer you live with things, all these little artifacts of our life, the more precious they are. Every chair, every plate and picture. And then the shock of seeing them spread out on the lawn and all your neighbors inspecting them: suddenly your belongings look shabby and raggedy out there in the light—your whole life spread out for all to see. Like being dissected.

But it's time to go. We start out making a home on our own and we have nothing, and we get a few sticks of furniture here and a few there, and the years go by, and we go to a few auctions and suddenly late in life you feel like you're the owner of a warehouse. It's time to get rid of it and resume our pilgrimage.

"Queen of the Autoharp," Stevie Beck.

Autoharp

A simple instrument, many people's first, but capable of lovely music in the hands of a dedicated harpie. Autoharpists on the show have included GK; Stevie Beck, Queen of the Autoharp, now associate producer of PHC; Jeanette Carter of the Carter Family; and Bryan Bowers.

Autumn

Here on an autumn night in the sweet leaf smell,
Sitting in a pile of leaves under the starry sky,
Oh, what stories we could tell
With this starlight to tell them by.

October night, and you, and paradise,
So lovely and so full of grace,
Above your head, the universe has hung its lights,
And I reach out my hand to touch your face.

I believe in impulse, in all that is green,
Believe in the foolish vision that comes true,
Believe that all that is essential is unseen,
And for this lifetime I believe in you.

All of the lovers and the love they made:
Nothing that was between them was a mistake.
All that is done for love's sake,
Is not wasted and will never fade.

All who have loved shall be forever young
And walk in grandeur on a cool fall night
Along the avenue,
They live in every song that is ever sung,
In every painting of pure light,
In every pas de deux.
Oh, love that shines in every star
And love reflected in the silver moon.
It is not here, but it's not far.
Not yet, but it will be here soon.

Bats

Before the World Theater was renovated, bats occasionally swooped through the hall during a show. Producer Margaret Moos made it clear to performers that no one was to mention the word "bat." She didn't want the audience to freak out. Once Butch Thompson was playing the piano, and he suddenly stopped, and said to the audience, "Excuse me, but a bird just flew over my shoulder." Bird, indeed. GK knew Stevie was terrified of bats, so he gave her the role of a bat in a script, flapping her wings and making high-pitched peeping sounds. Another time she played an over-the-road trucker hauling a load of bat guano.

Battle Hymn of the Republic

Down with all the East Coast liberal aristocracy,
Down with all the anchormen who live in
 luxury,
Down with all the lobbyists in Washington DC
Run them up a tree.

Glory, glory, liberation.
Let it spread across the nation.
Down with corporate criminals who swindle
 and pollute
And poke them in the snoot.

It's time for all you working stiffs and
 ordinary joes
To overthrow the lawyers in their fine imported
 clothes
And the bankers and the brokers and the hosts
 of radio shows
And poke them in the nose.

It's time for working people now to rally
 and defeat
The wealthy and the powerful and haul
 down the elite
And all the educated bums in paneled
 office suites
And throw them in the street.

Glory, glory, revolution,
Income redistribution.
Take away their vintage wines and let 'em
 all drink beer
And stick it in their ear.

We'll snatch them from their country clubs
 and from their big resorts.
We'll snatch them from the sailboats and from
 the tennis courts
We'll take them out of first class and with
 a mighty cheer
We'll send them to the rear. ➥

And then we'll get the media, those mighty
    millionaires
Who weave their little fictions sitting on
    their derrieres,
We'll grab them by their flabby hands and
    make them say their prayers
And kick them down the stairs.

Glory, glory, liberation,
Let us seize communication.
Let us all rise up and conquer public radio
For it is ours, you know.

The Prairie Home Companion—yes,
    it shall be overthrown!
We'll pull the host right off the stage and grab
    his microphone,
And instead of his dull stories we will stand and
    tell our own—
The truth will soon be known!

Beck

Stevie Beck (associate producer), born in Dallas,
daughter of an Air Force general, grew up in nine Air
Force locations, winding up in Omaha. She attended
the University of Nebraska, went to Minnesota for
graduate school in the history of art (specialization,
18th-century French painting), got off the plane, said,
"This looks fine. I'm never moving again." Started
playing old-time music in college, worked as a
stringed instrument repairperson, came to Minnesota
Public Radio in 1988, and joined PHC in 1992. Still
concertizes, playing the Autoharp.

Bebopareebop

. . . brought to you by Bebopareebop Rhubarb Pie.

It's a cold rainy day (THUNDER, LIGHTNING).
You kiss your wife (TWO DRY PECKS) and out the
door you go (DOOR SLAM) and you get on your
bike and ride to campus (TRAFFIC PASSING) and

Stevie Beck's warren at Minnesota Public Radio. Here, the booker works at her computer screen (left, behind lamp) and listens to CDs. To far right (not shown), sits a crate of unsolicited tape cassettes, all of which get heard eventually.

you don't see the car come racing through the puddle (CAR, BIG WAVE OF WATER, CRY OF ALARM) and you're drenched. Soaked. You get to the English Department office smelling like an old dog (SOGGY COAT DROPS) and you take off your coat and Sheila, the department secretary (**Sheila:** English Department—how may I direct your call please?), she's all dressed up in a black suit with a string of pearls (**Sheila:** Good morning, Professor Hawker). What a peach she is. And today is her last day. She's leaving to go into corrections work so she can be with her boyfriend. And now you suddenly realize (**Hawker:** Which button makes it go?) you don't know how to work the copier, you don't have a clue. (**Hawker:** Maybe this one. CLICK. RAPID, HIGH-SPEED PRINTING, WHIRRING. **Hawker:** Sheila!) The coffee machine. The fax. You don't even know how to get your E-mail (**Hawker:** I think I just click on here—KLAXON—uh oh). You shut the computer down (CLICKS) and then it won't go back on. (SHAKING COMPUTER, SHORTING) And now the screen is doing crazy things.
Hawker: Sheila!! What's wrong?
Sheila: There. (CLICK) All better.
Hawker: Gosh, thanks. What are we ever going to do without you?
Sheila: Want me to tell you, Professor Hawker?

You go to the farewell lunch and Sheila has three glasses of wine. (**Sheila:** Let me tell you clowns something...you're all unemployable. You know that?) Cruel words. Everyone sits there lacerated (SOFT SOBBING) and to console themselves they all have flaming desserts (POOF OF FLAME) and (**Hawker:** My eyebrows!) your cherry flambé burns off both your eyebrows (FAST FOOTSTEPS) and you dash to the men's room and (GROAN) you look strange without them so you take a felt tip pen and color them in (**Hawker:** There. Better) and then you come back to the table (**Hawker:** Hello?) and you're all alone with the check (**Hawker:** Three hundred and—oh my gosh!) and it takes a while to settle up (**Waiter:** Your credit card has been declined, sir. **Hawker:** I have one in the car, I think). And you sneak out back. (TIPTOE STEPS) And you dash across the parking lot (FAST STEPS) and you get to your three o'clock class with moments to spare (PANTING, BELL RINGS) and the students are staring at you like trout in the butcher case (**Hawker:** Good afternoon, class)—

and suddenly you have no idea what class this is, if it's the 19th-century Novel or Chaucer or what. (**Hawker:** So...who'd like to stand up and talk about this week's reading assignment?) Nobody says a word. (PERSPIRATION) And somehow you talk your way through the hour without being too specific about anything. (**Hawker:** The aggregate banality of the paternalist consensus of sensibility consequences and legitimates the modernity of the derealization of the dichotomy of myth and mass narrative as ethnocentric periodization—or should I say, the politics of gender?) Fifty minutes in which you never mention a specific work of literature, and then you hustle home (**Wife:** Honey? The Dean'll be here in half an hour) and then you notice (ANXIETY)—Sheila's blue silk garter is in your shirt pocket. (**Hawker:** Where'd that come from?) Must've been when she stood on the table and threw it. (**Wife:** Honey???) (FAST TIPTOE FOOTSTEPS, EASE DOOR SHUT) It was there all during your lecture? (**Hawker:** Oh boy.) You sneak into the bathroom and you try to (FLUSH) flush it down the toilet. It comes back up (BLOOP). You throw it in the wastebasket. And then (WOOF) there's Rex. With something blue and frilly in his mouth. (**Hawker:** Rex!) (WOOFS) (DOG GROWLING)
(**Hawker:** Gimme that, you stupid dog.) You grab the garter—(FOOTSTEPS, GLASS CRASH) (**Hawker:** Oh no!) And the entire glass cabinet full of your wife's toiletries is falling toward you (CLATTER, GLASS) and you throw yourself against it—thousands of jars and bottles and tubes—(GLASS BREAKAGE, CLATTER, CRASHING, THEN SILENCE)
Wife: Chuck? Is something wrong?
(ONE OBJECT DROPS AND CLATTERS)
Wife: And what is this that Rex has? It looks like—an armband from a banjo player—
Hawker: Yes! Exactly! (ANOTHER OBJECT DROPS) I used it in a lecture on the cognitive foundation of the fragmentation of paternalist alienation.
Wife: But why does it say "Angel Baby"? (ANOTHER CRASH)

(THEME)
Wouldn't this be a good time for a piece of rhubarb pie? Yes, nothing takes the taste of shame and humiliation out of your mouth quite like Bebopareebop Rhubarb Pie. ➡

Butch Thompson at the Fitzgerald Theater piano. A Steinway nine-foot grand (Model D), a gift of Mr. and Mrs. Robert Sivertsen in 1986. "It has an easy action, a beautiful tone; it speaks but not too loudly for radio; everybody who has played on it has liked it," says Rich Dworsky.

One little thing can revive a guy,
And that is homemade rhubarb pie.
Serve it up, nice and hot.
Maybe things aren't as bad as you thought.

ALL:
Mama's little baby loves rhubarb, rhubarb,
Bebopareebop Rhubarb Pie.
Mama's little baby loves rhubarb, rhubarb,
Bebopareebop Rhubarb Pie.

Blizzards

Back in January of 1983, we got a couple of feet of snow on a Wednesday in the Twin Cities and more on the following Friday. It was bad, even by Minnesota standards, five-foot drifts. Stevie Beck started digging early Saturday morning, but it was no use. It was like a prison movie, in which the convicts tunnel to freedom, only to discover they've come up a few feet short of the wall. She called a cab. It finally came. Driving was so bad, Stevie couldn't imagine how anyone would make it to the

theater; but in true Minnesota fashion, they all did, and the show played to a full house.

The most memorable blizzard was Birmingham AL, in March 1993. The cast flew in on Friday, when it was raining; the rain changed to snow, and that night they realized, impossible though it seemed, that they were in the midst of a blizzard. Thirteen inches of snow. The town was paralyzed. The radio station called to say that they couldn't get into the theater in the morning, because none of the crew could get there. The chief of police called to say there was no way to do a show the next day because nobody could move, and besides, nobody would come.

Friday night in the hotel room, GK wrote all this stuff about Southerners and how they couldn't bear up under a little cold weather, and then Russ Ringsak came in from his rounds, a six-pack in hand, snow on his Stetson, and said, "This is a blizzard that'd make Bemidji proud." GK threw out all that material and rewrote the show.

Chris Tschida knew, of course, that the show had to go on. Minnesotans don't go all the way to

Alabama to be defeated by a blizzard. The crew shoveled out the satellite dish and towed it to the theater through the deserted streets. One stagehand had skied to work, and luckily he was the one with the keys. He got the building open and the lights turned on. An hour before broadcast, none of the guests were there. Emmylou Harris phoned from her bus on the road. They were fifty miles out of town and at a dead standstill, and the Birmingham Sunlights, a gospel quintet from five different parts of the city, were trying to find a way into town. Russ went out in the equipment truck to pick up a Sunlight whose wife was immensely pregnant, and the show started at five with no guests and about five hundred brave souls in the audience. At 5:20, the wind rushed through the back of the theater when Emmylou came through the stage door. She went right on stage and sang a duet with Garrison, no rehearsal, no soundcheck. By the end of the mono-logue, the Sunlights had all assembled, too, and they closed off the show. A big finger-popping finale.

Blount

Roy Blount Jr. has appeared often on the show, act-ing in scripts and reading his own work, including the following from his book *One Fell Soup*:

Song to Oysters

I like to eat an uncooked oyster.
Nothing's slicker, nothing's moister
Nothing's easier on your gorge
Or, when the time comes, to dischorge.
But not to let it too long rest
Within your mouth is always best.
For if your mind dwells on an oyster...
Nothing's slicker. Nothing's moister.

I prefer my oyster fried.
Then I'm sure my oyster's died.

Bob

"The Story of Bob, a Young Artist" was sponsored by Rainbow Motor Oil and the Rainbow Family of Automotive Products. A typical episode began with Bob, Berniece, and Pops and his dog Rex sitting around the lunch table:

Roy Blount Jr. in Austin TX, spring 1998.

Berniece: You care for another helping of cheesy noodles, Bob?
Bob: No, thanks, I feel pretty full.
Berniece: I put extra paprika on them just for you. You care for more, Pops?
Pops: I'll take a rain check. My stomach's a little gassy today. How about you, Rex? Huh? you care for some more cheese noodles, boy? (DOG THUMPS HIND LEG AS NECK IS SCRATCHED, COLLAR JINGLES, PANTING) (SNIPPING)
Bob: Would you mind trimming your nose hair someplace else?
Pops: You don't like it, look the other way. What do you want me to do with it? Comb it over my shoulders? (SNIPPING)
Berniece: So whatcha been workin' on all morn-ing, Bob? You were quiet as a mouse in your little studio. Didn't hear a peep out of you.
Bob: I'm working on a motet, Berniece, called "The Motif Motet 23."
Berniece: I see. What's that about?
Bob: (SIGH) A work of art is not "about" some-thing, for crying out loud. It *is* something. It exists on its own terms. Cripes.
Pops: Is it about sex then?
Bob: If you must know, it's about rebirth. (SNIPPING) Do you mind not doing that in front of me while I'm eating?
Pops: Wouldn't be doing it in front of you if you'd turn the other way. Don't get your undies bunched up over it.

Berniece: Speaking of undies, who's gonna run over to the laundromat and put that load in the dryer?

Pops: Not me, not with this heartburn, I better not. So when are you going to write a big hit, Bob, so we can clear out of this dump and move to someplace nice like Tampa, huh?

Bob: I don't know how many times I have to tell you, Pops. I'm an artist and an artist does not sell his soul just so he can earn a snootful of money and buy a home in Tampa. That's not who I am.

Pops: Well, why not create something that people want to buy?

Berniece: Now, Pops, don't you go getting Bob all up in a lather now—anybody care for some coffee?

Bob: No, thanks. I've got to get back to my motet. It's due on Tuesday. The choir's supposed to sing it in two weeks for Memorial Day

Pops: It'll be Memorial Day for you, if there's any critics around.

Bob: You are so cruel. You know that?

Berniece: All right you two. Enough bickering. Pops, you better take your medication. You get cranky when you don't take it when you're supposed to.

Pops: What's wrong with cranky? (SHAKES PILL CONTAINER) Dang these childproof caps!

Berniece: That's wonderful that the choir's going to perform your motet, Bob!

Bob: We still haven't worked out the contract. They're asking for 50 percent of the film rights.

Pops: Ha! The chance of your motet being made into a movie is about the same as the chance of me getting a sex change.

Bob: It's not right. I'm not going to allow it.

Pops: What do you have to say about it?

Bob: This just makes me furious.

Pops: If I want to have a sex change, I'll go ahead and have it—I don't need to ask you—

Bob: I am sending Mrs. Zimmer a very terse note.

Pops: Just have to get me a wig is all.

Bob: I'm not going to let them walk all over me.

Pops: If you put a sex change operation in that motet of yours, maybe somebody would make it into a movie.

Berniece: What are you two arguing about?

Pops: If I want to become a woman, dang it, I will. I'm sixty-seven years old. Maybe it's time to cut loose. (HE CLEARS PHLEGM)

Bob: Could you please not do that?

Pops: That'd give 'em something to talk about at the senior citizen center.

Berniece: Pops, what are you doing! Not the hammer! Don't! (POPS SMASHES CONTAINER)

Bob: Oh, for pity's sake!

Pops: Only way to get the dang thing open!

Berniece: Pops, I think it's time for your nap.

Pops: You want to sit on my lap, go right ahead.

Bob: You know, I am at the end of my rope! I can't even hear myself think around here. If I could just get a moment of peace and quiet, I'd be able to finish things!

Bob Elliott and Ray Goulding, April 1987.

Bobs

The name "Bob" comes from the Anglo-Saxon name "Hreodbeorght," which was shortened to "Robert." The first famous Robert was the Scottish king Robert the Bruce—later called "Robert the Bob." Nonetheless, the name "Bob" was what linguists refer to as "a dumb name," as the Scottish poet Bob Burns found out. ("Dear Sir: I enclose the stupid poems you sent to our literary magazine. Poems by a guy named Bob? Be real. Signed, Robert Browning.")

Men of science and industry were forced to use aliases: B. F. Goodrich, B. F. Skinner. Both hid their Bob behind an initial. And also, a little known fact—Susan B. Anthony. In our time, a boy from Minnesota gave a boost to the Bobs, the Bob who wrote: "The times, they are a-changin'."

But the times haven't changed—not for Bobs, they haven't. In the White House, we've had two Franklins, a Millard, a Rutherford, a Chester, a Grover—but no Bob. As Bob Dole found out.

This year the Bob Foundation is looking for a Bob to run for President. America needs a Bob. If you're a native-born American over forty, with some experience in elected office, call us. Do it for all those Bobs across the country. The Bobs who have to go out every day and say, "My name is Bob." A message from the Bob Foundation for the working Bobs.

Body

Joyce Sutphen appeared on the October 24, 1998, show. This poem was published in her book *Straight Out of View*.

Living in the Body

Body is something you need in order to stay
on this planet and you only get one.
And no matter which one you get, it will not
be satisfactory. It will not be beautiful
enough, it will not be fast enough, it will
not keep on for days at a time, but will
pull you down into a sleepy swamp and
demand apples and coffee and chocolate cake.

Body is a thing you have to carry
from one day into the next. Always the
same eyebrows over the same eyes in the same
skin when you look in the mirror, and the
same creaky knee when you get up from the
floor and the same wrist under the watchband.
The changes you can make are small and
costly—better to leave it as it is.

Body is a thing that you have to leave
eventually. You know that because you have
seen others do it, others who were once like you,
living inside their pile of bones and
flesh, smiling at you, loving you,
leaning in the doorway, talking to you
for hours and then one day they
are gone. No forwarding address.

Booking Acts

The staff recalls first noticing the Exwhyzed Band tucked into the record reviews of a British trad-music magazine. Their name had popped up a time or two—scuttlebutt on the folk grapevine—but now comes this rave review of the quartet's latest offering on a small indie label called Dented Boot Records, warranting further investigation.

The associate producer, in charge of all guest talent, got the new CD, listened, liked, and passed the disc on to GK, who agreed they should come on the show. The associate producer tracked down the group's management by calling Dented Boot and following a chain of phone numbers that covered the better part of the British Isles. The good news: their manager was familiar with Prairie Home Companion. Even better news: Exwhyzed would be touring the States in the spring and still had an open Saturday. Best news of all: another U.S. promoter on their tour would take care of the U.S. Immigration and Naturalization Service Petition for a Nonimmigrant Worker—the dreaded O-1 visa application, a process that could squander an entire week and leave the most hard-boiled talent coordinator racked with sobs and suffering otherwise inexplicable tics.

I'LL SHOW YOU MINE; YOU SHOW ME YOURS

We settle on a date. The associate producer sends Exwhyzed's management Prairie Home Companion's standard Letter of Agreement, in which Minnesota Public Radio agrees to produce the PROGRAM at the determined THEATER, and to pay PERFORMER the established fee, and to provide a travel allowance, lodging, ground transportation, and per diem (not to exceed two days); and in which

> "PERFORMER agrees that MPR may initially distribute this program nationally for broadcast on approximately 460 public radio stations in the United States, but may further broadcast, distribute for broadcast and place on the MPR Web site, the PROGRAM pursuant to all terms and conditions of, and financial compensation required by, the American Federation of Musicians (AFM) National Public Radio Agreement, or The American Federation of Television and Radio Artists (AFTRA) Public Radio Agreement (whichever is applicable), in effect at the time of the performance."

There are a few additional slugs of legal twaddle, including a clause wherein

> "PERFORMER affirms neither they nor anyone acting for them has agreed to give Producer or anyone associated with the PROGRAM any portion of their compensation, or anything else of value, for arranging for their being engaged in connection with the PROGRAM, and PERFORMER understands that it is a federal offense, unless disclosed to the Producer prior to the distribution of the PROGRAM, for a person to accept or agree to accept anything of value, other than their regular compensation, for promoting any product, service or venture on the PROGRAM."

Exwhyzed's management signs the three copies and returns two (as requested) along with four copies of the band's standard Concert Contract and Rider (not really appropriate to our show, but it's all they've got), in which they request "eight monitor wedges, bass amp, four graphic equalizers, deli tray, case of Amstel Light, and four clean bath towels," and in which they note that the band's appearance is "subject to detention by sickness, accidents, riots, strikes, epidemics, acts of God, or any other legitimate conditions beyond their control."

After some negotiating (no towels, no beer), the contracts are signed AS AMENDED, and the deal is done.

THE WHEELS ARE IN MOTION

Thousands of details are mowed down one by one: from publicity to travel and hotel arrangements to technical requirements—the PHC staff is humming like a well-oiled Briggs and Stratton. Finally it's the day of the show and a weary Exwhyzed Band arrives at the Fitzgerald Theater around noon, having driven for seven and a half hours following last night's Chicago booking. They appear dazed and apprehensive, and you really can't blame them. From the guest-artist point of view, this gig has calamitous earmarks: it's not their venue, it's not their tech crew, it's not their audience, it's not their show. Crimony! But the PHC staff is friendly and makes them welcome. And the Fitz is a beautiful hall—a fully restored 1910 Shubert theater with two balconies and four grand opera boxes at each side of the proscenium. The backstage area is comfortable with spacious dressing rooms and a greenroom chock-full of catered good-

ies. Things are looking up.

After a snack and a cup of pretty good coffee, Exwhyzed takes the stage and begins their soundcheck. The tech crew and stagehands focus mikes, push monitors into position, "roll a little off the low end," "put a little more me in my monitor." The band runs through their numbers, the associate producer timing each one and discussing which the band would prefer to start with, what would come next, and so on. Later, the producer and GK will take all these details into account when deciding on the show's running order.

HURRY UP AND WAIT

Between the soundcheck and the on-air light, there are a few hours of downtime. The PHC staff and crew are still moving fast, but the guest talent's day has coasted to a stop. Some welcome this interlude, stealing a catnap, seeing to merchandise sales, maybe taking a walk through the skyways of downtown St. Paul. And, of course, the late-afternoon meal whipped up by Prairie Home's legendary caterer breaks the monotony.

Suddenly it's showtime, and after barely twitching a muscle all afternoon, Exwhyzed has to leap onto the stage, play their numbers, and leap off again. There's no inching into this, just hit the ground running, zero to sixty in five flat. Prairie Home regular Peter Ostroushko used to call this "guerrilla picking"—race out of the bushes, fire off a tune, and disappear into the forest. It plays havoc with the blood pressure, but when it's over, you think, "Hey, that was great, let's do it again." Kinda like the Wild Mouse ride at the State Fair.

The Exwhyzed Band played their hearts out. The Fitzgerald audience, customarily a staid bunch, went nuts. Back in the greenroom, thunderous applause still ringing in their ears, the band told the associate producer, "Hey, that was great, let's do it again."

—Stevie Beck

Brain Capacity

I know I shouldn't be talking about my problems on this show, but frankly, it's depressing to get to my age and realize that probably this is about as smart as I'm ever going to be. Probably I'll just go on doing what I do now, which is brain surgery. I've always been interested in the brain, and the recent changes in health care aimed at controlling costs have opened up the field of brain surgery to people outside of medicine, and what can I say? I've been the low bidder on a number of operations.

GK: How're we doing there? He looks asleep, doesn't he?

Tim: Looks asleep to me.

GK: Well, I guess we'll know in a moment. Say, when it says "right side of the brain," does it mean his right or our right?

Tim: His right, I think.

GK: I think you're right. (POWER DRILL REVS UP, DRILLING) Boy, there's a lot of loose gunk in here. Give me that vacuum. (DRILL STOPS) See if you can't get that stuff there. (VACUUM HUM) Good. How old is this guy?

Tim: Fifty-something. Fifty-four.

GK: No wonder. (VACUUM OFF) Lot of trivia in there. Give me the water pic.

Tim: Here you go.

GK: Thanks. (SPRAY OF WATER) There. That ought to help.

Tim: What does this guy do for a living anyway?

GK: I don't know. Let's find out. Put the electrode right there.

Patient: (IN A TRANCE) So if you value the programming you hear on this station, won't you call now and pledge your support—

GK: He's one of us.

Tim: A radio guy.

GK: So I guess my brain must look like that, too.

Tim: You want me to take a look?

GK: No, thanks. (MUSIC)

Brevity

Whenever you write, whenever you sing:
Don't be too much of a good thing.
Keep your song to just one verse.
Don't go on, it just gets worse.

Brevity is the soul of wit.
Go out and sing, then quit.
If people clap and shout Encore,
Just remember: less is more.

Less is more, what more can I say?
A hero is a man who went away.
Today your praises would be sung
If only you'd died when you were young.

Brown

Greg Brown first appeared on the show on May 31, 1980. He was a regular from 1983 to 1985, and wrote his song "Cheapest Kind" to sing on the show.

We travelled Kansas and Missouri spreading
  the good news
Preacher's family in our pressed clothes and
  worn out polished shoes
Momma fixed us soup beans and served them
  up by candlelight
She tucked us in and I know
She worried through many a sleepless night
Dad and me would stop by the store when
  the day was done
Standin' at the counter he said, "I forgot to
  get the peaches, son."
"What kind should I get?" I said to him there
  where he stood in line
And he answered just like I knew he would,
  "Go and get the cheapest kind." →

Greg Brown in Red Wing MN, August 1986.

Philip Brunelle rehearsing
his Ensemble Singers
for PHC.

[CHORUS:]
But the love, the love, the love
It was not the cheapest kind
It was rich as, rich as, rich as, rich as, rich as
Any you could ever find

I see the ghost of my grandfather from time
    to time
In some big city amongst the people all dressed
    so fine
He usually has a paper bag clutched real tight
His work clothes are dirty
He don't look nobody in the eye
Oh he was little, he was wiry, and he was lots
    of fun
He was rocky as roadside dirt back where
    he came from
And they were raisin' seven children on a
    little farm
In not the best of times
The few things that they got from the store
Were always just the cheapest kind

Fancy houses with wealthy people I don't
    understand
I always wish I could be holdin' on to my
    grandpa's hand
So he could lead me down that long road
    somewhere
To that little house where there's just enough
    supper
For who's ever there
My people's hands and faces they are so dear
    to me
All I have to do is close my eyes and they're
    so near to me
I have to laugh I have to cry
When I think of all the things that have drawn
    those lines
So many years of making do with the
    cheapest kind

Brunelle

A contemporary of GK's at the U of M, a music
major and famous campus overachiever (pianist,
organist, carillonneur, percussionist in Minnesota
Orchestra), Philip Brunelle was enlisted for the first
live PHC (July 6, 1974) because he could play
hymns. (A preacher's kid, he knows the first verses
of several hundred hymns, and many of their paro-

dy versions.) Has appeared often since, conducting
his choir or accompanying Vern Sutton or Janis
Hardy, and once to sing his Latin version of
"Rudolph the Red Nosed Reindeer," "*Rudolphus
Rubrinafus.*" Founding father of the Plymouth
Music Series of Minnesota, now in its 31st season
of presenting eccentric and ornery concerts of
lesser-known and neglected works, plus commis-
sioned pieces. Music director of Plymouth Church,
Minneapolis. Guest conductor, Swedish Royal
Opera in Stockholm, Aldeburghe Festival, Chicago
Symphony, St. Louis, Seattle, and elsewhere.

Buster

Buster the Show Dog, sponsored by Scotty's Cough
Syrup for Dogs, began with Buster in his radio
career. After losing and regaining his job and then
going on strike, Buster gets an eyeball transplant.
He's sent to Hawaii with Father Finian (whose life he
had saved a month earlier) and Timmy, the sad rich
teenage boy, by Timmy's parents. Here their adven-
tures get wild, and every week's story ends in a crisis.
Rescued from half-naked men with long knives, they
find themselves in an African game preserve. Sheila
the Christian jungle girl joins the group as they try
to make their way back home. Timmy lost their air-
plane tickets, so they first take a boat, but it sinks;
they grab a ride in a truck, but it crashes; and they
continue by train, rocket, and bus, with each
week's episode ending in a cliff-hang-
er. Timmy finds his credit card and
buys air tickets for them, but they are
bumped from their seats. They walk
through the Salt Lake City terminal
until they reach Denver. Finally getting home to St. Paul, they want to
take a souvenir picture. While they

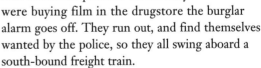

were buying film in the drugstore the burglar
alarm goes off. They run out, and find themselves
wanted by the police, so they all swing aboard a
south-bound freight train.

Buster ran for twenty-four episodes December
1986–June 1987 and starred Tom Keith as Buster the
dog, as Tommy the sad rich boy, and as the warmhearted Father Finian from St. Paul. Kate
MacKenzie played Sheila. Dan Rowles played assort-
ed villains. Occasional roles were taken by guests,
such as when the Everly Brothers played passengers
on the bus trying to get home to see their mother.

Café Boeuf

Typically, GK enters the café to find Maurice, the French maître d', prepared to lord it over him.

GK: *Bonsoir*, Maurice.

Maurice (Tom Keith): No, this is not a bar. Do you smell beer? Do you smell the mothballs in the toilets? Eh? Non. It's a restaurant.

GK: I didn't ask if it's a bar. I said: *Bonsoir*.

Maurice: No, I cannot park your car. I am a maître d', not a parking attendant. Am I wearing a white coat? No, I am not.

GK is leery of café specialties such as pâté of pancreas of pigeon and sautéed trout throats, or the armpit of a young sheep stuffed with spinach, so he orders boeuf, very rare, with French fries.

Maurice: Monsieur, all of our potatoes are French. Whether they are fried, boiled, mashed—it is not necessary to refer to them as French. This is assumed. The potatoes do not need your recognition in order to be French potatoes. They are well aware of it themselves.

Camping

When you visit our great national parks of the west, you naturally want to be comfortable. At your age, certainly. Yet there's a certain embarrassment in rolling around in a forty-eight-foot motor home with a satellite dish on top and an air conditioner the size of a wheelbarrow. It's time for the Grand Teton Road Tortoise, the forty-eight–foot motor home equipped with everything, including infrared scope for the driver. You come into the campground by night, park, and move the camouflage shield into place, and in the morning when the other campers wake up, they see an immense gray boulder and a tiny pup tent in front of it. That's your escape hatch. You crawl into the pup tent and crawl through the hatch into the Road Tortoise and there's your coffeemaker, your blender, your microwave, your color TV, your king-sized bed with magic fingers, and of course your cellular phone. The Grand Teton Road Tortoise motor home. Thousands of them are parked in Yellowstone, Glacier, and Yosemite parks this weekend. See if you can identify them. And if you do, walk over and knock and say hello.

Canaan's Land

Over the course of twenty-five years we've lost some friends. Long live their music and the memory of them.

Red Maddock,
    drummer, Butch Thompson Trio
Ray Marklund, stagehand
Jethro Burns, mandolinist
Minnie Pearl, comedienne

Merle Watson, guitarist
Charles Kuralt, journalist and author
Charles Brown, blues pianist and singer
Charles Sawtelle, guitarist, Hot Rize
W. L. "Preacher" Richardson and Walter Settles,
    Fairfield Four
Gamble Rogers, singer-songwriter
Bessie Jones, Georgia Sea Island Singers
Joe Williams, jazz singer
Jaki Byard, jazz pianist
Kate Wolf, singer-songwriter
Lonnie Pitchford, Mississippi bluesman
Rose Maddox, singer
Joe Val, bluegrass artist
Carl Martin and Ted Bogan, singers and guitarists
Carl Perkins, singer
Jim Ringer, singer
Craig Ruble, fiddler
Bill Crofut, singer, banjo player
Jimmy Driftwood, singer-songwriter
Allen Ginsberg, poet
Roger Miller, singer-songwriter
George Fenneman, actor-announcer
Sonny Terry and Brownie McGhee, blues artists
Bob Gibson, singer-songwriter
Roy Huskey Jr., bass player
Ray Goulding, radio comedian
Doc Cheatham, jazz trumpeter

The Prairie Home Cemetery in Moorhead MN, near Concordia College. An old Norwegian graveyard in the Red River Valley that GK saw after a reading at Moorhead State University in 1971, which was followed by a wild party at Mark Vinz's house, after which the partygoers took GK to the train station and sang "Red River Valley" on the platform as the eastbound Empire Builder pulled in about 2 A.M. The name of PHC came from that memorable evening, as close as GK can remember: "You couldn't name a show Prairie Home Cemetery, so I substituted Companion for cemetery, in honor of the people on the platform."

Cats

Cats May Safely Sleep

Die Katzen dürfen sicher schlafen
(music: "Sheep May Safely Graze," from the Birthday Cantata, No. 208, by J. S. Bach)

Here in the room where the sun is shining,
Two little cats on the rug reclining,
Slowly their eyes are closing,
Now they are sweetly dozing,
Curled up together in a heap,
Two little cats are fast asleep. →

God in His grace has given us cats so that even
 the lonely can love and admire
Creatures so light, so graceful, so elegant—
 we are inspired
By them to know our own perfection and
 the love and grace that fills this life.

There in the square that the sun is making,
Two little cats from their naps are waking,
Yawning and stretching slowly,
Washing their face in holy
Pleasure of warm and sunny days,
Purring a little song of praise.

Cigarettes

Once I lived a life of some renown
People looked up to me in this town
They listened to what I had to say
They named a sandwich for me at the café
And then I began my slow descent
I discovered what misery meant
I found rejection and regret
All because I smoked a cigarette.

Nobody knows you
When you take a smoke
You pull out a Marlboro or even a More
They look at you and point to the door
You stand on the sidewalk and take your drag
Next to the lady with the big plastic bag
I tell you young people, and it is no joke,
Nobody knows you when you take a smoke.

Cleaning

There's a general mood of improvement in town.
People are on the verge of spring housecleaning,
which in most homes is a major effort. Everything is
hauled out and given an airing, the storm windows
are taken off and the screens put on, and the windows opened up and the house aired out.

 Especially in homes with smokers in them, with
the windows shut up tight since last November, the
air gets stale to the point where even the smoker
notices it. He may wake up in the middle of the night
and say, "I smell smoke." Well, he should. Add to
that the cooking smells and dog smells and fuel oil
smells and the ordinary exhaust that we all give off,

and by the end of March, you feel as if you're living
in a tomb. It's time for Mrs. Krebsbach to go into
action. One of these Saturday mornings she decides
to do the spring housecleaning. She's up at 6, gets
Wally out of the rack and puts him to making pancakes, rousts up six kids and by 7:30 they're at it, like
sheep with a dog on their tails. Off come the storm
windows, out come the mattresses and blankets and
pillows, teams of kids moving at a slow trot hauling
out chairs and sofas and carpets, and the Mrs. darting
from one area to the next, directing them, urging
them on, going after the kid who was sent down the
basement for the carpetbeater a half hour ago and
who is lying behind the furnace trying to visualize
where it might be. She's amazing, and when she
moves in to beat carpets, people come out and watch.
It's awesome. One hundred and nine pounds, but
when she lays into those carpets, she's laying into
ignorance and sloth and filth and squalor in general,
she is taking on corruption and apathy and lack of
ambition and everything that is dull and lifeless.

 After the beating, the kids move faster and
Wally too. They're done by mid-afternoon. That
house is clean. Floors wet-mopped and waxed.
Curtains washed. Walls washed. Clean air blows in
the windows, the curtains blow, the house is clean.
Wally is exhausted and goes to bed. The kids drift
away, too tired to do more than just walk out of
earshot. Her, she looks great. Amazing woman.

Clock

I liked the clock that hung in the Orpheum, so we
took it with us to the World. Some would call it
theft; I call it preservation. Dan Rowles held the
clock and I removed the bolts. It's big, with neon
hands, so you can see it in a dark theater. We keep it
on stage where the audience can see it.

Columbia

O Columbia the gem of the ocean
The home of the brave and the free
The home of Jergens Hand Lotion
That keeps skin soft and heavenly.
Round thy banner let heroes assemble
When Liberty's flag stands in view
Thy perfume makes my heart tremble.
Ramona, I'm longing for you.

O Ramona, I'm longing for you
O Ramona, I'm longing for you
Round thy banners let heroes assemble
And Ramona, I'm longing for you.

The ark then of freedom's foundation,
Columbia rode safe through the storm.
And thanks to foam insulation,
Mom and Buddy will be warm.
With her garlands of victory around her,
When so proudly she bore her gallant crew,
Let democracy triumph and flower
You've got something stuck to your shoe.

The star spangled banner bring forward
O'er Columbia's true sons let it wave
Look at the underwear we ordered.
It's amazing how much you can save.
May thy service united ne'er sever
But hold to their colors so true
The Sears Roebuck catalogue forever
Three cheers for the girls at the U.

Comet

Every four thousand years it swings on by,
Flying through the western sky
A hundred-twenty-three million miles high:
Hale-Bopp.

It's big and bright as a comet can be.
Don't know much about gravity
But I feel it pulling on me:
Hale-Bopp.

The night Hale Bopp came overhead
You and I sat up in bed.
"What is going on?" you said.
Hale-Bopp.

A comet twenty-five miles wide,
Nothing but ice and dust inside,
But its magic cannot be denied:
Hale-Bopp.

On April first it approaches the sun,
Achieving its perihelion.
I'll dance with you and I will not stop:
Hale-Bopp.

And then in May it'll fade away,
Heading south to Uruguay.
Life is short. Things disappear.
Got to catch them while they're here.
May I have this dance, my dear?
Hale-Bopp.

Cowboys

(WESTERN THEME)
Announcer (Tim Russell): THE LIVES OF
THE COWBOYS... stories of the men who made
the West the West... brought to you by Western
Lubrication... and now here's today's story...
(HORSE HOOVES, OUTDOOR AMBIENCE,
CATTLE)
Dusty (Tim): Heeya. Kkkkk. C'mon, big girl.
(WHINNY)
Lefty (GK): Giddup.
Dusty: Hey! Look. Over there!
Lefty: It's a boy—and there's a school bus after
him! They're just about to grab him!
Dusty: Maybe we can head it off. Giddup! (GAL-
LOPING HOOVES AND GUNSHOTS. BUS
PULLING AWAY FAST)
Lefty: Ha! Guess we showed him.
Dusty: (WHINNY) Whoa! (HORSE COMES TO
A STOP) Howdy!
Kid (Jeffrey Goddell): Hi.
Lefty: What's your name, son?
Kid: Gene.
Dusty: Looks like me and Lefty come along just in
time, Gene. One minute later and that school bus
woulda had you.
Kid: How come he drove away without picking
me up?
Lefty: Because we drove him off, Gene.
Dusty: Saved you from slow death at the hands of
educators, ain't that right?
Kid: But now I'm going to be late for school.
Lefty: You're not going to be late, you're going to
be free, son. Big difference.
Dusty: Now you can ride and be free—like us!
Kid: Like you?
Lefty: Like us.
Kid: *Just* like you?
Lefty: That's every little buckaroo's dream, to be
free like a cowboy.
Kid: But I want to grow up and be a psychologist.
Lefty: A psychologist! That's crazy. Cowboyin' is

the good life, son.

Dusty: Psychologists don't do nothin' but sit around and read tea leaves. That ain't no work for a man. You want to get into cowboyin', like me and Lefty.

Lefty: Look here. First thing is you got to learn to whoop. Can you whoop? You go like this— WHOOO. HEEEE YA. HI. WHOOO WHOOOO WHOOO. HEE YA. You see how it goes?

(Kid AND Dusty AND Lefty TAKE TURNS WHOOPING)

Lefty: Well, I reckon you learned to whoop pretty good, now let's try shootin'. You see all those empty beer bottles me and Dusty left out on the fence rail last night? Watch the one on the left. (GUNSHOT, DISTANT BOTTLE BREAKAGE. HE BLOWS OFF GUN MUZZLE) Pretty good shootin'. Okay, your turn, Gene.

Kid: This is like a video game—(FIVE GUN-SHOTS, EACH FOLLOWED BY A DISTANT BOTTLE EXPLOSION).

Dusty: Hey hey hey. Now that's what I call shootin'!

Lefty: Boy, you can ride in my gang anytime you want.

Dusty: All you got to learn now is spittin'.

Kid: That's easy. Anybody can spit.

Lefty: No, it ain't. Watch carefully. You get all the juice out of your wad and get it in position on your tongue just behind the teeth and—(Lefty SPITS, LONG PAUSE, DISTANT DING)—hit the old water tank pretty good. Here, kid. Take a chaw of tobacco in your mouth.

Kid: (MOUTH FULL) Boy, this is gross.

Dusty: You get used to the taste.

Kid: (MOUTH FULL) Tastes like dirt.

Dusty: Tastes worse'n dirt, Gene, that's what makes a man out o'ya.

Kid: (MOUTH FULL) This isn't spitting, this is more like projectile vomiting!

Lefty: Go ahead now. Let her fly. Give her a good ride now, Gene. C'mon!

Kid: (HE SPITS) (LONG PAUSE) (DISTANT DOG ARFING)

Lefty: Why, you spit right in Rin Tin Tin's eye there, son.

The cast doing "Lives of the Cowboys": Tom Keith (hooves, mooing), Tim Russell (Dusty), Sue Scott (dance hall floozy, or waitress, or schoolmarm), GK (Lefty).

Dusty: That's what I call spittin'!

Miss Peterson (Sue Scott): Hold it right there, mister. Don't move a muscle. (CLICK OF HAMMER IN SHOTGUN)

Kid: Miss Peterson!

Lefty: Why, Delores—

Miss Peterson: *Miss* Peterson to you, saddle bum.

Dusty (to Lefty): You been foolin' around with the schoolmarm?

Lefty: We dated a couple times. Nothin' much.

Miss Peterson: Nothin' much—ha. *Zero* is more like it. Come on, Gene. I got here just in time.

Kid: I'm glad you came, Miss Peterson. I did my homework!

Miss Peterson: Good. I'm not going to waste my time on you two tramps except to say, Don't let me catch you upwind of this school again, you hear me? Look at you. Drunk, filthy, your clothes aren't washed, your hair is stuck to your heads, you got bugs in your ears, you look like death on a cracker. Kids take one look at you, they wouldn't *want* to grow up.

Dusty: Just one minute, Miss Peterson. You're trying to teach all the wildness out that boy.

Lefty: That's right. You've got to let that boy discover the wild man inside him, his inner cowpoke, Miss Peterson.

Dusty: We were teachin' him shootin' and whoopin' and spittin'.

Miss Peterson: You want to see some spittin', mister, I'll show you some spittin'—(SHE HAWKS. DOG GROWLS) What's that? (DOG SNARLS) This your dog? (DOG SNARLS, TEETH BARED)

Lefty: That there's Rin Tin Tin, ma'am. He's got spit in his eye and he's pretty riled up about it. (DOG LOW GROWL) I'd put that gun down if I was you, otherwise that dog's liable to bite your hinder. That dog dropped out of obedience school and he's discovering his inner timber wolf.

Cruise

Lynne Cruise, technical director 1974–1985, designed the sound for PHC, and gets a lot of credit for the early success of the show. She always was amused when crews at locations away from St. Paul expected her to be a man. Speaking of soundmen, here's Pat Donohue's song, sung to the tune of "Mr. Sandman."

Lynne Cruise and Doc Watson in August 1986.

Mr. Soundman

Mr. Soundman, Turn up the sound
So they can hear me for miles around
Use all the volume that you can manage,
I wanna do a little hearing damage.
Mr. Soundman, you know what I need
Keep on a-crankin' till their eardrums bleed.
I'm gonna terrorize this crowd,
Mr. Soundman, turn me up loud.

Mr. Soundman, I'd like there to be
Lots less of everyone and lots more of me.
If you could take me up a little higher
To just before you blow your amplifier.
Mr. Soundman, cause me some pain
I don't need earplugs or Novocain
I ain't too good, but I ain't proud.
Mr. Soundman, turn me up loud.

Mr. Soundman, what did you say?
I must have blacked out. I think I'm okay.
You really got me with that high-pitched
    squealin'
I can't hear nothin' but I like the feelin'.
Mr. Soundman, you got it right
My ears are ringin' for the rest of the night
It's always up and never down
Mr. Soundman turn up...
I wanna crash and burn up...
Mr. Soundman, turn up the sound!

Daddy

(to the tune of "You're the Cream in My Coffee")

I'm just your papa, happy to hop a bus and
   come home to see you
It gives me such a thrill, I know it always will.
And if it's noted your pants are loaded,
   I'd never holler, P.U.
No matter what you do, I'm still in love
   with you.

I'm the fruit in your oatmeal, I'm the swing
   on your tree
I'm your feeder, your cook and valet, you'd be
   lost without me.
I'm the man with your bottle, I'm your faithful
   old pa,
I'm your horsie, your mule, your punching bag,
   you'd be lost without moi.
Someday you'll meet guys who you'll
   romanticize

I can't say why, kid, but they won't do what I did
I'm the shoulder you burp on, I give you rides
   on my knee,
I'm your friend at three in the morning and
   you'd be lost without me.

Dakotas

Following Sunday's election in East Germany, reunification fever is spreading across the globe. Here
in the U.S. there's a movement afoot to reunify
North and South Dakota. Coming to us live now
with a late-breaking development in this story is
correspondent Mitchell Minot here at the border of
North and South Dakota. It's a jubilant scene—people are embracing, weeping, and leaping across the
deep ditch which formerly separated the two states.
They're drinking grape nectar and waving flags and
ringing cowbells and there's a bedsheet—somebody's written, "Not the worst that could happen.
Hey?" It's wild. The leader of the reunification
movement, Pierre Bismarck, says there never should
have been a North and South Dakota, but people
said if it was one state, it'd be too square, so they
divided it in two. Some people fear a United
Dakota, but exactly what this means remains to be
seen. Nobody could have predicted this. As for the
future, it's far too early to say. We'll keep you posted
on similar developments in West Virginia and
North and South Carolina.

Disgusting Things

Three episodes of "They Made Us Do It" in 1983
featured performers doing disgusting things requested by the audience. Stevie Beck ate a piece of
unwashed fruit, Peter Ostroushko played "The
Orange Blossom Special" and told an ethnic joke,
Pop Wagner said an unkind word, Hot Rize played
out of tune, and Greg Brown read aloud from a book
in poor taste. Butch Thompson objected to it all.

Deep Valley Bed

George Bridgman, a math professor at the University of Minnesota, Duluth, created Lake Wobegon math problems for his students from 1976 to 1979.

Lake Wobegon Math Problems

35.   Jack's Deep Valley Bed

The Mattress of a Jack's Deep Valley Bed is shaped with a cross section shown in the diagram. Find the area of this cross section, in square feet.

This area, multiplied by the length of the mattress in feet, equals the amount of stuffing, in cubic feet, needed to make the mattress.

The curve across the top of the cross section is the formula

$$Y = \frac{1}{3} X^2 + 1 \, ,$$ where $X = 0$, $Y = 0$ represents point 0 in the diagram.

Solution: (Calculus)   The cross sectional area of the mattress is found by calculating the definite integral

$$\int_{-3}^{3} \frac{1}{3} X^2 + 1 \, dX = \frac{X^3}{9} + X \Big]_{-3}^{3} = 6 - (-6) =$$

$= 12$ square feet of cross sectional area.

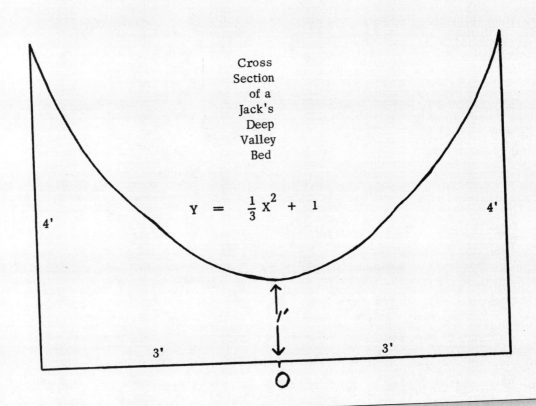

Cross Section of a Jack's Deep Valley Bed

$$Y = \frac{1}{3} X^2 + 1$$

4'

4'

3'

3'

O

Donohue

Pat Donohue, finger-pick guitarist, country blues
songwriter, and a Guy's All-Star Shoe. His songs are
featured almost every week on PHC, and as a Shoe
he backs up gospel, folk, pop, plays Lefty's guitar on
"Lives of the Cowboys," and rocks out on a
Stratocaster in the Love Shovels. Albums on the
Bluesky label include *Life Stories*, *Two Hand Band*,
Manhattan to Memphis, and *Backroads*.

"Would You Like to Play the Guitar?"
(to the tune of "Would You Like to Swing on a
Star?")

Would you like to play the guitar,
Take your money home in a jar
From a coffee house or a bar,
Or would you rather get a job?

A job is the thing that makes you get out of bed
And work every day until you're dead.
Your back is breakin', and your brain is numb,
And you just can't wait until the weekends come,
But if you don't want to starve or beg or rob,
You'll probably have to get a job.

Would you like to play the guitar,
Drive for miles and miles in your car,
And pretend that you're a big star,
Or would you rather book the gig.

The agent's the guy who gets his twenty percent.
What he said ain't exactly what he meant.
He'll clean you out in ways you never thought,
'Cause he's good at business, and he knows
  you're not.
And then he'll sue you if you finally make it big,
'Cause he's the guy who booked the gig.

Would you like to play the guitar,
For a living, hardy-har-har.
I admit it's kind of bizarre.
But would you rather be the wife?

The wife is the one who has to rescue our butts.
She's either a saint or else she's nuts.
She gets impatient, and she gets annoyed,
'Cause she's the one who must remain
  employed,
And by the way, if you want to wreck your life,
Become a guitar player's wife.

'Cause all the monkeys aren't in the zoo
They can be trained to play guitar too.
Some do a whole lot better than you,
But even if you don't go far,
You could be worse off than you are,
At least you're playing your guitar.

Drinks

Wendy's beer; Guy Noir's martini with a soybean; Guy's namesake drink at the Five-Spot: vodka and Slimfast: you don't lose weight, but you don't care. The Baptist martini: vodka and lemonade. For the cowboys, two kinds of whiskey: layin'-down whiskey and fallin'-down whiskey.

Duct Tape

Hi. Supermodel Cynthia Maxwell here, with a tip for women like me who must be devastatingly beautiful at all times or else die. Fashion changes, you know? Sometimes four or five times in the course of one evening. You work on a look, black lipstick, white eyeshadow, a look of blanched fragility and psycho-pathic angularity that is so *now*, so *here*, so *us*, and you go to the club and you're with your people and suddenly you get the feeling that that whole fragility look is over, so you run to the ladies' room and you've got fifteen seconds to do a total makeover, you don't want to give your people time to start talking about you and about how *over* that whole look is now—and that's why my choice for makeup removal

is duct tape. Press the strips of duct tape tight to your face and rip off the old look, and now you have the bruised waif look that's always in—pink hair, a stripe of lipstick down your nose, a white plastic fork in your ear—fantastic. Duct tape...it's almost just about the only thing you need sometimes. A message from the American Duct Tape Council.

Duct Tape 2

Geezer: I do pretty well here at the Home. Go down to breakfast every morning and there's a big piece of duct tape across the door, it says "Remember Your Cane," so that's good and then I take my medication and if I drop a pill, I just use a strip of duct tape to pick it up, and that's okay, and then over to the activity center and we make things, I'm making a billfold out of duct tape, it's pretty good, I got six of them, and then I take my nap and then I get up and have me an eye-opener. This is a Baptist Home so they don't allow that here, but I keep mine taped to the bedsprings with duct tape. So I have a snort and then it's time for supper and I'm usually in bed by ten-thirty. As I say, it's pretty good. What was I talking about?

Rich is never dysfunctional.

Dworsky

Richard Dworsky, music director of PHC, pianist, and the Big Boot in the Guy's All-Star Shoe Band. A gentle, soft-spoken man, a veteran freelancer, composer of children's musicals (including *The Marvelous Land of Oz*, shown on HBO and Showtime), recording artist with two solo CDs, enthusiastic Latin dancer, vegetarian, raconteur, and, on PHC, the complete musician: parodist of New Age, accompanist of anything from grand opera to hoedowns, arranger, and instant improviser of dramatic underscores. PHC scripts simply indicate (MUSIC) and Rich figures out something understated and appropriate; sometimes GK, having forgotten to indicate it on the script, turns and makes pianistic finger motions and Rich plays.

Dysfunctional

Perennial cellar dwellers in the New Soo League, pathetic victims of the Melrose Hubs, Freeport Flyers, Avon Bards, Holdingford Oxen, St. Wendell Bungstoppers, St. Rosa Rangers, and Albany Allgemeinschaft, riding around in an old yellow bus on dusty roads, getting their butts kicked Sunday after Sunday, smirked at by small-town teenagers who yell, "Hey, when's the baby due?" at Fred Schue and Milkman Poquette and Lyle Dickmeier, the beer belly boys, and cheer for Boots Merkel when he bobbles the easy grounder and heaves the ball over Fred Frauendienst's head and when Rudy Schrupps or Orv Schoppenhorst or Marv Mueffelman or Larry (The Looker) Lienemann, all-time league leader in called third strikes, go down on strikes and walk chopfallen to the dugout, shout cruelly in unison, "Left, right, left, right, left, right": the Lake Wobegon Whippets (who else?). Captained by first baseman (a.k.a. First Basement) Wayne (Warning Track) Tommerdahl, nicknamed for the long flies he hits for outs, and famous for his immobility—Wayne is late even when he is already there.

Economy

The factories where Minnesotans used to manufacture things have all been turned into malls full of specialty shops. You want a hardware store? They don't have any. For vacuum cleaner bags, you go to a theme shop called The Bag Lady. Vacuum bags, shopping bags, duffel bags, burlap bags. For a wood saw you try The Cutting Edge down next to Strings 'N' Things. For glue there's a shop called Get It Together. They carry every kind of adhesive. You head down there, turn left at Socks In A Box and go past Hangers Unlimited and Four Floors of Drawers—there's a Little Jack Horner Pie Shoppe there—don't turn there but look for the Y where Kangaroo Lane splits into Wallaby Lane and Koala Court. We all know what kind of mall that is—old factory buildings where honest workmen turned out well-made cars and appliances and railroad engines now are the home to shops specializing in designer children's clothing and restaurants where you pay $30 to get two lamb chops the size of an immature chickadee.

Ecstasy

It's a good piece of work for someone my age who feels as depressed as I do sometimes. I try to eat the right foods and get exercise and relax and enjoy my family, but sometimes I still feel crummy. I read articles on health hoping to find the answer—the secret that everyone else knows—a tiny gland just below your kneecap called the hermer, which produces a thin golden fluid that enables the brain to feel pleasure and if you would only quit the bad habit of crossing your legs your hermer would recover and life would become wonderful. So far all I read is stuff I already know, like drink plenty of liquids and get your rest. I need something more miraculous than that. I need the secret of happiness. What as a child I thought Christmas would give me and as a youth I thought that sex would give me, now as a man I am still looking for it. I used to think I'd find it in art but then found out that art is work, it's like auto repair except more professional.

I remember when I switched from Christmas to sex as the secret of happiness, when I saw a dirty magazine at Krebsbach's garage. Never mind that the most explicit photo in it is nowadays the sort of thing you might see in newspaper advertisements, back then it excited me to the very core of my being. Now I knew which part of my being that was and I began to enjoy a fabulous rich imaginative life that eventually settled on a lovely person. I remember how those thoughts of her used to keep me awake. After years of thinking them, after courting her and getting engaged to her and the date of our marriage was fast approaching when I would cross over the river into the land of bliss, the excitement was almost unbearable.

Nowadays young people cross over into the land of bliss pretty much whenever they want to. There are bridges, there are islands in the river, some places you can jump across, some years the water is low and there are sandbars, getting over and back is no problem, but back then where I come from, the river was wide and deep and fast and the church owned all the boats. The church ferried you across to the land of bliss and you stayed there.

Three days before she and I were to walk up the aisle and into a motel room, I went for a long walk around the lake, from Ralph's out past the grain elevators and around by Hansen's, thinking the bitter cold would take my mind off carnal thoughts, but cold is an aphrodisiac, as we all know. I rehearsed in my mind exactly how I would go about making love to her, changing some details, tossing in a couple of improvements, and halfway around the lake I began to practice ecstatic cries.

I'd never made love before and so had never cried out in an ecstatic way, except maybe when I got a Lionel train when I was eight, but somehow that cry ("Oh boy, Mom and Dad") didn't seem appropriate during sex, and I wanted to do everything right. I stood on the shore, looking across the ice toward our little hometown, rehearsing outbursts of sexual passion—loud ones like Tarzan, soft sighs, grunts and some growling. I tried yipping and wahooing, I even tried something like yodeling— and then it suddenly occurred to me: what if sex for her and me turned out to be not this exciting, not the sort of thing that you'd yip or wahoo about, but something that during it you'd just say, "Are you having a good time?" or "As long as I'm up, can I get you anything?" It also occurred to me that a guy practicing ecstatic cries is probably so repressed and inhibited that perhaps he will have tragic problems as a lover that years and years of high-priced psychiatry cannot solve. I walked the rest of the way home full of trepidations and went over to see my true love and her parents weren't home and one thing led to another and we slipped across to the promised land and we both made some sounds. When we faced Pastor Tommerdahl at the altar I was pretty sure he knew what I'd done and maybe my parents and my Scoutmaster and I would have felt guilty except for the fact I was so happy to be marrying someone so wonderful, so funny and smart and so sexy.

Eephing

Pronounced with a long "e," eephing is one of the forms of mouth music performed in the third and fourth Mouth-Offs. Mouth-Offs occurred in January 1976, September 1976, January 1979, and November 1981. Contestants played the jaw harp, the jug, whistled, made loon calls and sound effects, droned, eephed, lilted, dolted, gargled, chortled, tapped their teeth, and slapped their cheeks. Other contests on PHC included a Love Song Contest; the New Birthday Song Contest for songwriters, won by Randall Davidson; the New Christmas Carol Contest, won in December 1989 by fourteen-year-old Carrie Mallonee of Baltimore with "The Carolers at My Door," a fine work performed many times since on the show. (She grew up and went off to study music at Harvard.) There was the New York Subway Musicians Contest, for which the prize was a trip to St. Paul in January, and money collected from the audience. And there was the three-round Pianists Show-Off when Butch Thompson, Rich Dworsky, and Julia and Irina Elkina played (1) music to get a date, (2) the most music with the fewest notes, and (3) music to impress their mothers. There was an Evil Laugh Contest, too.

Elegance

I grew up on the frozen plains of Minnesota, where my family lived in a sod hut with our animals. The animals ate with us and slept with us, and then we sold them to rich people. When I looked in a client's window and saw the chandeliers and crystal and candles and people eating poached fish and jasmine rice and arugula and not on hubcaps but on china plates, I promised myself someday I would be like them. Elegant. It was sure better than living in a dim squalid dirt hut with livestock and people whanging you on the head with farm implements.

I borrowed books about elegance from the library and learned that it is the art of proportion. But low-down crude talk ("Boy, the dog threw up on my shoe, I about barfed in the Jell-O") is not so far away from high-class talk ("I threw my shoe up in the air for the dog, and my scarf got caught in my cello"). Often the difference is slight. "Boy, talk

Mary Hartnett "cheek-thumping" at the PHC Mouth-Off, January 23, 1976.

about your plumbing problems, we had a toilet overflowed, it stank to high heaven, I about lost my lunch" can easily become "The plum blossoms are so fragrant, like toilet water, they smell heavenly, let's have lunch."

Elvis

I remember, '54, I was in Memphis. Hanging around Sun Studios. Had my band there, Scotty and Bill, and we were going over that line, "Treat me like a fool," me and El did it as a duet. Elvis. I called him El. We grew up together. You didn't know that? Yeah, we learned guitar together, listened to the same records, even combed our hair the same way. A lot of people thought we were twins. In fact, Elvis

did have a twin, a brother, born in the same hospital I was born in. Same exact day, even. Anyway, El was as close to me as a person could be. Seemed to know what I was thinking. Finished my sentences for me. He was the one who told Sun Records about me. He was going to sing backup at that session. And then I went to brush my teeth, which I always did before singing, and reached for the toothpaste and it was shampoo. Prell. I spat it out but there was, like, this film on my teeth and when I sang, bubbles came out. I turned to Elvis, I said, "Hey, man, you know this song." So he sang it. I moved to Minnesota a few weeks later. No regrets. It's hard being on top and trying to stay on top. I never had that problem, I must say, and I'm grateful.

Editing

During the Friday script rehearsals, GK rewrites his scripts. Note his changes penned onto the script the actors have been reading, that the script is for the February 20, 1999, show, that this is the first of eleven pages, and that the sketch plays for ten minutes and thirty-five seconds.

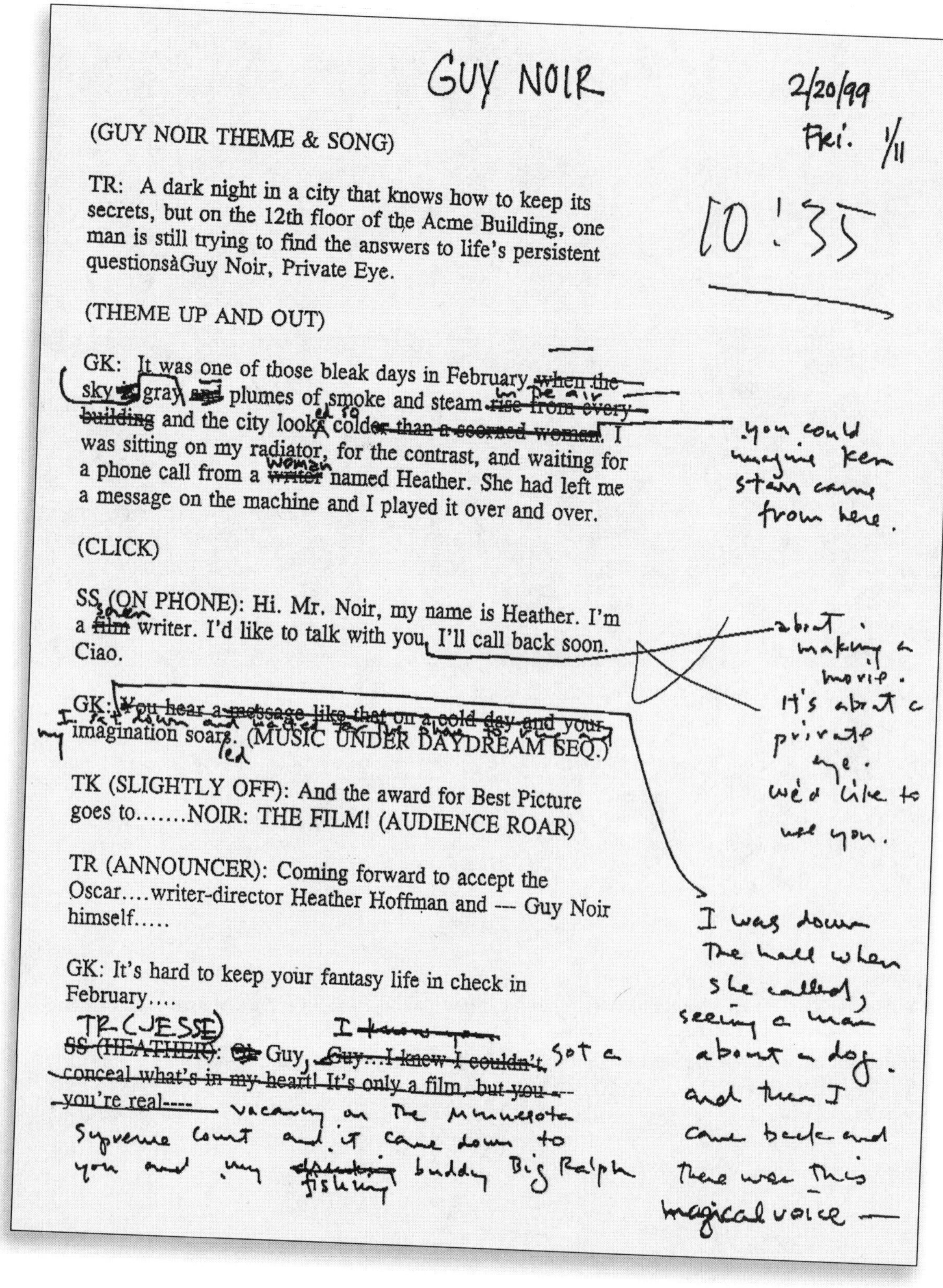

GUY NOIR

2/20/99

Fri. 1/11

10:35

(GUY NOIR THEME & SONG)

TR: A dark night in a city that knows how to keep its secrets, but on the 12th floor of the Acme Building, one man is still trying to find the answers to life's persistent questionsàGuy Noir, Private Eye.

(THEME UP AND OUT)

GK: It was one of those bleak days in February ~~when the~~ sky ~~is~~ gray, ~~and~~ plumes of smoke and steam ~~rise from every building~~ in the air and the city looks colder ~~than a scorned woman~~. I was sitting on my radiator, for the contrast, and waiting for a phone call from a ~~writer~~ woman named Heather. She had left me a message on the machine and I played it over and over.

you could imagine Ken Starr came from here.

(CLICK)

SS (ON PHONE): Hi. Mr. Noir, my name is Heather. I'm a ~~film~~ screen writer. I'd like to talk with you about making a movie. It's about a private eye. We'd like to use you. I'll call back soon. Ciao.

GK: ~~You hear a message like that on a cold day and your~~ I sat down and waited for her to call and my imagination soared. (MUSIC UNDER DAYDREAM SEQ.)

I was down the hall when she called, seeing a man about a dog. And then I came back and there was this magical voice —

TK (SLIGHTLY OFF): And the award for Best Picture goes to.......NOIR: THE FILM! (AUDIENCE ROAR)

TR (ANNOUNCER): Coming forward to accept the Oscar....writer-director Heather Hoffman and --- Guy Noir himself.....

GK: It's hard to keep your fantasy life in check in February....

~~SS (HEATHER)~~ TR (JESSE): ~~Oh~~ Guy, ~~Guy...I knew I couldn't conceal what's in my heart! It's only a film, but you --- you're real----~~ I got a vacancy on the Minnesota Supreme Court and it came down to you and my ~~drinking~~ fishing buddy Big Ralph

GK with Bill Kling in the MPR studios, 1978.

Enchilada

The big one, so far as PHC is concerned, is William H. Kling, president of Minnesota Public Radio ever since it began at St. John's University in 1967. Two years after that, he hired a bearded GK as a morning announcer. "It was my last job interview, knock on wood. Terrifying. To sit on a couch and try to impress a very cool guy in a dark suit who was my same age. And probably still is. In 1974, having written about the Grand Ole Opry for *The New Yorker*, I came into Kling's office and said I wanted to do a show like the Opry for MPR. He said, 'Fine. When?' He was the coolest management guy I ever met. He made decisions quickly, did all the backstairs stuff like raising money, and he listened to everything I did and would drop a comment every so often to let me know he was there. And he's a real entrepreneur, a rare animal in public broadcasting, which has its roots in academia, which is notorious for negativity. I'm a gloomy academic. Bill is a builder. He was a mover and shaker behind the satellite uplink system of 1980 that made it possible for people outside Washington and New York to produce shows, PHC and also *Fresh Air* and *This American Life* and *Car Talk* and *Marketplace* and all the stuff that comes from the hinterlands. A very quiet guy who revolutionized radio and a terrific hands-off manager. I once got up at an MPR party and gave a big speech about what a great manager he was and he looked as if someone were shoving hot needles under his fingernails. A real midwesterner."

English

The story of English is a story of success.
A thousand years ago, who would've guessed
This obscure unpronounceable Germanic
   tongue
Would someday become No. 1.
Almost a billion people in the world today
Turn to English when they have something
   to say.
Oh, some of them speak another language,
   I know.
Like some nights you might get Chinese to go,
And there are languages that more
   people use,
Certainly, but we should not confuse
Quantity with quality. English
Is magnificent, distinguished
By richness and grace,
Both elegant and commonplace,
Both lyrical and humorous,
And very precise thanks to its numerous
Vocabulary, the official tongue of sea and air
Spoken almost everywhere,
The language that I speak to you,
Mon cher, in every rendezvous.

Evil

Sponsored by the American Council of Remorse, a nonprofit organization working for a greater sense of contrition, four sketches in May and June 1990 with the Broadway Local Theater Company dramatized the hidden history of evil. In "Adam and Eve" the snake tells Eve that he had been a friend of Adam's old girlfriend, Janet, and then gives Eve an apple to make her feel better. In "Sodom and Gomorrah," Lot's wife becomes a pillar of salt when she turns back to see where Lot dropped his keys. Noah, in "The Flood," gets heckled for building his ark in the middle of 640 acres of winter wheat in North Dakota, with no water for miles around. In "The Prodigal Son," Wally returns with the five foolish virgins from his debaucheries and his elder brother Wayne complains, "Ever stop to think who fatted that calf, Wally? That was our best calf, Dad, the best one."

Facts and Figures

There have been 941 live performances of the show and 864 live broadcasts as of July 1999.

Close to one million people have attended Prairie Home Companion.

Three thousand feet of microphone cable are on the stage during each performance in St. Paul.

Ten thousand feet of tape were used per show when the show was broadcast and recorded analog.

Technical staff use over 7,200 feet of gaff tape (cloth cousin to duct tape) per season.

In its twenty-five years, PHC has used over thirteen million feet of quarter-inch recording tape, which is 2,470 miles, almost enough to reach from New York City to Seattle.

PHC has broadcast over 2,600 hours of programming in twenty-five years.

When the World Theater was renovated in 1985, over twenty-eight miles of new audio wiring circuits were installed.

In the last twenty-five years, the truck has traveled over 230,000 miles; show personnel have flown or driven over 385,000 miles.

PHC has toured to forty-four states, all except Arkansas, Delaware, Kansas, Maryland, New Hampshire, and West Virginia.

Minnesota Public Radio started sending analog recordings of the show on reel-to-reel tapes to Australia and Sweden in 1985, and sent digital audio tapes to Taiwan in 1990. Since 1996 the show goes direct to the satellite for broadcast worldwide. The show also goes out on Armed Forces Radio. Listeners write back from many countries, including Japan, Israel, England, Germany, Switzerland, and France.

As of July 1999, the first PHC signal uplinked to the satellite has traveled 146.6 trillion miles into outer space, a long way from Lake Wobegon.

About eight hundred entries each year come in for the "Talent from Towns Under Two Thousand" (TUTT) shows.

In 1999, listeners sent over five thousand submissions for the annual Joke show.

PHC audio was delivered live over the Internet for the first time on October 5, 1996.

In one week in April 1999, computer users clicked 256,645 times looking at the pages in the Prairie Home website <http://prairiehome.org>.

Families

Musical talent frequently runs in families. Families who have performed on the show include Edwin and Bruce Johnson and Paul Dahlin, three generations of Swedish fiddlers; the Everly Brothers; Ricky Skaggs with his parents, Hobert and Dorothy; Sally Dworsky with her brother Richard; and the Cox Family from Cotton Valley LA, with dad Willard on fiddle, sisters Evelyn on guitar and Suzanne on mandolin, son Sidney on dobro, and Dennis Sunderman on bass. Families have also appeared on the talent contests, including the Griffin family, son Buddy, daughter Pam Chapman, father Richard, and mother Erma, from Flatwoods VA, and the accordion-playing Emter family from Glen Ullin ND.

GK with Griffin family from the second TUTT contest, 1996. Ricky Skaggs with parents, Hobert and Dorothy, April 1987.

Famous Celebrities

In "Famous Celebrities, a look at the private lives of the illustrious, sponsored by AmRan, makers of NarCon," Tim Russell played Bob Dole, Bill Clinton, George Bush, Julia Child, Mr. Rogers, Henry Kissinger, Ted Koppel, Tom Brokaw, Luciano Pavarotti, and Jack Nicholson. GK asked questions such as what disguises they would wear on Halloween, or what they would have for Thanksgiving dinner, or what they wanted for Christmas. For Halloween, George Bush was "thinking choices, really. That whole fairy thing, the hobo thing, and so forth. And your cowboy of course. Texas. Boots, hat." For Christmas, Jack Nicholson wanted the names of the naughty girls on Santa's list. Bill Clinton wanted peace in the world and greater understanding between peoples and a greater sense of cooperation in Washington, but thought he might get a little dog that would come running in, be happy to see him, and love him no matter what.

Asked about Mother's Day, he said: "Well, I just think that mothers are so important. And I think that of all the things this Administration has accomplished, the things I'm most proud of were things we did for mothers. On the other hand, fathers are important too, and so are cousins. The President's Advisory Commission on Cousins is looking at some proposals right now."

Bob Dole spoke in short flat sentences and Ross Perot in folksy non sequiturs ("Now that's what I call pulling out the driveway after the trailer's been unhitched. Or passing the peas after the table's been cleared") and Henry Kissinger declined to speculate and insisted his refusal be off the record. Ted Koppel spoke in endlessly modified sentences ("Let me tell you frankly—and I say this not only as a journalist but also as a man who has, on occasion, stuffed a turkey or two—that Thanksgiving, for me, and perhaps for people like me, as well as others, including those who feel that this is a self-serving comment, and to them I would say 'If it is, so be it,' is a holiday when, in a sense, if one can refer to sense in this context, and I believe that I just did, we—or at least many of us—those of us who do, and I have—and now I seem to have forgotten the question").

Mr. Rogers had a gentle but spooky voice reminiscent of Peter Lorre. "My mother? She lived in a big pink apartment building in Las Vegas. Yes, she did. Mother went to work as a blackjack dealer every night at ten and came home at seven in the morning. And that's how Mr. Rogers started to talk like this. Because he had to be very quiet while Mother got her rest. Yes, he did. But sometimes Mr. Rogers would go and move Mother's hands while she was sleeping. Yes, I did. And I'd move her lips and make her say, 'I like you just the way you are. I like you even more the way you are than I like Dad the way he is.'"

Fear

The Fearmonger's Shoppe (serving all of your phobia needs) pays particular attention to the danger of poisonous snakes. Snakes like to come indoors at night to get warm and thanks to their flexible skeletons can squeeze through an opening just big enough for a pipe cleaner. Many people have reached for what they thought was a belt or sat down on what looked like a lovely pillow and gotten bit in the butt (where do you put the tourniquet?). Some safety tips:

1. Always step back as you open a closet door.

2. Before using a toilet, check for ripples in the water. They may indicate the presence of a water moccasin. Flush.

3. Always shake a drawer before opening.

4. Never leave cupboard doors open.

5. Before entering a room that has been unoccupied for more than half an hour, lob a shoe in.

6. Before climbing into bed, look for odd wrinkles or bulges. Whack the bed with a baseball bat carefully from head to foot, leaving no area unwhacked. Then ease bedcovers back slowly.

Follow those rules, and nine times out of ten, you'll have no problem with poisonous snakes whatsoever.

Fisher

Rob Fisher. Musical director of PHC in its New York incarnation and founder of the Coffee Club Orchestra, PHC's sixteen-piece house band (an eight-piece reduction was called the Demitasse Orchestra). From PHC he became musical director of the Encores series at NY's City Center, producing concert versions of classic Broadway musicals such as *Chicago*, the Encores revival of which went to Broadway, with Rob as m.d. and the C.C.O. in the onstage bandstand, ran forever, and earned Walter Bobbie (Pete on the early Guy Noir episodes) a Tony for Best Director. Rob has returned to PHC since as solo pianist, interpreter of Gershwin and Zez Confrey, once in his native Norfolk.

Fisher's Coffee

If you suffer from inattention, chances are you're not getting enough coffee.

Barbara: Al?
Al: Hmm?
Barbara: Al—this is me. I'm your wife. Barbara. Remember? The wedding? 1983? I was the one in the white dress, Al. You spoke to me afterward. Remember?
Al: Mmmhmm.
Barbara: Al, if you don't speak to me in words in ten seconds, I'm going to hit you over the head with this valuable lamp. Do you hear?
Al: Mmhmm.
(BIG CRASH)
Barbara: That was a lamp, Al. I hit you over the head with it
Al: Mmhmm.
Barbara: Now I'm going to hit you over the head with this coffee thermos, Al. This is really going to hurt.
Al: Coffee...*Coffee.*
Barbara: Yes. You care for—a cup of coffee?
Al: Yes.
Barbara: Oh, Al. You spoke. You said words, Al. Oh, Al. I've been so worried. You came home from the office and you picked up that magazine and now it's Wednesday.
Al: Mmmmm. Great coffee, Martha.
Barbara: Barbara. But never mind. It's just good to have you back. Talking and drinking coffee. Just like it used to be.
GK: Fisher's Coffee...if someone you love isn't listening, don't yell...give 'em a cup of Fisher's. That'll bring them around.

Fitzgerald Theater

Formerly the World Theater, and before that, the Shubert, the Fitzgerald was renamed in September 1994, in honor of F. Scott Fitzgerald, born in St. Paul on September 24, 1896. A parade wound down the hill from Summit Avenue, led by the University of Minnesota marching band, with FSF's granddaughters and great-grandchildren riding in an open car and Senator Eugene McCarthy and novelist J. F. Powers in another. After speeches, the building was christened with buckets of Mississippi River water. The night before, a series of readers had given a five-hour reading of *The Great Gatsby* in the theater. As a boy, FSF came downtown to the theaters along Wabasha Avenue to enjoy the Saturday matinees and may have attended this one. A bust of him by sculptor Michael Price sits on a ledge in the lobby, looking over the audience as they arrive.

The Finn Who Would Not Take a Sauna

In northeast Minnesota, what they call the Iron Range,
Where a woman is a woman and some things never change,
Where winter lasts nine months a year, there is no spring or fall,
Where it gets so cold the mercury cannot be seen at all
And you and I, we normal folk, would shiver, shake, and chatter,
And if we used an outhouse, we would grow an extra bladder;
But even when it's coldest, when our feet would have no feeling,
Those Iron Rangers get dressed up and go out snowmobiling
Out across the frozen land and make a couple stops
At Gino's Lounge and Rudy's Bar for whiskey, beer, and schnapps—
And then they go into a shack that's filled with boiling rocks
Hot enough to sterilize an Iron Ranger's socks
And sit there till they steam out every sin and every foible
And then jump into a frozen lake and claim that it's enjoible—
But there was one, a shy young man, and although he was Finnish,
The joys of winter had, for him, long started to diminish.
He was a Finn, the only Finn, who would not take a sauna.
"It isn't that I can't," he said. "I simply do not wanna.
To jump into a frozen lake is not my fondest wish.
For just because I am a Finn don't mean that I'm a fish."
His friends said, "Come on, Toivo! Let's go out to Sunfish Lake!
A Finn who don't take saunas? Why, there must be some mistake."
But Toivo said, "There's no mistake. I know that I would freeze
In water colder than myself (98.6°)."
And so he stayed close by a stove for nine months of the year
Because he was so sensitive to change of temperature.

One night he went to Eveleth to attend the Miner's Ball.
(If you have not danced in Eveleth, you've never danced at all.)
He met a Finnish beauty there who turned his head around.
She was broad of beam and when she danced she shook the frozen ground.
She took that shy young man in hand and swept him off his feet
And bounced him up and down until he learned the polka beat.
She was fair as she was tall, as tall as she was wide,
And when the dance was over, he asked her to be his bride.
She looked him over carefully. She said, "You're kinda thin.
But you must have some courage if it's true you are a Finn.
I ain't particular about men. I am no prima donna.
But I would never marry one who would not take a sauna."

They got into her pickup, and down the road they drove,
And fifteen minutes later they were stoking up the stove.
She had a flask of whiskey. They took a couple toots
And went into the shack and got into their birthday suits.
She steamed him and she boiled him until his skin turned red;
She poured it on until his brains were bubbling in his head.
To improve his circulation and to soften up his hide,
She took a couple birch boughs and beat him till he cried,
"Oh, couldn't you just love me now? Oh, don't you think you can?"
She said, "It's time to step outside and show you are a man."

Straightway (because he loved her so, he thought his heart would break)
He jumped right up and out the door and ran down to the lake,
And though he paused a moment when he saw the lake was frozen
And tried to think just which snowbank his love had put his clothes in—
When he thought of Tina, Lord—that man did not think twice
But just picked up his size-12 feet and loped across the ice—
And coming to the hole that they had cut there with an ax—
Putting common sense aside, ignoring all the facts—
He leaped! Oh, what a leap! And as he dove beneath the surface,
It thrilled him to his very soul!—and also made him nervous!
And it wasn't just the tingling he felt in every limb—
He cried: "My love! I'm finished! I forgot! I cannot swim!"

She fished him out and stood him up and gave him an embrace
To warm a Viking's heart and make the blood rush to his face.
"I love you, darling dear!" she cried. "I love you with all my might!"
And she drove him to Biwabik and married him that night
And took him down the road to Carl's Tourist Cabins
And spent a sleepless night and in the morning, as it happens,
Though it was only April, it was absolutely spring,
Birds, flowers, people put away their parkas and everything.
They bought a couple acres around Hibbing, up near Chisholm,
And began a life of gardening and love and Lutheranism.
And they lived happily to this day, although they sometimes quarrel.
And there, I guess, the story ends, except for this, the moral.
Marriage, friends, is a lifelong feast, love is no light lunch.
You cannot dabble round the edge, but each must take the plunch.
And though marriage, like that frozen lake, may sometimes make us colder,
It has its pleasures, too, as you may find out when you're older.

Flies

GK: The studio where I write is a big room with high windows, very quiet, and some days I write quite a bit, and other days I only write seven words, such as, "The tall man got up and left." When you sit in a quiet room so long, concentrating, you begin to hear everything in the room—floors creak, dust falling, flies dying in the windows.

Floyd: I feel so listless—like I just want to sleep and sleep and sleep. Maybe it's the flu.

Flo: Flies don't get flu, dear.

Floyd: I have no appetite. No interest in breeding whatsoever.

Flo: I know.

Floyd: Maybe we need fresh air.

Flo: It's too cold. We'd die.

Floyd: Do you think we're *dying*?

Flo: No, no, no—

Floyd: I sure hope not. I've got a busy schedule all of November and December. (HE FLIES AGAINST THE GLASS) Why can't I get out of here?

Flo: That's glass, Floyd. Glass is transparent. You can't fly through it.

Floyd: How do you know all that?

Flo: I was crawling across an encyclopedia once and I read about it. Save your strength.

Floyd: I'd rather die trying to escape! (HE FLIES AGAINST GLASS)

Flo: Floyd! Look! He's getting up—he's coming this way.

Floyd: We've got to flee!

Flo: He's got a rolled-up newspaper. This is it, Floyd.

Floyd: I love you, Flo.

Flo: They were good months, Floyd. Both of them. The best.

Floyd: One last try. (HE FLIES AGAINST GLASS) If only I were strong enough to break the glass!

Flo: If you were strong enough to break the glass, we never would've been able to mate, Floyd.

Floyd: Here he is!

Flo: Goodbye, Floyd. One last kiss—oh, that thrills me when you touch my thorax like that!

Floyd: Goodbye, Flo.

Flo: Goodbye. So go ahead and kill us, God! What are you waiting for? Kill us. Put us out of our misery. We're just a couple of flies. What do you care? Huh? You don't care. You'd be glad to see us both dead. So why don't you do it? You've been murdering us flies all summer, left and right. So what's two more? You don't care.

GK: I do care, I just don't care for you.

Flo: Well, I think you're the lousiest God I ever saw in my life. You put us here in this beautiful world and just when life starts to get good, you kill us. I hate you.

GK: But I'm not God.

Flo: You're not? Oh, my God! Floyd, listen to this. What do you mean, you're not God? Is this a joke?

GK: I am not God. Someone else is.

Flo: Oh, boy—oh, boy—We busted our tails worshiping you.

GK: You worshiped me?

Flo: All those times we landed on you and walked up your face? You didn't know that was worship? And we brought up four hundred children believing in you—every one of them confirmed—except the one you swallowed. So, if you're not God—if you're not God then what gives you the right to kill us?

GK: You're a pest.

Flo: Oh, my. A pest! Listen to him, Floyd.

GK: You spread germs.

Flo: Oh, listen to him. "You spread germs." Boy, look who's talking. You spread such filth, such poisons, your car, your house—don't tell me about *germs*—flies are saints compared to you!

GK: I'm sorry you're so bitter.

Flo: It's a terrible thing to lose your religious faith at the end of your life—to die without that sense of consolation.

GK: Have you heard of Christianity?

Flo: I crawled across a Bible once. I didn't get much out of it.

GK: Maybe it was turned to the wrong page.

Flo: It was in the book of Revelations.

GK: Yeah, that isn't a good place to begin.

Flo: I feel so confused. I have no idea why I'm here or anything.

GK: We're here because we're meant to be here. We're meant to live and to be aware of life. That's the meaning of life, to know that you're alive.

Flo: You're not a great philosopher, are you?

GK: No. I do a radio show.

Flo: I thought so.

The Friday night read-through of scripts, after which GK goes home and rewrites, sometimes entirely. "There has to be a first draft before there can be a second or third. And you have to hear the words out loud to get a clear idea of what to cut."

GK: I think your husband is dead, ma'am.

Floyd: Nope. Not dead, just resting up for the next big push.

GK: If you want to go out, I can open the window for you, sir.

Floyd: No thanks. I prefer to do it my way.

GK: Okay. Ma'am, you want me to take you outside?

Flo: No, I'll stay here with Floyd.

GK: Okay. Anything I can bring you?

Floyd: If you'd spill some more of that Chianti, that'd be great.

GK: Okay. Anything for you, ma'am?

Flo: I'd like a last book to read.

GK: Okay. What?

Flo: I started reading that book, *The Bridges of Madison County.*

GK: But that's garbage—

Flo: So? I'm a fly.

GK: I can't believe that even a fly would go for that.

Flo: It's a short book. I'm not going to live long enough to read *Lord of the Flies.*

GK: Listen, honey, you're not going to live long enough to read anything. (SLAM)

Floyd: Why'd you kill Flo?

GK: I suddenly didn't like her anymore. Even for a fly, she seemed shallow.

Floyd: She's dead. And I'm so tired, I can't even cry.

GK: You want to join her?

Floyd: Yes.

GK: Okay. (SLAM)

GK: (SLOW TYPING) "They were gone. Gone forever. The room was still. Leaves fell from the trees outside, and a sharp chill in the air announced the coming of winter. The sky was gray. The tall man stood up and left."

Flood

Mrs. Deeanna Brower of Grafton ND was interviewed by telephone during the Red River flood. She spoke over a cellular phone, the phone lines having snapped when her home floated away. She was in the upstairs bedroom and her husband, Arlen, was about a quarter mile behind her, floating in the barn. She was burning her dining room table for heat. The Holsteins were with her ("We have a lot of extra room now with the children grown up and moved away") and she was feeding them spinach linguini. And meat loaf ("I told 'em it's soybeans, so they're okay with it"). She was miffed at Arlen because she saw another woman with him in the barn.

GK: Are you sure?
Mrs. Brower: They're up in the copula together.
GK: You mean the cupola.
Mrs. Brower: What did I say?
GK: Never mind. Where'd this woman come from? You're adrift in the middle of the river.
Mrs. Brower: Well, I can't wait to ask Arlen that very question.

Nonetheless, she was in good spirits. "The house rides real well in the water, so I'm sleeping okay, and I've been keeping busy getting my spice rack organized and going through recipes. I'm doing fine. Starting to miss my TV shows, but it's okay. And if we float into the Atlantic and catch the Gulf Stream, I think we might go all the way to Norway. We've been talking about going for years, so maybe this is our chance. You got to look on the bright side."

Flu

A lot of people have gotten sick in Lake Wobegon, and it might be due to the weather. So many of these people are from Norway, a seafaring country. If you're Norwegian, you're happier and you operate best if you're cold, wet, and sick to your stomach. Misery keeps a Norwegian going. In warm sunny weather they get sick and go to pieces with a case of Swedish flu caused by weakness on account of a lack of suffering. Swedish flu is like Asian flu, but in addition, you feel like it's your fault.

Folksong, Dept. of

"The Dept. of Folksong" ran on PHC for forty-five editions between August 1983 and January 1987. Listeners were asked to send in songs "you have heard from someone else" and "to which you remember the words mostly." Each week, GK and his guests would select several songs to perform. The first week Greg Brown, the "chairman," sang "Ain't We Crazy." Eighteen hundred listeners sent songs in letters, sheet music, and on tapes. Songs tended heavily toward parodies ("I'm Looking Over My Dead Dog Rover"), summer camp or school chestnuts ("Greasy Grimy Gopher Guts"), and school children's naively anti-authoritarian "folklore" of rebellion. A collection of three hundred listener submissions was published in 1988 as *A Prairie Home Companion Folk Song Book*.

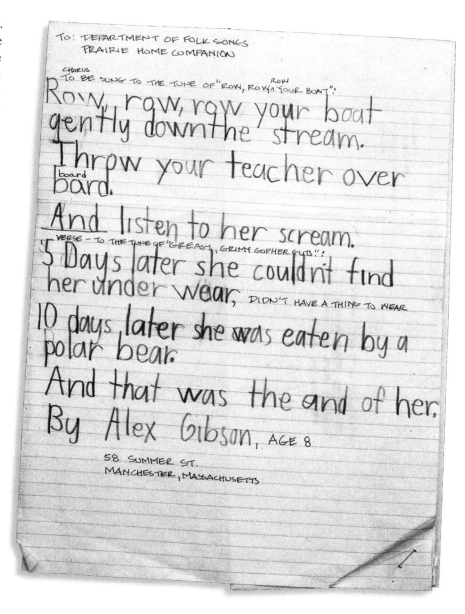

TO: DEPARTMENT OF FOLK SONGS
PRAIRIE HOME COMPANION

CHORUS
TO BE SUNG TO THE TUNE OF "ROW, ROW, ROW YOUR BOAT":
Row, row, row your boat
gently down the stream.
Throw your teacher over
bard. (board)

And listen to her scream.
VERSE — TO THE TUNE OF "GREASY, GRIMY GOPHER GUTS":
5 Days later she couldn't find
her underwear, DIDN'T HAVE A THING TO WEAR
10 days later she was eaten by a
polar bear.
And that was the and of her,
By Alex Gibson, AGE 8
58 SUMMER ST.
MANCHESTER, MASSACHUSETTS

Fred Farrell

Fred Farrell Animal Calls ("the name to trust when it comes to animal calls") manufactured calls that kept cats off your lap, repelled rodents, attracted fish, and taught the Five Pillars of Clear Communication (Snapping, Snorting, Snarling, Barking, and Bellowing). Also Telepets, for busy people. And deer calls to drive deer away, that said (in deer talk), "There are forest rangers shooting hypodermic needles into deer's butts and they sure won't have any trouble hitting yours, wide ride. You hang around here, you're going to wake up with a radio transmitter in your armpit."

For each animal call you ordered, you got, free, a ten-in-one set of Fred Farrell Animal Calls, e.g., moose, mouse, mollusk, mosquito, merganser, muskrat, muskie, musk ox, water moccasin, mastodon. Or tree toad, timber wolf, wood duck, snow goose, prairie dog, mountain goat, water spaniel, water buffalo, polar bear, and sea lion. Or the twelve-in-one: lizard, leopard, Lipizzaner, lamprey, lamb, llama, lemur, lemming, Labrador, longhorn, leghorn, and loon.

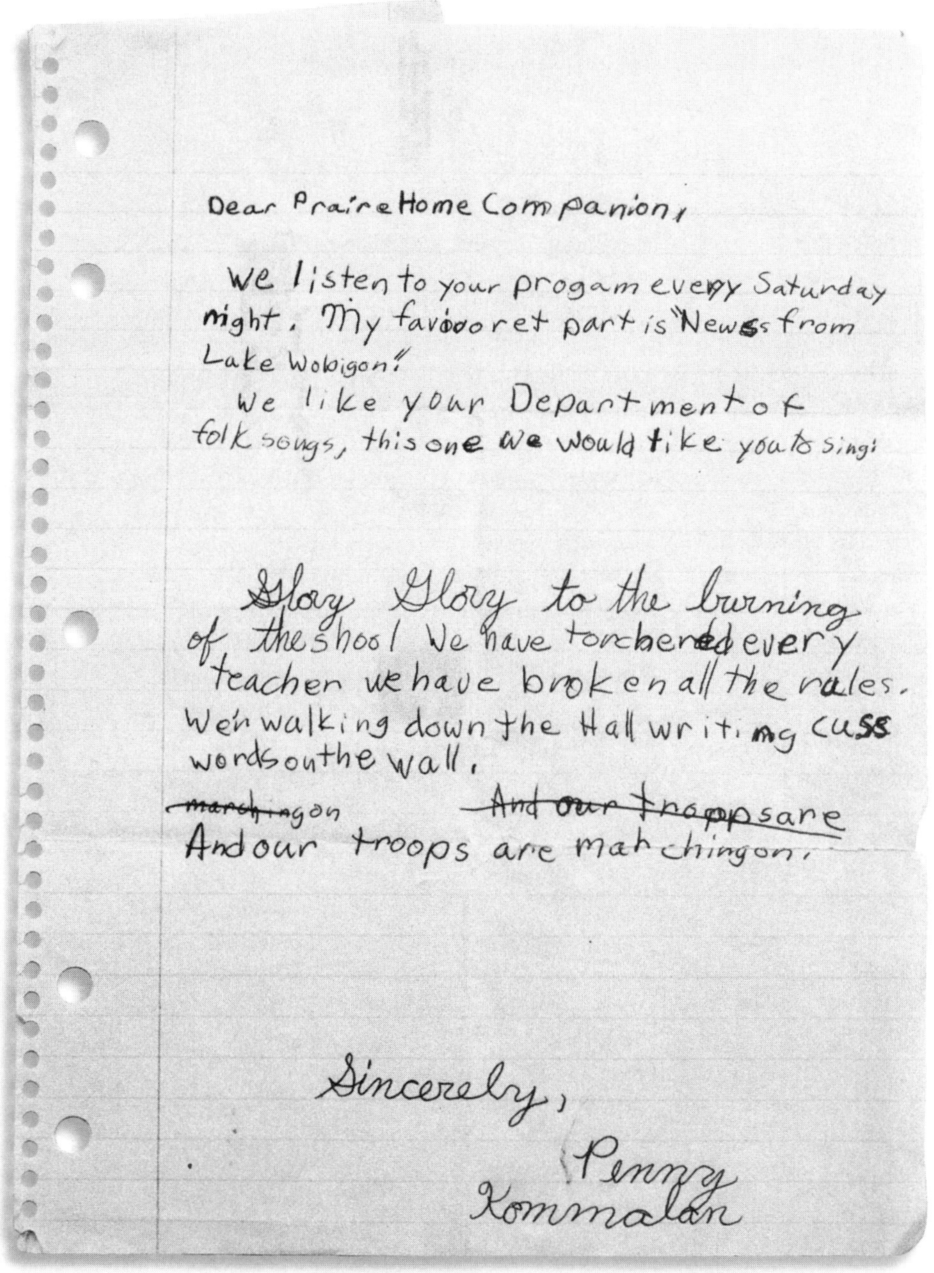

Fritz Electronics

Child Tracking System

Minitransmitters clip to children's collars, emit constant signal via mitten-string antenna for pickup by home tracking station. Bright blips give accurate fix on tiny tots' location, velocity, direction, up to six blocks away. Four transmitters included. For additional children, simply wire in pairs. Easy to use. No license required.

"Everything you need is on the Fritz."

Dear Prairie Home Companion,

We listen to your progam every Saturday night. My favooret part is "News from Lake Wobigon."
We like your Department of folk songs, this one we would like you to sing:

Glory Glory to the burning of the shool We have torchered every teacher we have broken all the rules. We'r walking down the Hall writing cuss words on the wall.
And our troops are marching on.

Sincerely,
Penny Kommalan

Garbage

The Town Council met on Tuesday to discuss the dogs who've been getting into people's garbage.

They decided they would issue warnings to the owners, which didn't satisfy the people whose garbage had been got into. They figured it would do about as much good to warn the dogs. They wanted stern measures. But Lake Wobegon isn't ready for stern measures against dogs who run free. People who own dogs there don't chain them up—you don't buy a dog and treat him like property—you buy a dog and that dog runs off and joins a fraternal lodge of other dogs and runs with them, and hangs out with them and now and then as a part of initiation, this dog has to go dig out somebody's garbage and spread it around. It's part of being a dog.

Of course, you can see how the people with garbage look at it. When you find your garbage spread out in the backyard and down the alley, it's not only a nuisance, it's an embarrassment. Garbage is stuff you don't care for the neighbors to see. In this sense, a dog is something of a journalist. It's a revelation.

Gear

PHC travels with a substantial amount of equipment required for the live broadcasts that is not always available where the show travels, including: sound-effects props for Tom Keith; microphones, stands, and cables; forty-eight-channel microphone splitter to split the stage microphones to broadcast mix and house sound mix; fifty-six-channel broadcast mixing console; five digital effects generators; two Codecs for transmitting the program on ISDN digital lines; stage monitor system of ten speakers with amplifiers and graphic equalizers for performers; supplemental sound reinforcement speakers and amplifiers; two-hundred-amp power distribution system; music stands with lights and rugs for the stage; Hammond B3 organ with Leslie rotating speaker; Yamaha DX7 keyboard synthesizer; acoustic bass in hard case; miscellaneous stage support equipment and spare parts; tools; loudspeaker fly hardware; some wardrobe, including ironing board and iron; and a fourteen-foot-long aluminum loading/unloading ramp.

Occasionally PHC is performed from a site where ISDN digital lines for transmission are not available. Such sites also need a portable satellite uplink to feed the program to the network. For larger stages we bring a twenty-five-foot-tall, two-story house with a front yard lamp post. In all, it takes nine tons of equipment hauled in a forty-eight-foot semitrailer to do a show. This equipment is also used at the Fitzgerald Theater. —Scott Rivard

Georgia

Georgia is a state of towns with names like
  poetry:
Towns like Mystic, Dewy Rose, Coffee,
  Ogeechee,
Chickamauga, Chickaswatchee, Cisco, Oconee.
I love driving through Georgia.

Chehav! Mayhaw! Bogart, Mayday, McBean.
Louella! Cornelia! Roberta and Kathleen.
And I'll bet the town of Loving is the sweetest
  ever seen.
I love driving through Georgia.

And if you want to see the world, you need not
  go so far.
Georgia's got everything, just jump into
  your car,
You'll find Jerusalem, Jordan, Delhi, Damascus,
Waterloo, Scotland, Vienna, and Dallas.
Hollywood, Woodstock, Monticello, and Juno.
Dublin, Mount Vernon, Washington, Fargo,
Macedonia, Montezuma and I swear it's the
  truth:
In Georgia, you can even find a place called
  Duluth.

I'd love to drive through Florence, Athens,
  and Rome,
Experiment, Center Post, Subligma, or Free
  Home.
Social Circle, Chattahootchee, Gratis, or Naom-
I—wonderful driving through Georgia.

Hurrah! Hurrah! for Temperance and Ball
  Ground!
Hurrah! Hurrah! for Lumpkin and Hentown!
But you won't find a place named Sherman
  anywhere around
As you are driving through Georgia.

Gloria

"The Story of Gloria: A Young Woman of
Manhattan" ran for twenty episodes between
November 1989 and June 1990 as a Brechtian soap
opera, in which the characters break from dialogue
into sung commentary set to music ranging from

Ivy Austin in rehearsal 1990.

"Three Blind Mice" to an aria from *Aïda*. Ivy Austin
starred as Gloria, a girl from Iowa living on New
York's Upper West Side who yearns for meaning in
her life and relationships, as well as a nicer apartment. Gloria, her friend Tony, and her faithless
boyfriend, Victor, have conversations mixing the
New York obsessions with career, self-fulfillment,
and the right address with a love of New York's
beauty and vitality. The series followed Gloria on a
futile trek to rebirth in Seattle, a mandatory family
stopover in Iowa on the way back to New York, and
her eventual hope of subletting the desirable
Riverside Drive apartment of a wealthy Republican
played by Bob Elliott. Rob Fisher and the Coffee
Club Orchestra provided the music.

Graduation Speech

Members of the school board, faculty, parents,
Class of ____.

As you end these four years of endeavor, I
remind you that the word "commencement" comes
from the Latin "to begin or start" and so this is a
beginning, not an end. As you cross this threshold of
opportunity on your way to the highway of life, it is

you who must decide whether to go with the flow or march to the beat of a different drummer.

Life is no bed of roses. It's what you make of it, and in the words of the philosopher, an unexamined life is not worth living.

Remember to take chances, but don't throw the baby out with the bathwater. It's not a perfect world out there, but it's the best one we have, and my challenge to you is to make a difference.

As we pass the torch on to you, the new generation, I challenge you to light that darkness that comes before the dawn and leave the world a little bit better than how you found it.

If you give a man a fish, you feed him for a day, but if you teach him to fish, you've fed him for life. Which is to say that a man's reach should exceed his grasp. With your feet on the ground and your eyes fixed on the stars, you'll be able to look in the mirror and know you've done your best. That's all we can ask.

—Phil Bosakowski

Grand Ole Opry

In June 1994, PHC broadcast from the Ryman Auditorium in Nashville, the legendary home of WSM's Grand Ole Opry from 1941 to 1974. GK had made a pilgrimage to see the Opry in 1973, and returned in 1974 to write an article for *The New Yorker* about the last Opry broadcast at the Ryman, the writing of which inspired the invention of PHC. In honor of the connection, twenty years later, GK wrote a ballad and sang it on the broadcast, backed up by Chet Atkins, with Phil Everly singing harmony:

I remember when I took the train back in '73
To see the Grand Ole Opry in Nashville,
   Tennessee.
I didn't know you had to pay, and the tickets
   all were gone that day,
So I stood in the parking lot and heard the show
   for free.

It was the Ryman Auditorium, it rose up proud
   and high,
And it was in the summer, the windows open
   wide,
And I scooched down behind a wall and I could
   almost see them all,
The sequins and the smiles, the announcer to
   the side.

There was Porter and Dolly, Ernest Tubb, and
   Bill Monroe,
Roy Acuff and Grant Turner who announced
   the Opry show,
And dressed up like a country girl, from
Grinder's Switch came Minnie Pearl,
She was just so proud to be here, and the people
   loved her so.

And the music came pouring out the windows
   and it found you,
Songs full of sorrow, longing for home,
You'd like to cry but music seems to put its arms
   around you
Music, sweet and low.

There were dusty cars and pickups in the
   parking lot that night.
The sun went down and the air was cool and the
   stage seemed twice as bright.
We ran and stood by a silver bus and Loretta
   Lynn walked right by us,
Her long black hair and her dress pure white.

There were pickers by the back door, waiting to
   be found,
And singers who were getting lost in Tootsie's
   Orchid Lounge.
And little children in the cars lay asleep in
   Daddy's arms,
Listening to the music and that sweet lonesome
   sound.

I took the train next morning, and I went back
   up north,
I don't recall just what it was I came here
   looking for,
But I remember that romance, the country music
   and the fans
Standing in the parking lot outside the
   Opry door.

And how the music told us, with every sweet
   guitar,
That everyone is on the run and none of us
   gets far,
So you may as well pull in and park and hear
   the music in the dark
And think of those who loved you and
   remember who you are.

And the music came pouring out the windows
   and it found you,
Songs full of sorrow, longing for home,
You'd like to cry but music seems to put its
   arms around you
Music, sweet and low.

Greetings

The greetings began with members of the audience calling out the names of their hometowns.
People attending the show of February 4, 1978,
in St. Paul, for example, came from Eagan,
New Haven CT, France, Hopkins, Silver Bay,
Lincoln Ave. in St. Paul, Pittsburgh, Boulder
CO, River Falls WI, Houston TX, Duluth,
and Winnipeg. The greetings, read at the
top of the second hour of the show to allow
the audience to settle down, have carried
birthday and anniversary wishes, announced engagements and births, have
proposed marriage, and have conveyed
to listeners at home reminders to turn
off the oven, put out the dog, and pick
people up at the airport. Nancy
Kmonk wrote remembering the
greeting from her mom and dad in
the summer of 1985. Nancy worked and
lived in a Forest Service fire lookout tower at
Hershey Point ID. Immediately after hearing the
greeting, her Forest Service radio began to buzz
with calls from other lookouts sitting on far peaks
on the horizon, asking if she'd heard the message
from her parents. A single greeting multiplies.

**Audience members in the lobby of the Fitzgerald
Theater, writing messages for GK to read on the air.
"Listeners often ask, 'Are those greetings real or
made up?' I don't know: I didn't write them, people in
the audience did. If it's fiction, it's their fiction."**

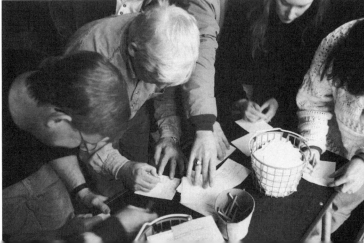

Guy's All-Star Shoe Band: Andy Stein, violin and sax;
Rich Dworsky, leader and piano; Pat Donohue,
guitarist; with Vince Giordano sitting in on sax.
Greg Hippen, bass, and Arnie Kinsella, hidden in
the percussion.

Groups, Invented

Stevie Beck had her Stevedores. There was the
Driftwoods, a folk trio. The Chenilles, a girl group
who sang about boyfriends. The Love Shovels
appeared on their Bummer Summer Tour, crazed
and dangerous, traveling under armed guard, to
sing, "Marilyn Manson, step aside! / Ozzie
Osbourne, run and hide! / Jesse Ventura and
Howard Stern! / Shut up! You've got lots to learn! /
The Love Shovels come to pillage and burn!" And
of course Marvin and Mavis Smiley in their green
motor home, promoting their crossover Broadway

Bluegrass album, making "Tonight" (and everything
else) sound vaguely like "Rocky Top."

Guy's All-Star Shoe Band

A handpicked bunch, diverse, like the bomber
crew in an old war movie—an Upper West Side
violinist, a St. Paul Jewish pianist, a New York
Irish-Italian drummer, a St. Paul Irish guitarist
and a German bass player. They play so great,
they make the old dead heroes stand up and walk.

Guy's Shoes

Guy's Cash Shoes, the shoes that dispense cash
through a slot in the toe. How do they work?
Simply place your deposits in the Cash Shoe sole,
and when you need to withdraw some, enter your
PIN number on the keypad on the tongue and
out comes the money. Cash Shoes are cheaper
than ATMs and they're more convenient.

Gym

I hear the squeak of shoes on a gym floor, and I
feel faint and nauseous, remembering the humili-
ations of phy-ed class. When you're fourteen and
6-2 and weigh 135 pounds and have size thirteen
feet, you should not be expected to do cart-
wheels. Walking on level ground is challenge
enough. But you must put on your gym shorts
and shirt and shoes and socks, which have been
fermenting in your locker since fall, and do flying
somersaults over the horse and chin yourself on
the bar and climb a rope as fifty other boys
watch, most of them compact and muscular.
There were two of us incompetents in the class,
Sheldon and I, and each of us could see from the
other how dumb we looked, a tall guy running
forward toward the mat like a wounded moose
and then stumbling and pitching forward and
falling. Phy-ed class made me feel I did not come
from this planet. Phy-ed made me fear I would
never be able to marry and have children. Thank
goodness for English, which made me feel that I
could marry a couple hundred women all at once.
"Come live with me and be my love and we shall
all the pleasures prove." I thought, "Yes, there
are many women that could apply to."

Handmaidens of Literature

In 1991, PHC did a live broadcast from the Reading Room of the New York Public Library, at 42nd Street and Fifth Avenue, dedicated to "the handmaidens of literature." It began: Every spring, at better liberal arts colleges around America, the graduating English majors are suddenly struck by a terrible thought. They can't spend the rest of their lives in the library, much as they would love to. They are going to have to find a job. Unless—maybe they could get a job in publishing, be paid to read and think and write, and to talk about writing.

So the slim, beautiful, intelligent young woman comes to New York with stars in her eyes and finds herself—a Slave of Literature. At the Port Authority Bus Terminal, publishers' reps meet the buses arriving from Ithaca, Charlottesville, Cambridge, New Haven, Chapel Hill. They can recognize the English majors by their sallow skin and earnest expression.

Young grad: New York! I'm here! I'm over-whelmed with impressions! I must sit down and enter them in my journal!
Recruiter: Hey, beautiful—I'm with Simon and Schuster.
Grad: Simon and Schuster! Why, they publish books—hundreds of books every year by wonderful writers such as Neil Simon and Isaac Bashevis Schuster.

Recruiter: That's right. You wanna be in publishing? Can you type? Work a Xerox machine? Work like a dog from 9 to 6 and then go to the women's lavatory and by 6:15 transform yourself into a femme literaire and attend cocktail parties and publicity soirees in the evening and glitter and be care-free and alluring? And then go home and read page proofs until 4 in the morning?
Grad: Yes—oh, yes! I can and I will.
Recruiter: Want to know how much money you'll be earning?
Grad: No. It matters not a whit. I am a handmaiden of literature, passionately in love with books and writing, even at wages less than that of a parking lot attendant. Take me. Take me to your office.
Recruiter: (OFF) Let's go. Get her on the truck! C'mon, Larry. You grab her ankles and I'll take her arms. One, two, three—

And that's how people get into publishing. They get hauled in a truck to the publishing house, and they're sorted into piles—editorial, business, publicity, sales—and the ones who don't have nice curly hair are sent to magazines to become checkers and mail boys.

Reading unreadable manuscripts, hoping for signs of talent, that's what slaves of literature do—and what would we do without them? The editorial assistants, the checkers, the librarians, the English teachers—this show is in their honor.

The Hopeful Gospel Quartet: GK, Linda Williams, Kate MacKenzie, and Robin Williams, posing for a publicity picture for the First Annual Pre-Millennium Tour in 1998. Which one looks the friendliest? Which one looks the most like a special prosecutor?

Hanging

"He that is born to be hanged will never be drowned," I thought was a hopeful adage. I was afraid of drowning and Minnesota has thousands of lakes and rivers, but there's no capital punishment here. "He who is born to be hanged will never be drowned" is more or less a promise of long life to a Minnesotan of my character.

Heaven Survey

It's a time of widespread dissatisfaction in America, as we know from the newspapers, and in the news this past week we heard that this dissatisfaction does not end with death. Americans who have died and gone to heaven are not entirely satisfied with it either. Twelve hundred dead Americans were interviewed in a survey. These tended to be older than average. Older, or else more careless. About 36% found heaven better than they expected, and about 21% thought it was about the same as they expected, and 43% were disappointed. Of the 1200 Americans surveyed, 31% feel it's poorly run and 17% feel that govern-

ment is not paying attention to their needs. If I were God, I'd be concerned about it. Those are pretty high negatives. Those who are disappointed with heaven say the food is good, and they like not having winter and all that, but they feel a lot of uncertainty about the future. You get there and it's not as perfect as you think. The hardware is a different size. So you can't do home improvements or anything. No yard work. The selection of reading materials is limited. So is cable reception. It's poor. They don't care for the people all that much. The blessed, the meek, they get on your nerves. And the pure of heart, they tend to be hard to get to know. Women especially, they're just real standoffish.

High School

"Go Whippets," said the sign. It didn't say where, but it said, "Go Whippets." And a bunch of girls did the Whippets Cheer, which has never come true in the past. But they did it anyway. "W-O-B-E-G-O-N, W-O-B-E-G-O-N. I've said it twice, I'll say it again. W-O-B-E-G-O-N, Wobegon, Wobegon. That's our town. We'll beat you up and knock you down. That's our town, that's our team, you're the curds, and we're the cream. So pick up your trash, get out of the way! Lake Wobegon's gonna win today! W-H-I-P-P-E-T, I said W-H-I-P-P-E-T, Whippets, Whippets! Yea, Whippets!"

Hippen

Greg Hippen first played bass on PHC in 1984, in the Night O' Rest Orchestra on the tenth anniversary show. Greg studied bass at Indiana University, graduating in 1974. He has played in rock and roll bands, rhythm and blues bands, jazz groups, for Broadway musicals, at the Children's Theatre Company, the Minnesota Opera, and the St. Paul Chamber Orchestra. Now one of the Guy's All-Star Shoe Band, by day Greg is a systems programmer.

Horse hockey

The Flag Day celebration will have a parade and a potluck and a drawing and a dance and all the rest of it. The parade is going to be nice, have the high school band, have antique cars and vehicles out there, including a wagon that I doubt any of you have seen before. It's the Lake Wobegon Ladies' Carriage, invented by a great-uncle of Mr. Swenson. Back in 1898, he invented this, at the time of the Spanish-American War, back in Victorian days. He was concerned about young, delicate ladies, sitting in a carriage and having to watch the beasts relieve themselves as they pulled the carriage. And so he solved this problem by putting the horses behind the wagon. Put the wagon tree back there, hitched the collars to it, harnessed them up. Never realizing that with the horses behind the wagon, it would make steering more exciting. It's hard to rein animals in when they're behind you. So some delicate young ladies suffered serious injuries as a result of their sensibilities. It was the only one ever made, and therefore was the first of its kind. The first rear-drive, horse-drawn wagon in America. That'll be in the parade on June 14th, pushed by a car.

Hotel Minnesota

Desk clerk: Oh, hi there. Real good to see ya again. Yeah, I was just telling Rudy, I wonder if he's going to come, or should we send out a search party, but it's real good to see you, and you come in then. I got your room all ready for you, and we got supper on, so you wash up right away then, okay? Real good.
GK: At the Hotel Minnesota, from the moment you arrive, you feel you've been there a long time. The smell of old rubber boots in the hallway, the pale wallpaper, the closet full of boxes, many labeled "MISC," the blond maple headboards on the twin beds, the bedside lamps, everything is familiar. And your room, not an empty hotel room, but a real guest room with golf clubs, old winter coats, and a sewing machine in the closet. Your own room cat. And remember: no tipping. There's no big lobby at the Hotel Minnesota, everyone just goes and sits in the kitchen and asks, "What's new?" "Not much, about the same. And yourself?" When you leave, you know it won't be long until you come back.
Desk clerk: Okay, then. We'll be talking to you soon then. Real good. Bye now.

How The Mind Really Works

Sponsored in 1986 and 1987 by Standard Sandpaper, seven segments explored the mind. In "Dreams," a therapist tried for weeks to help the wife interpret her dream of an empty casserole dish,

Greg Hippen

until she accidentally dropped it, which dispelled her guilt. In "Naked," a timid guy went to an X-rated movie to learn about the human body and found himself in the midst of naked people at a seminar on sexuality. In "Memories of Pain," a guy driving down a street hears an eye operation over the radio, invoking memories of earaches, dental appointments, and a vasectomy, and he has to pull over to the side of the road and put his head between his knees. One segment looked at the tiny people who run the cerebellum and the optic nerve to see why we use only a small part of our brain. Another, "Adversity," explained that bad times, like a harsh winter in St. Paul, make you feel good, and good times, like a vacation in California, can make you sick. "Country Music" showed the power music exerts when people became what the songs described. The last of the series dramatized people spending large sums for high-tech electronic equipment they never figure out how to use, while the manufacturer of the $14 pencil sharpener that lasts a lifetime is in danger of going out of business. Amazing how the mind works.

Huck and Jim

In February 1996, James Earl Jones played Jim and GK Huck in a reunion of the old raftmates many years later. Jim had found his way to New Orleans and sailed to Paris and went into the theater. ("Slavery is good training for a life in the theater, Huck.") He learned French and earned a fortune playing kings and dukes.

Huck: You played kings and dukes! Just like the Duke and the Dauphin . . .
Jim: I'm better than they were. Much better. I have to tell you, I'm not particularly nostalgic about our trip down the river, Huck. I did read your book though. I didn't care that much for it. Look here. Page 53. You're quoting me here. "I hear Ole Missus tell de widder she gwyne to sell me down to Orleans. I lit out mighty quick, I tell you."
Huck: I remember that passage, yes, I do, Jim—
Jim: Huck, I didn't talk like that. I was very particular about grammar and enunciation. You've got me saying "gwyne" about two hundred thirty-eight times in that book. You got one thing right, though.
Huck: What's that, Jim?

Jim: You almost turned me in that one time. You took the canoe to town and I hid in the wigwam and I heard some men call out to you. They were in a skiff, and they said they were looking for runaway slaves. They said, "Do you have any men on that raft yonder?" And you said, "Yes. I've got one." And they said, "Is he white or is he black?"
Huck: I remember that.
Jim: It took you awhile to decide to lie and protect me.

The two reminisced about the Duke and Dauphin and the play they put on in Arkansas that didn't draw a big crowd until they added a line to the poster, "Ladies and Children Not Admitted," and then it drew a full house three nights running. Jim recited the Duke's version of Hamlet's Soliloquy. Huck borrowed a few hundred dollars from him. And the sketch ended with a duet of "Red River Valley."

Human Sacrifices

Men in suits were often thrown off high cliffs, and once, for a Fall Harvest show, one hundred guys were thrown off the railroad trestle into the Mississippi River. "The Mayans discovered that when you kill off a certain number of people in management every year, productivity shoots up," GK explained. The sacrifice was held up momentarily by the state Pollution Control Agency, which thought that a hundred guys in suits might have an adverse affect on the carp population, but they studied it and decided it would be okay.

The hundred guys were all management people, department heads, directors, managers, assistant managers, and about twenty vice presidents, chosen for their use of buzzwords. Big buzzword agenda. It was how they interacted. And it doesn't take a rocket scientist to recognize buzzwords, it's a no-brainer, and arguably, these guys at the end of the day had the lowest signal-to-noise ratio of anybody in their organizations. Whatever the buzzword, these guys had been there, done that. They felt empowered by buzzwords. So the proactive solution was to administer tough love, and put these guys on a glide path toward the bottom line and after they impact the water the healing process could start and have some quality time. It was pushing the envelope but it was a reality check and it humanized the workplace.

Ice Fishing

Swanny has the first two-room fishhouse on the lake. It's twenty feet long and ten feet wide, a mansion. He hauled his out on Tuesday and by Wednesday night, there were forty houses out there, a little city of men who know that this is the alternative to divorce. In the dead of winter your home gets smaller and smaller, the walls close in, and a man's natural tendencies become more pronounced. Some days she looks at you and wonders if it was worth the $15 for the license, and then one day she finds you surrounded by empty beer bottles and dirty plates and she shrieks in horror and you look down and dangling from your mouth is the tail of the dead rodent you're eating for dinner. At this point in the marriage, discussion is no good. You need a place to hunker and that's your fishhouse: a little plywood room with a stove and a sleeping bench and table and chairs and a floor with a couple holes in it to fish through the ice. Sit there, say what you like, scratch yourself, and feel free.

Iditarod

From a show in Anchorage in 1996, an interview with the lead sled dog in the Iditarod race in Alaska, forced to miss the race because of a foot injury.

Dog: Tail injury.
GK: Tail injury knocked him out of the race—

Dog: Yeah. Busted my tail.
GK: Sorry to hear it, and welcome to our show, Ranger.
Dog: Thanks. Good to be here.
GK: You're a husky, right?
Dog: Well, you're not so small yourself. (He chuckles) Just an old dog joke.
GK: Do all huskies become sled dogs here in Alaska, Ranger?
Dog: No, I'd say that most dogs are content to make their mark on the world in other ways. On trees, mainly. But I went into sledding because it seemed like a way to get ahead. Sled dogging is basically like corporate life. You start at the back, and you get pretty tired of looking at the hind end of the dog ahead of you and having his tail in your face, so you work your feet to the bone, and you become lead dog, and you have to pull, and you have to show the guy in the sled which way to go, and then there's all the social obligations—gotta keep the young pups in line and there's a lot of butt sniffing involved.

Impeachment

People were walking heads down into the wind in Lake Wobegon. They gathered in the Chatterbox Café for long coffee hours this week talking about the impeachment trial in the Senate. My people are in contact with the real world so it's hard for them to get a handle on unreality. It's difficult for them to talk about something as surrealistic as this. There have been times, goodness knows, when Congress has been out of touch, but this impeachment process has been a long trip down the rabbit hole and it's lasted for a year now. It's odd to come out of the real world in which most of us conduct our business and go down into the dark guided by the rabbit. And come upon this Republican confederacy, the old Republican confederacy, rising up again to bring down the Presidency. You just wish it would be over soon and the whole long sorry line of characters who promulgated this would find some other work, perhaps pest control. And begin with themselves.

People in the Chatterbox said that it reminded them of when they were boys and they used to go out into the pasture when they could get their hands on a few M-80 firecrackers, the big ones with the fuse coming out the side. They would go out and they would blow up cow pies. And you'd find a cow pie that was of just the right age, so it was a little bit crusty on the top and would hold the M-80 with the fuse sticking up out of it. It wouldn't be swallowed up by the pudding, but the heart of the cow pie was viscous enough so that it really would explode. You'd set it in very carefully, you and all of your pals. And you would light the fuse and then you'd turn and run fast to get outside the perimeter of fallout, but you'd turn so you could see the thing go up and enjoy it. Sometimes a person would miscalculate. You'd go to what you thought would be outside the perimeter but you saw the explosion and suddenly there was incoming. There was flying shrapnel coming at you, flying dung coming directly at you. You ducked down but some of it got in your hair and a big chunk of it got in your ear. That's what is happening to the people who are putting on the impeachment. They think that when they put this firecracker in the cow pie, they can run fast enough to get away from it. But they're not as fast as they imagine. And out there in the pasture are all sorts of other cow pies in their path that are a lot fresher, that they passed up in order to put the firecracker where they put it.

Irish Envy

We Minnesota Lutherans envy the Irish for their sweet accents and their colorful sayings ("May the wind always be at your back but not coming out of you yourself personally") and their freckles and windblown red hair and twinkly green eyes. And for St. Patrick's Day. All we've got is Syttende Mai and Svenskarnas Dag and nobody else can pronounce them. They got great movies like *The Quiet Man* and *The Bells of St. Mary's*. We've got *Fargo*. They've got names like Megan, Sean, Ryan, Caitlin. We've got Elmer and Gladys. They've got Irish coffee, we've got Sanka. They've got Baileys Irish Cream, we've got Cool Whip. They've got neighborhood pubs, we've got the church basement. The Irish are poets and dreamers. Lutherans are dairy farmers and actuaries. They've got nine-hundred-page stream-of-consciousness novels in which people wrestle with their souls, and we've got call-in shows where people talk about road conditions.

Jason's Song

When I was just your age I looked at Papa,
And I wondered how it felt to be so old,
Work so hard and come home gray and tired,
And worry about the money that you owe.

Now we're driving home I see you dreaming,
You aim the old blue Chevy toward the sun,
Pull back on the lighter and we're flying.
I remember how it felt to be so young.

Child, your mama worked so hard to have you,
Two long days of labor 'fore you came.
I thanked the Lord to see that you were living,
And I knew my life would never be the same.

I think about that night we almost lost you.
The doctor stood by helpless and afraid.
Your father could do nothing then but want you,
But oh, the wondrous journey that you made.

Now I see you hold the neighbor's baby.
Your hands are just as gentle as can be.
Someday when you have your own to cradle
I know, my boy, you'll often think of me.

Child, when you were born, I was a young man,
I thought of all the things I'd never do,
Lands I'd never see, but I've forgotten.
There's none of it so sweet as having you.

Jason Keillor, 18, squeezing out a blues riff on his Fender Telecaster on a PHC broadcast, May 1987. GK's son, he attended the first shows, sold popcorn as a child and took tickets at the door, and made his debut, at 16, playing rock guitar in a comedy sketch.

The times that I looked down and saw you
   trembling,
To feel your father's anger in the air,
And suddenly it was my papa shouting,
And I became the child standing there.

All the times I carried you upstairs, child,
And tucked your grandma's quilt around
   your head,
And kissed you as you lay there sleeping,
And each one was a blessing that I said.

It's just a song I wrote for you in April,
Knowing you'll be eight the first of May,
To tell you once again how much I love you,
And think of you on that amazing day.

Julia Child

Julia: *Toujours, mon ami! Toujours—*
GK: Good to see you. You look well.
Julia: Strong as a horse. That's what mixing puff pastry will do for you!
GK: So what are we going to make today?
Julia: Today I'm here to promote my latest book, *Menus for Tête-à-Tête*—those romantic dinners for two where you may not stay at the table very long. Hmmmmm? So maybe you serve a lovely *A la Recherche de Turqui Perdu*. That's French for leftover turkey. Or have some Moo Goo Gai Pan delivered. Eat it right out of the pan. You and that guy. Or how about this roast duck—*Le Canard la Moins Chère*?
GK: Roast duck—that's pretty complicated, isn't it?
Julia: No, you only start two days ahead of time and partially roast the duck, take a straw and blow air under the skin and remove the skin, remove the legs and wings, and press them for the juice—
GK: That sounds awfully involved.
Julia: Yes, it does, doesn't it. To heck with it. Let's have a nice *Pasta Fromage*. It's simple. We just boil the pasta and add fromage.
GK: What kind of fromage?
Julia: I have no idea. It's a powdered fromage and it's in this little bag that comes right inside the box of pasta.
GK: Sounds great.
Julia: It is, Big Boy.

Jumper Cables

Everyone has jumper cables. Jumper cables are basic equipment in Minnesota. Boys and girls get them for graduation presents. They come in leatherette cases, the attaché or the bag with the shoulder strap, and they come in all different decorator colors. What you do with them is this: you put the two clamps at one end on the positive and negative poles of the battery of the car that's running, and the two clamps at the other end on the positive pole and on the engine mount of the car with the dead battery, and she should start right up. You do this gingerly because there are stories of batteries that blew up like car bombs and stories of people who put one clamp on the wrong place and wound up with curly hair, but you also do it fairly quickly because it's so cold. If it doesn't work then you use the jumper cables to spell out SOS on a snowbank and you go indoors and crawl into bed and wait till you hear the helicopters.

Tom Keith does footsteps as Prudence Johnson, Chet Atkins, and Johnny Gimble perform a western adventure about rustlers and weight loss (April 26, 1986). The show was videotaped for television; thus the modernistic set.

Keith

Tom Keith started working with GK on the Morning Show in 1971, and then joined PHC in the St. Paul-Ramsey Arts & Science Sculpture Garden in 1976. He came on as Jim Ed Poole with Curtis, the Attack Chicken, in a cage, and sold photographs of himself to people, giving them more money in change than they paid for the photo.

The first sound effects guy you probably met was your brother who lay in the bunk bed below you and worked on his drip sound late at night, and wouldn't quit even when you dropped things on him. Or the kid who sat behind you in school and made sounds during physics tests and when the teacher left the room and when you reached down for a pencil. Sound effects are a child's art. It started when you were a little kid and got soldiers and lined them up on the living room floor behind barricades and they banged away at each other. The guys who weren't that good at making sounds, like me, we became authors, and the guys who could do mortars and dive bombers and hand grenades won the war and they became sound-effects men.

Ketchup

The Ketchup Advisory Board became a sponsor of the show in the fall of 1996, with commercials about the ill effects of ketchup deprivation—trees turning brown, chickadees avoiding your feeder, etc. The Barb and Jim dialogue commercials followed, in which, each week, the couple counted their blessings, discovered that despite everything they were still dissatisfied, and concluded that what they needed was ketchup with its natural mellowing agents.

Among the blessings they counted: The upstairs toilet stopped running. After six months the art finally downloaded on the computer. The kids' arrest records were sealed. What Jim thought was kidney stones was only the sharp edge of a rivet on his jeans. They discovered a new conditioning hair rinse that made their hair bouncy and fun-loving. The dog got his degree from obedience school (awarded posthumously). They took a test in a magazine that showed them to be reasonably happy and Jim lied on only a few answers. The couch that Barb's mother gave them finally reached the point where they could throw it out. The neighbors' wind chimes were stolen. Jim's hair implant, the one that caused numbness in his legs, was replaced at no charge. After the cat went on Valium, she didn't wake them up at night scratching at the door. Jim's dry cleaner used less starch in the shorts, so the burning sensation went away. The ugly brown growth on Barb's shoulder that

Edward Koren's poster art for GK's *Family Radio* album, back in the LP era.

she feared might be skin cancer turned out to be a refried bean. And so forth.

Richard Dworsky sang the jingle at the end in a fragile vibratoless voice. Either:

> These are the good years, in the golden sun,
> A new day is dawning, a new life has begun...
> The river flowing, like ketchup on a bun.

Or:

> Ballet and painting and the operas of Rossini
> Flowers and red wine and pesto and linguini
> Good things are flowing like ketchup on a weenie.

Or:

> Rocky mountain sunset, valleys filled with fog,
> Campfire blazing, sparks fly from a log,
> Red clouds at evening, like ketchup on a dog.

Kinsella

Arnie Kinsella is the drummer in the Guy's All-Star Shoe Band. A graduate of Brooklyn College, a percussion major, Arnie has played Broadway shows and recorded with Leon Redbone and Vince Giordano's Nighthawks. He played PHC in 1984 and in 1989 became a regular. When songs and sketches feature tap dancing, Arnie "plays" tap shoes.

Koehler Thanksgiving

The family rents the Lake Wobegon town hall and packs as many as a hundred and twenty Koehlers in, a great compression of people talking and food cooking, enough food to sink a battleship, turkeys and ducks and a goose and sinkholes of potatoes and squash and candied yams, pickles of every description, cranberries, six varieties of stuffing, a battalion of pies, and the ultimate dish—the dish every

Koehler expects to be served, otherwise what's the point in coming—Sharon's creamed onions. People spoon her creamed onions onto their plate and eat the first helping while waiting in line for seconds. The art of creamed onions is the art of combining sweet and sour so that one tastes both, so that each expresses itself individually and yet combines harmoniously, and of course that is the art of families. Some families, afraid of conflict, lay on too much cream, and others, afraid of compromising individual integrity, are just a bowl of onions with some milk thrown over them.

The Koehlers sit around after dessert and sing, "Come and sit by my side if you love me, do not hasten to bid me adieu," and also "*Muss i denn, muss i denn, zum Stadtle hinaus, Stadtle hinaus und du mein Schatz bleibst hier. Wenn i komm, wenn i komm, wenn in wiedrum komm, wiedrum komm Kehr i ein, mein Schatz, bei dir.*" and of course, "I dream of Jeannie with the light brown hair, Borne like a vapor on the summer's air," and these grand old songs always cause hard feelings. "*Muss i denn*" is Evelyn's song and it is sung every year, and so is "Red River Valley," and why not something new for a change? Why not "Give Peace A Chance"? What's wrong with that?

But the hurt feelings are gradually healed by the administration of more creamed onions. After dessert. There is still lots left. Sharon always worries if she's made enough, but even though the Koehlers have been stuffing their faces with it all afternoon, there is always more left. It is the miracle of the creamed onions.

Kottke

Leo Kottke began on the trombone and wanted to be a "jazzer" to play in clubs and hotel lounges. He also wanted to be a radio announcer. When he was six he wanted to be Martin Agronsky, the journalist and commentator. When he was twelve, he came down with mononucleosis and his mother bought him "one of those little guitars with the cowboy on it," Leo recalls, to entertain him while he was sick. The guitar lasted about two weeks before the bridge came off, but that guitar cured him and headed him toward a career as a guitarist and composer. Leo has written scores for movies and television, and for a children's album of the story of Paul Bunyan narrated by Jonathan Winters, and has released more than two dozen recordings.

Professor Kinsella, playing the skins on a cramped stage at Town Hall in New York, and Commander Kottke, picking the twelve-string with a slide on his left pinkie, at the old World Theater.

Lake Wobegon Trail

In June 1998, a bike trail called "The Lake
Wobegon Trail" opened from Avon to Melrose MN,
along the old rail bed of the Great Northern line.
GK attended the dedication in Albany, and on the
following Saturday's PHC sang a song to mark the
occasion:

> When the storms of life assail you
> And you hit a stretch of bumps
> And your children chew your arms and legs to
>   little bleeding stumps
> And you're feeling depressed
> And weird thoughts cross your mind
> And you dare not take a Rorschach test
> For fear of what they'd find—
> Before insanity strikes
> Let us go and ride our bikes—

> On the Lake Wobegon Trail
> With the wind at our backs we will sail
> Straight on ahead
> Down the old rail bed
> Past the pond and field and peaceful homestead.
> Through St. Joe and Avon it goes,
> Albany, Freeport, Melrose—
> Past hog farms and dairy
> Across the wide prairie
> Along the Wobegon Trail.

> When you want to leave the hustle
> And get out of your car
> And go where there's no cruelty, no cares,
>   no Kenneth Starr—
> And you're tired of the blather,
> The rat race and the grind,
> And you keep getting farther and farther behind,
> Let us preserve our faculties
> And ride as slowly as we please—

> On the Lake Wobegon Trail
> Through farm and valley and dale
> In the autumn sunshine
> Oh, what is so fine
> As a ride with your pals on the Great
>   Northern line.
> In downtown Avon we will enter
> And go all the way to Sauk Centre.
> Get your bike and let's ride
> Twenty miles side by side
> On the Lake Wobegon trail.

Larry

GK: When this show started, I was the co-host
along with my twin brother, Larry, who was funnier
than me and better looking and could dance and
sing and play musical instruments. He was the star
of the show until the day he was hit on the head by
a sandbag and it knocked all his hair off.

Larry (Tom Keith): Yeah, I remember that.
GK: I'm sure you do, Larry. I felt tremendous guilt over it because when the sandbag fell on him, Larry was standing right where I had told him to stand and I was standing backstage by the rope that held the sandbag. But it wasn't so bad, there was no brain damage...
Larry: There was no brain damage.
GK: No brain damage. It just knocked all the hair off his head and he lost his confidence.
Larry: I just lost my confidence.
GK: But Larry still comes to every show—
Larry: Every show.
GK: And when we do a commercial for Bertha's Kitty Boutique, like this one, Larry gets to hold the kitty. (MEOW) Isn't that right?
Larry: I always hold the kitty.

Librarians

(to the tune of "Rocking Alone in an Old Rocking Chair")

> Sitting alone in a library chair, I saw a
>   librarian's silvery hair
> And I thought of angels as I saw her there,
> Sitting alone in a library chair.
> Her tweed skirt was dusty, from books she
>   had read,
> And the tips of her fingers were all stained
>   with lead,
> And her blouse was tucked down into her
>   underwear,
> Sitting alone in the library chair.
>
> She's waiting for someone to ask for a book,
> And she'd find it no matter how long it took,
> No matter how specialized, obscure, or rare,
> Sitting alone in her library chair.
>
> She's waiting to serve you, waiting to share
> The wealth of data and literature there
> And yet her budget was radically cut,
> Sitting alone on her skinny old butt.
>
> I looked at her and I thought, What a shame—
> She gave up money and glamour and fame,
> To simply be useful to everyone there,
> Sitting alone in a library chair.

Locks

Keith checks this door before each show to make sure it's ready to open and close on cue: "I learned the hard way that you have to make sure you don't get caught on stage with one of the locks actually locked."

Lighting

PHC Master Electrician Andrew Sullivan is one of
the few to light a radio show, which he's done for
seven years at the Fitzgerald Theater. (Alan
Frechtman handles lighting on PHC tour shows.)
Andrew took a BFA in Theater Lighting from the
North Carolina School of the Arts. He also does
lighting at the Guthrie Theater in Minneapolis.
The PHC is never rehearsed in sequence, so
Andrew must improvise sometimes, and because no
one in radio wears makeup, he uses rose or amber
gels so performers don't look pale and washed-out.

Limericks

There was a young fellow of Reno
Who lost his shirt in the casino,
And the kitchen sink
And most of his drink
Except for a small maraschino.

An upright bass player named Hippen
Said, "Frankly, for long-distance shippin',
I'd prefer a French horn: It's more easily borne,
And it's nice to put crackers and dip in."

A young architect of Nevada
Did a fountain in pink terra-cotta
That, six times a day,
Did the fall of Pompeii
And the sinking of the Spanish armada.

There was a musician named Schickele
Who could blow Finicula-Finiculi
On a tube of toothpaste,
Which was not in good taste,
Though rather amazing technically.

There was a producer named Tschida
So confident that she agreed a
Few moments ago
To stage, as one show,
Sleeping Beauty, *King Lear*, and *Aïda*.

A guitarist named Pat Donohue
Said, "Guitar is ideal, in my view.
I find it attracts
More girls than a sax,
And the neighbors are fond of it, too."

There was an old man of St. Paul
Built a laptop that won't run at all.
Expensive, not pretty, it's
Strictly for idiots.
If you'd like one, give him a call.

There was a conductor named Rob
Who had an impossible job
With singers so bold
They could not be controlled
Except by a man with a knob.

There once was a mezzo named Horne
Whose voice with such passion was torn,
When she played a theater,
About nine months later,
A number of babies were born.

The lovely Miss Totenberg (Nina)
Covers the political arena
With the elegant gloss
Of Diana Ross
And the wisdom of the goddess Athena.

There was an old man so embittered
At how he had wasted and frittered
His best years away
By listening all day
To reruns of *All Things Considered*.

There was an old lady of Knoxville
Who bought her brassieres by the boxful,
Which she stuffed with corn kernels
And old *Wall Street Journals*
And thus kept the front of her frocks full.

A liberal lady of D.C.
By day was tasteful and p.c.
And then after ten
She entertained men
Who were vulgar and filthy and greasy.
"A double life is not easy.
Stead of A.C. I wish I were D.C.
But liberal guys
Tend to theologize,
And I am not St. Francis of Assisi."

We don't talk about art or beauty or wisdom.
Art is our plumber, we called him, we
   missed him.
The toilet's not flushin', and so the discussion
Is all about when Art might get here.

And spring finally comes, but then the paper'll
Say that more snow's forecast the end of April.
We rise up like eagles and jump in our vehicles
And drive off to the store and buy stuff.

Oh, we don't care, we wear a smile,
We are folks who believe in denial,
We can't afford a trip down to Florida,
  So we're doing fine, no thank you.

Lodge

The Sons of Knute lodge is dwindling due to lack of interest in memorizing pages of ancient Nordic wisdom and ritual like the Little Finger Pull. A brother Knute taps your forehead, you say, "*Ost vest, hjemme bedst*" and walk five paces and he cries, "*Oya!*" and you turn and come back and hook your little finger with his and pull and both of you fart. An ancient meeting ritual of Nordic sages.

   Every January, on the coldest day, the Grand Oya and the High Chamberlain and the Keeper of the Keys and the Hooper dress up in the horned helmets and capes made from the skins of rainbow trout like a geezer glitter band and get out the golden walleye on the staff and the silver Hoop, and the Hooper cries, "*Hold op og vaer smuk*," which means "Shut up and be beautiful," and sing the hymn to winter:

   Sons of Knute we are, sons of the prairie,
   With our heads held high in January,
   Hauling our carcass around in big parkas,
   Wearing boots the size of tree stumps.

   Now the temperature's ten below zero,
   And according to the Weather Bureau
   The wind chill is minus one hundred, your sinus
   Is frozen, and your poor brass monkey.

Loyalty

Some people think a small town like Lake Wobegon is a model of free enterprise and the virtues of rugged individualism, but if they do, they haven't lived there. Lake Wobegon survives to the extent that it does on a form of voluntary socialism with elements of Deism, fatalism, and nepotism. It isn't a free-market economy, running on self-interest. It's socialism, and it runs on loyalty. You need a toaster, you buy it at the Co-op Hardware. Even though you can get a deluxe model with attachments for less money in the city, you buy it at the Co-op because you know Otto as you know the other merchants and you know the profit margin is thin as a worn dime. If people were to do comparison shopping, the town would go bust. Lake Wobegon cannot compete with other places item by item. Nothing in town is quite as good as it appears to be somewhere else. If you live there, you have to take it as a whole. That's loyalty, an act of imagination. You don't have to try all the options. You don't have to shop around or make continuous comparisons. Support your local merchants.

Dogs don't lie and why should I?
When strangers come, they growl and bark.
They know their loved ones in the dark.
Now let me by night or day
Be just as full of truth as they.

Love's Old Sweet Song

This song has been done on the show often, usually as a duet by GK and a guest singer.

M

MacKenzie

Kate began singing in public only in her late twenties. As a kid, she and her sisters sang together, pretending to be the Maguire Sisters. At night, Kate and her sister Lala would lie in their bunk-beds and sing their way through entire musicals. And she listened to wonderful singers—Ralph Stanley, Hazel Dickens, and Patsy Cline—as well as to jazz and classical music. But, as Kate says, she "came from people who didn't believe in drawing attention to themselves," so her early music making was limited to the bosom of the family—never in public.

Kate began her public career with the bluegrass band Stoney Lonesome. With them she recorded six albums and made her first performance on PHC on April 4, 1981. Her first solo CD, *Let Them Talk*, was in the Top 10 on the bluegrass charts for eight months. Her CD *Age of Innocence* (on the Red House label) received a Grammy nomination in 1998. She is one of the Hopeful Gospel Quartet.

Maps

A constitutional amendment on the November ballot in Minnesota would add this sentence to the constitution: "The aforesaid state, known and distinguished as the State of Minnesota, shall heretofore be defined and determined to be ipso facto those lands, properties and bodies of water, public and private, lying in toto or in partum within the boundaries of said state, whether known or unknown, and the official map shall so indicate forthwith and hereafter." It sounds reasonable but what they're talking about is a new survey of Minnesota. As students of Minnesota history know, the so-called Olson Survey of 1872 was full of mistakes, on account of the surveyors were paid in advance and so were in a mood to round off numbers. They surveyed more land than there was room for within the state boundaries, and about 180 square miles in the middle had to be dropped so that Minnesota could be scrunched in between Wisconsin, Iowa, Canada, and the Dakotas. Lake Wobegon lies in that middle part, and that's why it appears on no maps.

Now the state is preparing to correct the mistake, but at what price? Many towns will have to be relocated, particularly those that lie along rivers that will be rechanneled. Most of what is now Minneapolis will become part of St. Paul, which means that the alphabetical avenues of Minneapolis—Aldrich, Bryant, Colfax, Dupont, Emerson, Fremont, Girard—will become Hyacinth, Leona, Aster, Jonquil, Herman, and Rhododendron. It's no easy matter to rearrange a state, to drop in an extra 180 square miles—you may wake up one morning to find yourself living a hundred feet away from where you went to bed the night before. It'll be a bonanza for lawyers and misery for everyone else.

Marklund

Reynold (Ray) Marklund was an electrician with the Burlington Railroad, an old Swede from St. Paul's East Side who adopted our radio show. Ray came to every broadcast, watching from backstage. He loved musicians and he also knew about electricity. Ray had a trunkful of tools, and sometimes we suddenly needed him, and he was there. Once at the Arts & Science Center, GK introduced Butch Thompson at the piano, and Butch said, "The piano's locked." Ray rushed off and got a screwdriver out of his trunk and jimmied the lock. At the Walker Art Center, around 1976, at a show on the terrace on the roof, about an hour into the show, there was a loud pop and the power went dead. The sound went off, the clock stopped, everything stopped. Ray Marklund said, "I think that's a circuit breaker." He ran downstairs and he found that the museum guards had gone through the galleries at closing time flipping off all the switches. The show was off the air for maybe five minutes. Ray was a good man. He came to every show and wouldn't take pay. He came to the show until just before he died in 1992.

Microphones

For sound pickup Technical Director Scott Rivard uses many different models of microphones manufactured by companies including AKG, Audio Technica, Audix, Beyer, Sennheiser, and Shure Brothers. Each model has particular characteristics of frequency response, directional patterns, and proximity effect. Scott chooses a microphone for a particular instrument or voice to capture the essence of that sound in the most positive way, blending with the other sounds, but still maintaining separation in the mix. Sometimes, during the sound check, a microphone choice will not sound as he expected, necessitating a change to a different model. Once satisfied with the microphone choice, the audio engineers may further refine the sound by blending microphones, using equalization, filtering, expansion, compression, and reverberation.

Millionaire

How often we read in the papers
Or hear on the evening news
Of the death of a lonely old lady
Whom they call an eccentric recluse,
Who left behind five million dollars
Rolled up in her old Sunday hat—
Why do we shake our heads when we hear
That she left all the cash to her cat?

Nieces and nephews come out of the woods
The day her will enters probate.
Old second cousins three times removed
Sue for poor Mildred's estate.
Where were these people when she was alive?
Did they bother to visit or call?
Yet they would rob every penny she left
To her cat—Oh, the shame of it all!

Her friend and faithful companion
Who shared Mildred's trouble and care—
Should it be judged less deserving
Just because it is covered with hair?
Asking no luxury or privilege,
It happily lay at her feet;
And now that it's come to its earthly reward,
They would throw that cat into the street!

A millionaire cat! people cry in disgust,
What a scandal, a shame, and a waste!
It depends on the cat, if it's frugal or not,
And if it's a cat of good taste.
There's the home to keep up, employees to hire,
And Mildred must have a nice stone.
But how the cat spends its inheritance is
Its business and none of your own.

So if you should see a cat on the street
Driving by in a Mercedes-Benz
Or buying prime rib at the grocery store
Or going to shows with its friends,
Don't throw up your hands in utter disgust
Just bow very deeply and say:
"Good morning, O Cat, a pleasure I'm sure,"
And you may be rewarded someday.

Monologue

Also known as the News from Lake Wobegon, taking place in the second hour of the show, circa 6:20 (central time) and running approximately twenty minutes. A weekly feature on the show dating back to the late '70s though much changed in form and tone, from a series of rube jokes to something closer to a short story. The following is from the spring of 1998.

It has been a quiet week in Lake Wobegon. It was cold early in the week, like November, and it rained. Out behind the Sidetrack Tap was a lake fifty feet long, dammed up behind ice and mud put there by boys practicing the ancient boy trade of hydraulic engineering. The Easter egg hunt at the Lutheran church was moved indoors on account of wet ground, ninety-eight eggs hidden in the sanctuary on Saturday morning, fifty chocolate eggs and forty-eight hens' eggs dyed, and the kids tore around Saturday afternoon and found all but one. So there was a note in the bulletin Easter morning:

"Use caution when sitting. There may be an egg at your seat, perhaps under your cushion." But people never open the bulletin until they are seated. The egg was under Mrs. Val Tollefson.

The phoebes are back nesting beside Clarence and Arlene Bunsen's back door, up under the eaves, the mother on the nest and the father sitting watch in a spruce tree, ready to go for pizza or videos or whatever a pregnant woman would want. Whenever the Bunsens come out the door, the male flies up in the air, in a tizzy: Why do you keep doing that? What are you, deaf? We're trying to lay eggs out here. For crying out loud.

Out at the ends of driveways, people have parked things with For Sale signs on them, most of which look like sacrificial offerings. Big sedans for $700 or Best Offer, and you look at the car and the Best Offer might be to blow it up. Two snowmobiles sitting on a trailer, all three for sale. Farm machinery, old Allis Chalmers and John Deeres, old drills and corn planters, plows and discs and balers, harrows and cultivators. A couple of old manure spreaders.

Holy Week and everyone is in a contemplative mood, thinking about God's great goodness to us and our own unworthiness. The Catholics think of the unworthiness of the Lutherans, and vice versa. A beautiful day, Sunday, but cool. Carl Krebsbach went out to his parents' farm after Mass and got the John Deere and drove it back to town to plow up his garden and his sister's and her neighbor's. It was a good day to be out on a tractor. He wore a white cowboy hat and came chugging into town, the spring breeze in his face, and turned up his street and saw the cars parked alongside the Lutheran church and let up on the gas and the engine backfired going past the Lutherans, like artillery fire.

The windows were open in the sanctuary. Spring filled the room. Pastor Ingqvist was preaching about Job and about the tornadoes that left terrible destruction in southern Minnesota and how when we read about it the next morning over our scrambled eggs we were glad that it wasn't us. Job lost everything, his family, his farms, and sat covered with boils, and his friends Eliphaz, Bildad, and Zophar came to comfort him in his suffering and were so smug that God couldn't bear to listen them. "God preferred Job's honest unbelief to his friends' easy piety—God is not worshiped in platitudes!" cried Pastor Ingqvist, and then the tractor backfired and the organist, who had been working a crossword puzzle, dropped her pencil and reached for it and lost her balance and planted her left foot on a pedal and there was a deep bass note like a dying hippopotamus, and two of the altos burst out whinnying and Pastor Ingqvist directed a patient, long-suffering look their way, and then one alto got the hiccups.

The choir loft is well situated acoustically, and the hiccups rang out, one after the other, like someone dropping forks, and Pastor Ingqvist said, "We think it's our job to provide answers, but we don't need to find answers. We need to find God." And the poor hiccuping alto got up to go. Her high heels went clack clack clack clack clack up the steps of the choir loft to the door and then clack clack clack down the stairs to the entry hall and then clack clack clack down to the basement and clack clack clack clack the length of the basement to the women's toilet and the door closed. Pastor Ingqvist looked down at his sermon and the line, "We don't need to find answers, we need to find God." And he thought, "I'm just like Job's friends. I preach against platitudes and then I come out with a lulu like that." And meanwhile the hiccuping alto fled out the back door in her humiliation and went to the parking lot and got into her car. The congregation heard the door slam, and then the starter, and the engine coughing, and then it started. She backed up but someone had blocked her in. She pulled forward, then back, then forward, trying to maneuver past him. They could hear this through Pastor Ingqvist's prayer, the gravel

under the tires going back and forth, the front wheels turning, a car trapped, a sinner inside it.

Everyone knew who the alto was from the cadence of her walk and could imagine the long lanky legs and fascinating hips of Marilyn Tollerud, who, though the mother of six children, comes to church looking as if she were nineteen and hoping to catch someone's eye. When she turns and walks away, what goes through a man's mind is nothing you would discuss in detail in the Lutheran church.

Marilyn was working in her flower bed one fall day a few years ago when the garbage truck rumbled up the driveway to collect the trash. When the driver started to drive out Marilyn was bending over to press the tulip bulbs into the soft moist earth, and he hit the gas with the truck in reverse gear and backed into the Tollerud chicken coop and knocked it three feet off the footings, and three old laying hens shrieked and came flapping out the door, and the dog dashed in and ate two of the eggs and the garbage man went to look at the damage, and here came the old black Lab with egg yolk dripping from his chops and then there was Marilyn in her blue denim blouse and her jeans, saying, "Are you all right?" And no, he was not. His name was Arlen, he was twenty-three, he worked for his dad, he was a good boy, saving up so he could afford to have a family of his own one day, but his heart was filled with lust, and he quit his job that same week and bought a motorcycle and went to California and spent all his money on wine and wild women, and all because of those hips, those legs, those tulip bulbs.

Marilyn and her sister Audrey, back in their salad days, got a lot of young men excited. The fabulous Swenson girls. They loved to go to dances wherever there was one—wedding dances, 4-H, DeMolay, Elks—they'd borrow their dad's pickup and drive a hundred miles to go dancing, two big tall good-looking girls with strawberry blond hair, farm girls, full of self-confidence—women who grow up on farms walk and talk a certain way, the result of having driven tractors and handled a gun, slaughtered chickens, planted apple trees, an easygoing hands-on-the-hips confidence that is sexy in a way you can't achieve with a black lowcut dress and a string of pearls. They'd walk into Moonlite Bay or Fitger's or the Palace in Fergus Falls or the Arabian Nights ballroom in Alexandria, fresh and smiling, and in two minutes each of them was out on the floor waltzing with a young man, and other young men standing nearby, vitally interested, and after a few dances, you heard shouting in the parking lot and men slugging it out.

The Swenson sisters started plenty of fights in their day. They were full of fun and only wanted to dance, but young country men are charged with hormones up to their eyebrows, their brains are soaking in testosterone, and they interpret a woman's friendliness as avid sexual interest. If a woman says, "Hi, how are you?" the young man gets dizzy, so inevitably a couple young men came crosswise of each other and exchanged words and stalked out the back door, other men pouring out after them into the dark, and the two wrestled around and slapped at each other and ripped each other's shirts, and soon the others took sides, and then the whole crowd was wrestling and grabbing and gouging and pounding and kicking and cursing, and meanwhile the Swenson girls sat in a booth and sipped on a root beer and looked at each other and said, "Well, what's that all about? What gets into men anyway?"

The Swenson girls were ahead of their time: they liked music and dancing and appreciated dirty jokes up to a point and enjoyed flirting. They weren't demure. They looked straight at you with interest and appreciation, and plenty of young men thought that they were the chosen one and wound up grappling in the dirt with somebody else who had gotten the same idea.

Twenty-six years and six children later, Marilyn still makes a man's heart flutter. And when Carl Krebsbach, at the wheel of his John Deere, plowing his garden, looked up and saw her standing beside her car stuck in the mud beside the Lutheran church because she'd tried to drive across the grass to get out of the parking lot and had hit a soft spot, he swerved out of the yard and came chugging up the alley wearing his white cowboy hat. He pulled up and attached a chain to her front bumper and got back up on the tractor. Inside the church, it was the closing hymn—"Faith of our fathers, holy faith, we will be true to thee 'til death,"—and it sounded to the Lutherans as if they were under attack by a tank battalion, but it was only Carl Krebsbach, pulling Marilyn Tollerud out of the soft ground.

He was a little overeager. The rear tires of the John Deere got into a soft place, and by the time the Lutherans emerged from church, there was general desolation, turf dug up, big gullies where the tractor wheels had dug down, and Carl had gotten the chains out and there he stood, his arms full of chains, Marilyn beside him, beautiful, blushing bright red. A primitive scene. The earth ripped raw, the smell of dirt, the spring breeze, the man caught in the act, lust written all over his face, his tractor chugging and panting, the woman tall, smiling, hands on her hips, a woman who has slaughtered chickens and planted apple trees. And that's the news from Lake Wobegon, where all the women are strong, the men are good looking, and all the children are above average.

Moos

Margaret Moos (at right) produced PHC from 1974 to 1985, and the spring of 1987. Now Margaret Pick, she heads Pacific Vista Productions, Inc., in Petaluma CA, working with Lynne Cruise to produce the weekly "Riverwalk: Live from the Landing" and other public radio programs. She also runs the Vintage Jazz recording label.

Monback

Monback Brothers Trash Hauling is the only company in the trash trade that will come to your home and advise you on what to keep and what should go. Too many persons assess the value of their possessions by how difficult it would be to replace them. This is the standard that leads to those stacks of *Life* and *National Geographic* in the basement for truly it would not be so easy to find a copy of the July, 1948, *Geographic* with Pyrenees on the cover ("Spain, Land of Contrasts") A better test of value is: if this went away, would I miss it next week?

> We must fight our little battles against our goods
> and chattels,
> Simplify, simplify.
> All the useless apparatus and the paper they
> throw at us,
> Simplify, simplify.
> Choose what's practical and real, on reality rely.
> Keep this password your ideal:
> Simplify, simplify.

Mosquitoes

A thin high-pitched whine in the air, it's summer in Minnesota, and mosquitoes are part of our heritage, going back to Adam and Eve. They lived in the St. Croix valley (known then as Eden) and ate the apple (a Beacon) and swarms of mosquitoes descended on them and paradise became a memory. A couple weeks later it began to snow.

The Vikings came through in the 14th century and left a runestone in south Minneapolis, the Kenwood Runestone, that said, "Twelve of us on a fish fry and we're getting bit and we ran out of dill dip. God have mercy."

In the 17th century, French explorers searched for the fabled oilfields of northern Minnesota; they canoed through the swamps and streams, stopped and looked at each other—covered with insects and red welts and dizzy from slapping mosquitoes off their heads—and said, "What do you say we try Quebec first and leave this for later?" And so our fabled oilfields are still up there, safe and secure.

Mother's Thinking

My mother is a true Minnesotan. She knows it is bad luck to celebrate good luck, or to enjoy it too openly. We have been extremely lucky in our family, so to protect our good luck, my mother has always contemplated disaster. If you don't anticipate disaster, then your good luck will turn sour. This is an ancient religion that predates the Gospel of Matthew. It's like the winter freeze that enables the apple tree to bear blossoms in the spring. My mother has seldom driven away from the house in a car but what she could see clearly in her mind the house bursting into flames. An oven, an iron, the furnace—for whatever reason, the house went up in flames and she does not look into the rearview mirror because that might make it true.

And then later she comes home and the house is all right. A miracle. In this way she has kept us from harm over the years. But now my mother has used up most of her magic. Much of it on me, the black sheep of my family. My mother listens to the show with her magical sense of disaster. Every week she sees clearly in her mind a sandbag falling from high above the stage and dropping on my head and driving my head down into my chest cavity and leaving me a pitiful vegetable. By the power of this magical vision, she has kept me from all harm and enabled this show to endure. But now her magic is waning. She is eighty now. How much longer will her magic work? The longevity of our parents is a blessing; it gives us a luxurious long childhood, protected by their magic, and my mother often imagines me in a barroom, drunk, soaked in self-pity, bloated, and in this way, she enabled me to lead a fairly respectable and productive life. So far. But when she's gone, who will fear for me? Nobody. Everybody will tell me how good it's going, tell me how much they like what I do, how good-looking I am, and the next thing you know, that sandbag will fall.

Moving and Hauling

Monback Brothers Trash Hauling. What is this? Your Sunday *New York Times*? That's last Sunday's *Times*. You mean you're not done with it? You had six days to read it and you're not done with the "Week in Review" section? That's last "Week in Review." Today is Saturday. You got another Sunday *Times* coming tomorrow. You start getting behind on the *Times*, pretty soon you're gonna need your own personal ware house. Gimme that paper. We know what's trash. We're in the trash business. Monback Brothers.

Musicians

"Musicians' Fight Song" (to the tune of University of Michigan fight song)

> We are musicians and we play in the orchestra,
> We're gypsy artists and we're laughing at life
>   (ha ha ha),
> We get to sleep late and
> We don't work in offices
> We're in the music biz and you wish you
>   were too.
> We like to hang out and make fun of conductors
>   because
> They're so ridiculous—when they get mad
>   (ARF ARF ARF)
> We are musicians and we
> Like to act crazy cause if
> We don't act crazy, you would think we had
>   no talent.
>
> We play in musicals, at nightclubs and
>   wedding dances
> We play for funerals too—may we do yours?
>   (Just kidding.)
> We get to travel and we
> Stay in the best hotels and
> We never go to bed before two A.M.
> We wear black clothing so
> We never do laundry because
> We are bohemians and life is a song (la la la)
> We live on caviar and
> Champagne and oysters because
> We are musicians (yo!) and we are very cool.

Peter Ostroushko (left) with his Mando Boys, August 1986.

New Year's Eve Poem

Because I could not dance with you—
You kindly Danced with Me—
The Champagne Glass—Alas—inspired
An Awful Revelry.

You meant to dance—A Seemly Waltz—
I upward Kicked my Heels—
Showing how a Fox would Trot—
Across the Clover Fields.

I improvised—A Bumblebee—
I mimed—A Bobolink—
I did the Muskrat Ramble—
And never stopped—to think—

I danced—it seemed a Century—
And then I touched my Head—
And found that I was Wearing There
A Damask Blue Lampshade.

And I upon a Table Stood—
The Guests Arrayed Beneath—
Were looking in Amazement at
The rose—Between—My Teeth.

I sang a Song so Merrily
As Bird in Windowsill—
And then A Wave of Nausea—
A Yearning to—Be Still.
I Lay Down—in a Darkened Room—
A Washcloth—on my Brow—
Here have I lain—for Twenty Years
I'm feeling Better Now.

Nikolina

I fell in love with darling Nikolina,
And we decided that we should be wed.
But when I asked her father for permission,
He said, "Please wait until I'm dead."

Her mother wept so hard she broke her corset,
Her father reached out for his whiskey jug,
The dog jumped up and was so brokenhearted,
He had an accident upon the rug.

I said, "Is it because I can't support her,
Or is there something wrong I might have
        done?"
Her father said, "It's that you're Swedish,
I never met one who was that much fun."

"You only work, you never go to parties,
You never tell a joke when it's your turn.
You sit there silently and chew your roast beef,
It's like eating with a Boston fern."

He said, "You're boring, and I just don't get it,
What Nikolina ever saw in you."
And so I picked her papa up and kissed him,
"Boring, sir, it simply isn't true."

I danced a jig while telling jokes and riddles
And juggling knives till they were goggle-eyed
And sang an aria from *Rigoletto*,
Just to show I had another side.

NIKOLENA

A chart by Rich Dworsky

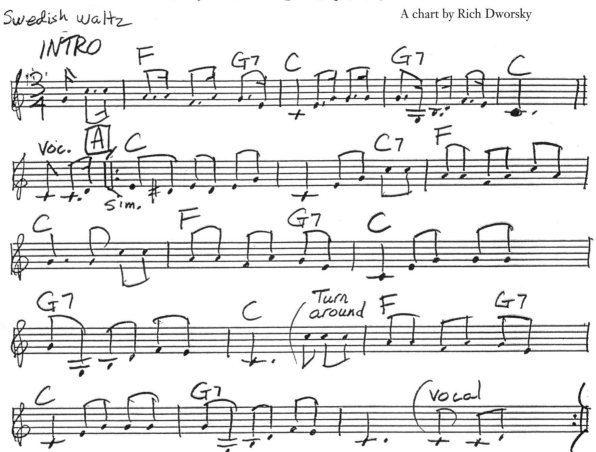

I took a match and lit some firecrackers
And somehow managed to burn down the joint,
And everyone leaped out the kitchen windows.
"Okay," her father said, "I get the point."

And so I married darling Nikolina,
We bought a little house right here in town,
We had a baby who we named Christina,
And every night to supper we sit down.

I toss the salad, and I wash the dishes,
I try to give them everything they need,
If you want comedy, go to the movies;
If you want marriage, you should find a Swede.

Noir

A dark night in a city that knows how to keep its secrets, but on the twelfth floor of the Acme Building, one man is still trying to find the answers to life's persistent questions—Guy Noir, Private Eye.

And there he is, feet up on his desk, waiting for the phone to ring, mourning for his lost Sugar, postponing his trek across the street to the Five Spot. The desk is piled with unpaid bills, one from the fumigator stamped "This bill is one year old." He scribbles "Happy Anniversary" on it and mails it back. It was one of those fall days when the rain against the window makes you imagine you're in

In "Guy Noir, Private Eye," Tim Russell (in light suit) plays Jimmy the bartender at the Five Spot, various Mafiosi and thugs, Guy's landlord Lou, and Jesse (The Body) Ventura. Sue Scott plays Guy's ex-love Sugar and various bombshells who walk into the Five Spot, accompanied by breathy saxophone. Tom Keith, far left, plays drunks, bozos, incoherent phone callers, and monosyllabic Mafia chieftains. GK is Guy.

England, in the officers club, it's 1944, your B-17 "The Shady Lady" is fueling up out on the tarmac, the crew is assembling in the ready room for another mission over Berlin, and you put down your cards—three aces—and scoop up the pot and say, "Well, gentlemen," and reach up to tighten your chinstrap, and all you find there is one of your chins. The rain was making my left knee ache, a reminder that I didn't have any place to go anyway. I studied a food stain on my left pantleg, thinking, If only I bought a new suit, it would give me the confidence I need to go out and earn the money to pay for it.

Or it's winter. It was the first week of February, a time when most Minnesotans have gone through the five steps of coming to terms with winter:

Anger, Denial, Bargaining, Depression, and Vacation in Florida. Myself, I was thinking of maybe checking into a Home for the Weak of Character and letting large sympathetic women nurture me for a few months. It was so cold that finally you could understand why Minnesotans talk that way. It was so cold, I felt like I was in an experiment and giant men and women in white lab coats were standing over me and looking down and saying, "Let's crank it down another ten degrees and see if he goes south then." I looked out the window. Gray snow, gray sky, and a large gray cloud in the middle of it, and then I realized it was the reflection of my face.

Or maybe it's spring. It was one of those cold rainy April days when it seems like spring is just around a couple more corners. I'd put on the wrong pair of socks, orange ones with little grand pianos, a gift from an admirer. And they didn't go with my green tie. A morning of disaster all around. I lost the key to my office when I was in the pawnshop getting a $3 loan on my answering machine and had to crawl over the transom, ripping the seat of my pants and revealing my mistletoe shorts, and then I discovered that the three bucks was gone. And the door was unlocked. A bad day and it wasn't even noon yet. I was thinking maybe I oughta lock up the office and go for a walk, and then I remembered how much I hate walks. I sat at my desk and examined a brochure for a cruise ship, the S.S. *Bellissima*, and imagined myself on it, in a white outfit, sailing the waters of Polynesia as beautiful women clustered around, listening spellbound to my tales of lonely courage in the fight against crime.

Then the phone rang. It was Mrs. Grady. I'd been looking for her missing husband.

Lady: Sorry. He was in the basement. He got engrossed in some old *National Geographic*s.
Noir: I been all over town looking for him, lady.
Lady: Maybe you shoulda checked the basement.
Noir: A whole day he was down there?
Lady: It was a good article. And he's a slow reader.

A knock on the door. Maybe it's a client.

Joe: You do surveillance?
Noir: Right. What you need surveilled?
Joe: I need you to go over to a family picnic and see if my dingbat cousin from Des Moines is there.
Noir: What does he look like?
Joe: He wears dumb clothes and he has a head like a pear and he stands around saying stupid things in a voice you can hear two blocks away. I need to know if he's there 'cause if he is, I'm not going.

The phone rings. It's a dad wanting Guy to swing over by the U and make sure his son Danny is going to class. It's a lady looking for her cat Pookey. Or a man who wants the answer to eleven down on this morning's crossword. Or it's a guy trying to think of the punchline to a joke his brother-in-law told him at Easter and he laughed so hard he felt like he'd had a facelift. Heck of a joke. Now he can't remember

it. Or maybe it's the cops, looking for help.
Sgt: Sergeant Hathaway from the SPPD.
Noir: The Saint Paul Police Department?
Sgt: Right. I'm engaged in an MPO right now.
Noir: A Missing Person Operation.
Sgt: Right. And I'm wondering if you could take a look at our RMPMF.
Noir: The RMPMF?
Sgt: Reported Missing Person Mugshot File. Mind if I sit down?
Noir: Sure, sit on the OAC.
Sgt: Uh—
Noir: Right there. The oak arm chair.

Or a phone call from a man in great need.

Man (on phone): You a private eye?
Noir: Yeah, right.
Man: I'm looking for my glasses.
Noir: (SIGH) Just look for them.
Man: I need some help.
Noir: Look in the bathroom. Look on your bedside table.
Man: I can't. I'm in my car, calling from a carphone.
Noir: You're driving without your glasses?
Man: I've got my reading glasses on. I can see shapes. (HONK) Hey!

His eternal hope, leaning back in his chair, is that a babe will walk in. And now and then one does. And just then she walked in. She looked a lot like the women in the swimwear catalogue except she appeared to be dry. She was tall and blond except she'd dyed the roots brunette, a nice touch. Her lips seemed to glisten, her eyes sparkled. She was wearing a black blouse which she had neglected to button all the way to the top. And jeans, preshrunk by somebody who must have measured her with a caliper. And the blouse was small—I mean, I've seen more cotton in the top of an aspirin bottle. It was so tight, it was more like a tourniquet. I watched carefully to make sure she was breathing. She was. So was I.

Babe: Hi. I'm Nichole.
Noir: Where have you been all my life, gorgeous?
Babe: Well, for the first half of it, I wasn't born.

GUY NOIR

Words G. Keillor
music R. Dworsky

In Cm

Lyrics (line 1):
They can | run a-way They can try to hide He'll find 'em wherever they are   He can see in the dark he's a private eye   He's, Guy Guy Noir He's

Lyrics (line 2):
smooth He's cool He's fast with a gun And a master in the boudoir   A man in a trench coat who gets the job done That's Guy Guy Noir

Tom Keith, Tim Russell, and Sue Scott. "Radio acting is a rare skill, not much in demand. It's all seat of the pants, hardly any rehearsal, and takes nerves of steel. And tremendous range. With these three, we've done the *Odyssey*, the *Iliad*, the Prodigal Son, the story of Job, and a lot of crummy commercials."

Norwegian Jokes

Lena: Norwegian men are emotionally challenged people. In the range of human joy and exultation, they're missing the top couple octaves. As for romantic, forget about it. A Norwegian guy likes to go to bed with two women so that when he falls asleep they can talk to each other. He would marry a pregnant woman just to save himself the trouble.

Ole: You're saying I'm not romantic?

Lena: Listen. When the sexual revolution came around, you were out of ammunition, Ole. You chase women like a dog chases a car, with no particular idea of what to do if you actually got one. The average Norwegian guy is so repressed, he blushes if someone says "Intersection." He only thinks about sex when he gets too drunk to go deer hunting, and then he gets up his courage and goes downtown and spends the night in a warehouse.

Ole: A warehouse?

Lena: They're terrible spellers too. I know Norwegian men, my father was one. He always came back from the dump with more than he went there with. Dad'd mow his lawn and find a couple new cars. And they were Norwegian cars, with rags for gas caps and a Hefty bag for the window on the driver's side because Dad broke it throwing out the beer bottles.

Ole: Your dad did that?

Lena: Yes, and you're a lot like him. Dad thought diarrhea was hereditary because he found it in his jeans. He and Mama had twelve kids because they lived near the train tracks and when the midnight train came through and woke him up, he'd say, "Well, should we go back to sleep or what?" and Mama'd say, "What?" And then he ran away and left her and she had six more kids. Because every so often he came back to apologize. He never sent her child support, he just wrote her letters saying, "I meant to enclose money but I already sealed the envelope." Then he went and got a vasectomy so he wouldn't get grandchildren.

Ole: I don't know what this has to do with me.

Lena: My dad wasn't that bright either. He wrote TGIF in his shoes to remind him that Toes Go In First. He was trying to count up to twenty-one, and they arrested him for indecent exposure. The house caught on fire once and he tried to call 911 and he couldn't find eleven on the dial. So he called the operator and she couldn't find it either.

Ole: That reminds me of the Norwegian counterfeiter who—how does that joke go?

Lena: He made two-dollar bills by erasing the zeros on twenties. And then he won the Norwegian lottery. That's the one where you get a dollar a year for a million years. To celebrate, he went to New York City. He called home, all excited, and said, "I went down these stairs in the street, down to some guy's basement, and you ought to see the trains he's got down there."

Ole: Okay, goodnight, Lena.

Lena: Goodnight, Ole.

Nouns

Guy: What's wrong, hon?

Wife: I can't find those little things with the hooks on them that you stick through the hangy part of the thing on the side of your head that you hear through.

Guy: I thought I saw them on that ceramic thing that has the metal things that you turn and stuff comes out that you can drink or wash up with.

Wife: I wore those last night, I need the ones with the little shiny stuff that comes out of the digestive part of those hard little whatchamacallits that sit on the bottom of that big you know—that's wet and covers almost the whole—what we're on right now.

Guy: Oh, *those*, sure I saw 'em over on the hard flat place that you put stuff on, in the room we sit in to watch that—you know—that you click the little thing in your—you know—and it shows you stuff?

GK: Life is hard without nouns—don't be caught short. Order some today, at The Noun Outlet. Many of the words I'm using right now are nouns, and I form them with my tongue, teeth, lips, and soft palate, and use them to give specificity to what I say. So can you. Contact The Noun Outlet. Use a phone, write a letter, send E-mail, or visit their store.

November

I'm always relieved when it comes and we can get on with the exhilaration of cold weather. Something in the human makeup requires cold weather. The need for winter is related to the need for sleep, and winterlessness makes people crazy as rats in a coffee can, but I suppose if you're around other people who all have the same symptoms, you don't notice it so much. And we outsiders are too polite to point it out. Southerners ask, "Why would anyone want to live in Minnesota?" It's like asking, "Why would anyone ever sail the sea?" Winter is an adventure. You can travel the world and pay thousands of dollars for it; in Minnesota you just walk out your front door.

Objects

Louis Jenkins, who lives in Duluth MN, appeared on PHC twice, October 9, 1976, and November 4, 1995, reading his poems.

A Place For Everything

It's so easy to lose track of things. A screwdriver, for instance. "Where did I put that? I had it in my hand just a minute ago." You wander vaguely from room to room, having forgotten, by now, what you were looking for, staring into the refrigerator, the bathroom mirror... "I really could use a shave...."

Some objects seem to disappear immediately while others never want to leave. Here is a small black plastic gizmo with a serious demeanor that turns up regularly, like a politician at public functions. It seems to be an "intregal part," a kind of switch with screw holes so that it can be attached to something larger. Nobody knows what. This thing's use has been forgotten but it looks so important that no one is willing to throw it in the trash. It survives by bluff, like certain insects that escape being eaten because of their formidible appearance.

My father owned a large, three-bladed, brass propeller that he saved for years. Its worth was obvious, it was just that it lacked an immediate application since we didn't own a boat and lived hundreds of miles from any large bodies of water. The propeller survived all purges and cleanings, living, like royalty, a life of lonely privilege, mounted high on the garage wall.

Odd

It happens unpredictably—the man and his wife are in a domestic setting, in conversation after Thanksgiving dinner, or eating at a truck stop, or getting ready to go to the neighbors'—and things go from bad to worse. On November 26, 1994, the husband went down to the basement to check on the lawyer they kept, and suddenly he disappeared, leaving only his shoes nailed to the wall. In April of the next year, the wife ordered chef's salad with chickadee strips, and the roast bunny rabbit, and suddenly all that remained of her husband was his watch, wallet, shoes, and belt buckle. More mysterious things happened in subsequent episodes in May 1995, November and December 1996 in "That's Odd," written for the Lonesome Radio Theater by Muriel W. Brubaker.

Ol' Man Winter

Ol' man winter, that ol' man winter
He comes in November and stays forever
He jus' keeps blowin'
Snowin' and blowin' along

He freezes our noses and kills our roses
We all get colds and then psychosis
But ol' man winter he jus' keeps blowin' along

You an' me from November to March,
Not enough salad and too much starch,
Push that car, shovel that walk
Sun goes down about three o'clock...

I am weary and I work like a fool I
Sure could use a couple weeks of July
But ol' man winter he jus' keeps blowin' along.

GK with Alan Frechtman playing "Chico," the stage-hand who becomes a famous crooner.

Only in America

Assistant Stage Manager Alan Frechtman's grand-mother, Eva Birkenfeld, a Jewish immigrant from Lodz, Poland, in 1920, lived in Brooklyn. When Alan worked with PHC in New York, his grandmother asked him to tune her kitchen radio to the public radio station carrying the show. She didn't always understand GK's allusions, but faithfully listened every Saturday. As Alan's mother tells

him, when she would hear her grandson's name mentioned in the credits, she would pound the kitchen table with her fist and shout out loud, "Only in America!"

Opera

Domino's Opera lets you order an opera to be delivered fresh to your door. You could order comic or tragic, with peasants or a masked ball or a sorceress, maybe extra sorceresses, and the delivery man arrived, proclaimed his love for you ("The night you spent with me / I remember what you said / Because your tongue was in my mouth") and aroused the jealousy of your husband, a sword fight ensued, the two of them killed each other, and sang a dying duet, during which the delivery man discovered that your Visa card had expired.

Orange Juice

Florida orange juice. You go along for years drinking it, and then suddenly your voice gets croaky.

Geezer: Wasn't that in '75 we went down and visited Val and Bob in Pensacola? That was the year Roger got married, wasn't it? Or was it in '78? Was Danny a baby then? Because Val passed away the year after that, didn't she? In '79? Or '80? And Bob in '84. Right?

You pour yourself a big glass of orange juice, and you start talking like this.

Geezer: They had a Subaru, I remember that, a blue one, and they drove us to a Perkins once for breakfast. Remember? That was in '78, and you had the Belgian waffle and I had a couple fried eggs with hash browns, remember? Because the waitress brought them with the eggs beside the hash browns and I had ordered them with the eggs on the hash browns, so I had her take it back and do it right. I forget what Val and Bob had. I think he ordered poached.

You're only in your late forties, but suddenly you have funny hair that you comb up from the side of your head and across the top.

Geezer: What did Val die of? Somebody was saying the other day it was liver cancer, but I think it was the pancreas. I forget who said that. It was over at your sister's. That guy from Tulsa, what's his name, he knew Val and Bob, and he said it was pancreas, but I think that's what Bob had. One of them did, I know that.

You can read great books, fill your mind with interesting things, travel, meet fascinating people, live a rich and rewarding life, but when you ingest citrus drinks, suddenly one day you'll look down and you're wearing plaid pants, white shoes, a white belt, and a golf shirt.

Geezer: No, it was Val who had the Belgian waffle, and it was in '75, it wasn't in '78, because I remember saying to her when the waffle came, I said, "Boy, I'd like to have one of those but I can't because I got to fit into my tuxedo for Roger's wedding," and Roger got married in '75, didn't he? What? '82? No, I mean his first marriage. She had the Belgian waffle and you had the fruit plate and the bagel, remember? And the bagel wasn't toasted and you had to send it back and then it was toasted but it was cold. Yeah, that was in '75.

Florida orange juice. Its role in accelerating the aging process is not exactly known, and until we know more, it's a good idea to limit your consumption of orange juice to a glass or two per month. A message in the public interest from the Minnesota Apple Growers Association.

Ostroushko, Marge

Marge Ostroushko, the associate producer from 1978 to1985, began by selling tickets for PHC in 1976. The St. Paul-Ramsey Arts & Science Center auditorium had 230 seats. Marge would go to MPR on Saturday at noon to answer the phone calls of people reserving tickets. Marge wrote their names and how many tickets, and when 230 seats were spoken for, she stopped answering the phone. One of her jobs was to call up St. Louis Catholic Church on Friday and remind them not to ring their bells on Saturday evening. Married to Peter Ostroushko. After leaving PHC, Marge worked for ten years for Public Radio International in program development and marketing. She now is a consultant and freelance producer of public radio programs and events.

Marge Ostroushko, 1980. Married to the borscht king, the Marlon Brando of the mandolin.

Ostroushko, Peter

Borscht

B-O-R-S-C-H-T, it's the sweetest thing this side
    of heaven Mama made for me,
I've eaten it all my life, or at least since I was
    three, this B-O-R-S-C-H-T.
B-O-R-S-C-H-T, and now that I'm an adult,
    I can make it just for me,
And if you've got a minute, I will share my
    recipe, for B-O-R-S-C-H-T.

First you get four quarts of water, put it in a pot.
You start a blaze beneath, add some salt, but
    not a lot.
Add some pepper, and some parsley, a bay leaf's
    optional
When the water starts to simmer then you know
    it's time to go.

Peter Ostroushko made his debut on PHC in 1974 and has appeared regularly ever since, playing bluegrass, old-time, Ukrainian, classical, and his own compositions.

And get a chicken, though my mama says a
    turkey tastes the best.
You chop it into pieces take the giblets
    and the neck,
Put it in the water, then turn the heat down low,
And let that chicken simmer for a half an
    hour or so.

When that chicken meat is cooked take it out
    with extra care,
Put it in a bowl inside your cold reFridgidaire.
While the meat is slowly cooling take a break
    and have a smoke.
While the soup it slowly simmers, you can
    watch your favorite soap.

Now it's time to get an onion, and two
    garlic cloves
Chop them finely then into a frying pan
    they'll go.
Sauté them in some butter till they're brown and
    kind of clear.
You put them in the soup and now tomato time
    is here.

If you can your own tomatoes, one quart is all
    you need,
But if you use the store bought kind, get two
    cans of Del Montes.
Add the 'maters to the soup let it simmer if
    you will.
Then add about a tablespoon of dried or fresh
    cut dill

Now it's time to get some carrots, potatoes five
    or six,
Three or four red beets, chop them into bite
    size bits,
Add the veggies to the soup, let it simmer there
    and thicken,
Go back to your Fridgidaire, and get that cooled
    off chicken.

Take the meat off the bone, take away the skin
    and fat,
Put the meat into the soup, give the rest to your
    old cat.
Now the soup is nearly finished; your race is
    almost run,
But don't forget the cabbage it's the last thing
    that is done.

One small head of cabbage, that you shred up
    fairly fine,
Once you put it in the soup it doesn't take much
    time.
You can start to set your table, and call your
    dinner guests,
But don't forget the condiments that'll put them
    to the test.

Get one loaf of rye bread that is full of
    caraway seeds.
You slice it nice and thick, use lots of butter
    if you please,
And next comes thick white sour cream that'll
    make them groan with pleasure.
You plop it in the soup, but now you're really
    under pressure.

'Cuz, the final step is garlic cloves that are nice
    and fat.
You peel them till they're naked, and you eat
    them just like that!
You dip them in a bowl of salt, and eat those
    puppies raw,
And now you're ready for the finest meal you
    ever saw.

And nirvana is at hand!! It's the best soup in
    the land!
And I'll spell it for you, one more time, to be
    sure you understand why:

B-O-R-S-C-H-T is the sweetest thing this side
    of heaven Mama made for me,
For breakfast, lunch, or dinner any day of any
    week it's B-O-R-S-C-H-T.
B-O-R-S-C-H-T, it's made me healthy, wealthy,
    wise, and unless I sound too meek,
It's made me what I am, and I'll continually
    always speak for B-O-R-S-C-H-T.
(and not clam chowder)
B-O-R-S-C-H-T!

Pans

"Keillor Should Take a Long Walk off a Short Pier into Woebegon," by Doug Mattson (*Mankato State University Reporter*, Wednesday, July 12, 1989):

> ". . .like bad morning breath he [keeps] coming back. . .it appears that the man [is] revered. But why? Try and figure it out. Could it be the way he emits his barely audible drawl into an endless series of stereotypes about Minnesota. For some, the stories never get old despite the same setting, same characters and same outcome. Spare public radio, put him on the Bat Channel."

"All The Music Is Above Average and Garrison Keillor Can't Take All the Credit. So What Makes 'A Prairie Home Companion' Sing?" by Keith Moerer (*Sidewalk Twin Cities*, March 1999):

> "Sorry to be blunt, but I can't stand the smug, self-adoring voice of Garrison Keillor, talking about the good folks of Lake Wobegon and their crazy Lutheran ways. . . .When I listen to 'A Prairie Home Companion'—broadcast live from the Fitzgerald Theater in downtown Saint Paul—I hope to hear Keillor shut up."

"Plenty Wholesome and a Little Perverse," by Spalding Gray (*New York Times Book Review*, October 4, 1987):

> "I would often force myself to stay tuned through all that tacky sexless music to try to find out why that golden voice was, if not better than, then at least more popular than mine. . . . But always somewhere at the beginning, just after Garrison Keillor got warmed up, my girlfriend, Renee, would charge into the room yelling, 'Turn that garbage off! It makes me want to swear!'"

"Post-Gorby Minnesota: Wobegon No More," by William E. Schmidt of the *New York Times* (in the *Saint Paul Pioneer Press*, June 7, 1990):

> "'In some ways, Garrison Keillor did more damage to the image of Minnesota than Stalin did to the Soviet Union,' Eisele said. 'We are more than a bunch of dumb Swedish farmers wandering around telling corny jokes.'"

"Rude Awakenings" by Mark Vaught (*The Downtowner*, January 29, 1986):

> "And as a midwesterner with rural roots, I see the show as an insulting, inaccurate caricature of rural and small town America."

Parents

After years of clawing your way to the top and doing ugly things you don't like to think about, you've finally reached the peak of your profession. You're hauling down a salary the size of the gross national product of a third-world country.

You're surrounded by underlings fawning over you and your P.R. people have convinced everyone that you're a genius and a living legend. Your only problem? Embarrassing parents, parents who say, "Yeah, it's gonna be a cold one tonight. They say it'll get down to twenty or so." "Izzat right?" "Yeah, that's what they say. Hey, where's that supper? I thought you was going to make supper." "I thought we were going out to Burger King." "What do you think I am? Made of money or what?"

Don't you deserve parents who reflect your taste? You can have them through Prestige Parents. Whether you want them for an evening, a weekend, or by the month, you can have the parents of your dreams through Prestige. Elderly but youthful Episcopalians from Minneapolis—a dad with handsome white hair, in a houndstooth jacket and slacks, with a pipe, and a mom, cheerful and spry, in her blue wool suit and Oxfords. You've got everything else you always wanted. Now it's time to get the right parents. Through Prestige Parents. Reserve yours now for the holidays.

Paris Review

Guy Noir (GK): It was February and the weather turned warm and I was thinking of going out for a walk when, (KNOCKS ON DOOR)—Yeah. (KNOCKS) Just a minute. (KNOCKS) (FOOT-STEPS) Coming, coming, coming...(DOOR OPENS)

Joey (Tim Russell): I come to see you about something. I'm here for Tony.

Guy: Tony Rigatoni? The capo primo de primo? Well. This is an honor.

Joey: He respects you very highly, Guy. And he hopes that he has your respect.

Guy: Of course. Always. Please convey my respect to Tony.

Joey: I will do that. In fact, he's here. In the hall. Mind if he comes in?

Guy: Tony—he's in the hall—what's he doin' there? Huh? Oh my gosh.

Joey: Hey—hey—hey—it's okay. No problem. No problem. Okay? Okay if he comes in? Come on in, Tony. (FOOTSTEPS) Tony, you remember Guy.

Tony (Tom Keith): Yeah.

Joey: Guy, you remember Tony.

Guy: It's good to see ya, Tony. It's been awhile.

Joey: Tony's been at Leavenworth for eighteen years, Guy. Tony got out on Tuesday.

Guy: Well. Congratulations. I'm happy for you.

Joey: And now Tony would like you to do a job for him. Tony spent eighteen years in Leavenworth and while there he got interested in writing poetry and now he wants you to get these poems published for him.

Guy: Aha. A poet. I'll see what I can do. I don't know much about poetry, but—

Joey: Tony has written some very fine poems, Guy.

Guy: I have no doubt about that, Joey.

Joey: I brought them with me. Tony wants these published right away. It means a lot to him. He wants them in the *Paris Review*. He liked the title. *Paris Review*. Classy, huh? And he wants to get a hundred grand for each one of 'em. Or else.

Guy: That's a lot of money.

Joey: You get a lot of poem for that money. And you get the name: Tony Rigatoni. Huh? That ain't chopped liver, pal.

Guy: I know that, but I don't think people get a hundred grand for a (SLAP)—

Joey: You're takin' a very negative attitude, Guy.

Guy: Is there going to be a lot of hitting here, Joey? Huh? I'm only asking.

Joey: You ain't even seen the poems and already

you're running down their cash value.

Guy: I'm sorry. Let me see it.

Joey: Which one you want me to show him, Tony? Huh? This one? "My love is like a red red rose"? Huh?

Tony: Yeah.

Joey: Here. (SHEET OF PAPER IS PASSED)

Guy: Okay. Thanks. Very nice typing job, Tony, let me congratulate you on that right away. Good neat margins. White paper, heavy stock. You're winning points right away with that.

Joey: Read the poem.

Guy: My love is like a red, red rose that's newly sprung in June. My love is like a melody that's sweetly played in tune. So fair art thou, my bonnie lass, so deep in love am I, that I will love thee still, my dear, till I see the gang go dry.

Joey: Whatsamatter?

Guy: Till I see the gang go dry?

Joey: He'll stop loving her the day he sees the boys give up beer and whiskey. Meaning, never.

Guy: Oh! Oh! Of course.

Joey: Something wrong with that?

Guy: No. Fine. Just was confused, because, you know, in the original, it reads a little different—

Joey: Original! You saying that Tony stole this? Huh? (WIND UP AND KONK OF PUNCH.) You saying this ain't original?

Guy: No, no—it's always been original. Great poem. Always was. You know, it's getting dangerous to make any statements about literature these days. It almost doesn't pay to be a critic. That was a compliment, Joey.

Joey: Well, it didn't sound like one. Did it sound like a compliment to you, Tony?

Tony: Yeah.

Joey: It did?

Tony: Yeah.

Joey: Okay. Tony says he took it as a compliment. My apologies.

Guy: Does that mean that I get to hit you now?

Joey: I dunno. Tony?

Tony: Yeah.

Guy: Thanks, Tony. Why you (HE SWINGS, KONK. **Joey:** OOF)—

Joey: Ohhhh. You hit me a lot harder than what I hit you, Guy—I think I got a freebie coming. Do I get a freebie, Tony?

Tony: Yeah.

Joey: Okay. (HE WINDS UP. KONK. **Guy:** OOF)

Guy: This is a rough business, poetry. I don't think I care to get into it.

Joey: You're in it, wise guy. Tony says you're in it, you're in it. You want I should show him another one, Tony?

Tony: Yeah.

Joey: Okay. Here. (PAPER PASSING) Read it.

Guy: You know, I think these poems are too good for me, in a way. I think you could find—

Joey: Read it.

Guy: Okay.

> Whose house this is I think I know
> He's gone into the village though
> He will not see me stopping here
> To write my initials in his snow
>
> Tonight I drank a quart of beer
> And now there is no men's room near
> I feel like I contain a lake
> Like I could stand here for a year
>
> Finally I give a shake
> And button up for goodness sake
> The only other sound's the sweep
> Of easy wind, you stupid flake
>
> The woods are lovely, dark and deep
> But I have promises to keep
> I've got to put some guys to sleep
> Including him, the little creep.

Joey: It's good, isn't it. Huh? It's good. You like it? That's his. Tony wrote that. Spent eighteen years writing poetry. Now he wants to see some money out of it. Anything wrong with that? Huh? Guy's a poet, he deserves to get something out of it. I figure a hundred thou apiece. *Paris Review*. Want you to take care of it, Guy. How soon can you fly to Paris?

Guy: Listen. *The Paris Review*! You don't need *The Paris Review*. *The Paris Review* isn't going to give you top dollar for these. French people—they don't read poems in English. These are in English. You want Tony's poems to go unread?

Joey: No, of course not.

Guy: You want New York.

Joey: *The New York Review?*

Guy: Naw. *The New Yorker*. That's where you get

top dollar. *The New Yorker*. These poems are perfect for them. The person to see there is Tina Brown. You go see her. Or ask for Roseanne.

Joey: Roseanne works there?

Guy: She's an editor.

Joey: Hey, Roseanne is going to love these.

Guy: You bet she will.

Joey: Tina Brown? How do you spell that?

Guy: B-r-a-u-n. (PENCIL SCRATCHES) Right.

Joey: Okay. That's better. Now we're getting somewhere.

(MUSIC)

Announcer (Tim): A dark night in a city that keeps its secrets, but one guy is still trying to find the answers, Guy Noir, Private Eye.

(MUSIC OUT)

Pest Sonnet

In autumn when the days get short,
The mice move into the davenport,
And settle in with great esprit
Deep in the upholstery.
And little worms and insects too
Quietly move in with you.
Beetles, crickets of all ages,
Some in egg or larval stages,
Tiny bug and rodent friends
Come to share your residence.
Try as you will to fill the cracks,
Set traps, mount poison gas attacks,
We creatures are meant to be together,
Especially in colder weather.

Plumber

When the ice comes and the snow and it's
    forty-eight below
And then the temperature begins to fall
And they hear the moan and whine of that
    frozen water line
Then the plumber is the man who saves
    them all.

Oh, the plumber is the man, the plumber is
    the man.
Down into the cellar he must crawl.
He is not sleek and slim and they all look down
    on him
But the plumber is the man who saves them all.

When the toilet will not flush and the odor
    makes you blush
And you cannot use the sink or shower stall,
Then your learning and your art slowly start to
    fall apart
But the plumber is the man who saves it all.

Oh, the plumber is the man, the plumber is the man.
With his wrenches and his pipes he comes to call.
They can take their sins to Jesus but when
    their water freezes
Then the plumber is the man who saves them all.

I supposed that in your youth, beauty, justice, truth,
Seem to be what life is all about,
But when the facts are faced, you realize life
    is based
On water coming in and going out.

They don't let him in their club 'cause he never
    dresses up
And he doesn't go for tennis or handball,
Or Mozart or Chopin, but when it hits the fan
Then the plumber is the man who saves them all.

Oh, the plumber is the man, the plumber is the man.
In his vest and rubber boots and overalls.
So don't turn up your nose at the aroma of
    his clothes
For the plumber is the man who saves us all.

Producer

The production schedule displays the producer's work on Fridays and Saturdays. On Tuesdays, Wednesdays, and Thursdays, she oversees details for upcoming shows, runs the weekly staff meeting, and negotiates contracts and arrangements for tour shows. She keeps track of incoming script submissions (rarely used but still worth looking at), listener complaints, audience surveys, and she speaks for the show to Minnesota Public Radio, to the underwriter Lands' End, and to the distributor, Public Radio International. All this, and make aesthetic judgments too. A woman's work is never done.

Powdermilk bands over the years: Bill Hinkley, Judy Larson, Rudy Darling, and Rod Bellville. At right: Adam Granger, Dick Rees, Mary DuShane, and Bob Douglas, 1978.

Powdermilk Biscuit Band

A band called the Powdermilk Biscuit Band played regularly on early shows. Its membership gradually evolved: first Bill Hinkley and Judy Larson, sometimes with Dakota Dave Hull, sometimes with Cal Hand on dobro. Fiddler Rudy Darling joined in early 1975. Bob Douglas, mandolin, joined in late 1975. Hinkley and Larson left, replaced by guitarist Adam Granger. Darling moved west, replaced by Mary DuShane in late '76. Dick Rees joined on bass, summer of '77. Molly Mason replaced Rees, fall of '78. Tim Hennessy for Adam Granger, summer of '79. The Powdermilk Biscuit Band dissolved, re-formed into the New Prairie Ramblers (Douglas, Hennessy, and Peter Ostroushko) in January 1980, joined by bassist Barb Montoro in February. Replaced by the Butch Thompson Trio the summer of 1980. In later years other regular musical groups formed and re-formed, such as the Coffee Club Orchestra, then the Demitasse Orchestra, Guy's All-Star Shoe Orchestra, and Guy's All-Star Shoe Band.

Public Relations

Curry, Varnish, Burnish & Shine, the public relations firm, is an occasional PHC sponsor. "If celebrities need the reassurance of PR, think how much more you need it—you don't earn as much money as they do," says CVB&S, which will send a PR person to your home to gush over your outfit, tell lies about your children and their bright future, tell you how much your colleagues respect your work, and even reassure you about your marriage.

Client: Uh, I'm kind of worried about my wife.
CVB&S: Your wife is crazy about you, she just doesn't know how to show it.
Client: She's seemed very quiet lately.
CVB&S: She's worshiping you.
Client: I've been a jerk to her.
CVB&S: Brilliant people do not have smooth lives.

Production Schedule

A PRAIRIE HOME COMPANION WITH GARRISON KEILLOR

Print Date 99/02/04 2:49 PM Page 1

Firm, FITZ, ST. PAUL

====== FRIDAY, FEBRUARY 5, 1999 ======

10:00a	Crew/Staff call at the Fitzgerald; JJ, JK, TC, AF, +;
	Tom Campbell + 2 assemble house;
Restore stage:	rugs, house, piano, music stands & lights, chairs, power, stage monitor, mics, headphones, audience mics, audience seating;
12:00n	Sam Hudson arrive and get house sound setup;
	Scott Rivard setup Broadcast;
1:15p	Systems testing;
1:30p	Lunch Break, 1 hour; Release some crew;
2:30p	Recall; Receive musicians and get them set up;
3:00-6:30p	GAS Band rehearsal;
tba	GK with GASB, Rehearsal;
6:00p	Actors call;
6:30p	Script Reading;
7:30p?	Wrap at the Fitzgerald;

====== SATURDAY, FEBRUARY 6, 1999 ======

tba	Piano tuning by Mark Humphrey;
8:00a	Lighting call; TC, AS, MW?; Focus & Color;
tba	Catering set-up and ready to serve by 10:00a;
10:00a	Staff & Remaining Crew call; Systems testing;
10:30a	APHC production meeting;
*******	
11:00a	GAS Band, Rehearsal/Soundcheck;
tba	Lighting crew Meal Break;
11:30p?	Phil Cunningham & Aly Bain, Soundcheck; (as soon as they arrive from airport)
12:30p	GASB returns, Rehearsal/Soundcheck;
1:00p	Leo Kottke, Soundcheck;
1:30p	Crew/Staff Break, 15 minutes;
2:00p	Actors & GK Call; GK features w/GASB;
3:00p	Script rehearsal onstage;
	GK with GASB as needed;
3:45p	Catered meal ready to serve;
3:59p	LIVE PROMO :30 seconds duration;
4:00p	Rehearsal ends; show presets; Hot Meal Break on-site;
******	
4:05p	Piano touch-up tuning;
4:10p	HOUSE OPENS;
4:29p	Start walk-in music
4:40p	GAS Band / crew in place; standby for warm-up
4:45p	GK & GAS band warm-up the audience
5:00p	LIVE BROADCAST BEGINS; 1hr 59min duration
6:59p	LIVE BROADCAST ENDS
7:00p	Complete Strike & Stow of APHC stage equipment; House knock down;
9:00p	Wrap at the Fitzgerald;

Q,R

Questions

1. Are women more realistic than men or just moody?
2. Do women weep more often than men?
3. Why do men think there's enough gas left when the needle is on E?
4. Why do men crave and then fear intimacy?
5. What causes men and women to argue all the time?
6. Why do men hate short hair on women?

These questions were analyzed in "The Difference Between Men and Women" (1990–1995).

1. Women aren't moody. They're just more in touch with their feelings than men. They experience negative feelings fully. Men postpone their emotions. They ignore reality so they can accomplish something.
2. Men weep internally. Their tears flow into the nasal passage and become phlegm. When you see construction workers spitting, they're trying to cry.
3. Testosterone. Or else a guy doesn't want to stop for gas until he has to use the bathroom.
4. A nodding acquaintance deeply satisfies men. They can imagine a wonderful relationship without having to bother with actual human intervention.
5. Because women are from Saturn, whose rings

represent circular thinking. Men are from Uranus, the distant cold planet enveloped in a haze of dense freezing gas. Women enjoy feeling like a part of a community. Men pride themselves on self-sufficiency. Women like to vent. Men like to find solutions.

6. Short hair is about power, and that's why men have shorter hair than women. When a woman cuts her hair she threatens patriarchal authority.

Quite Unusual Acts for Radio

- Angelo Rulli, organ grinder
- Harley Refsal, wood carver
- St. Paul Bouncing Team from the St. Paul Winter Carnival Blanket Toss
- Jack Hart, magician, Nicollet Island show
- Cowboy rope tricks by Pop Wagner

Pop Wagner's cowboy rope tricks and one of Harley Refsal's wood carvings.

- Old Faithful erupting at
  4:39:23 on the Yellowstone Park show
- "Manualist" John Twomey playing "The Star
  Spangled Banner" with his hands
- Alan Frechtman, taking a kid from
  the audience and a microphone down the slide at
  the St. Paul Winter Carnival, while on the air
- Serena Wong playing the carillon in the Cornell
  University Bell Tower
- Avner the Eccentric, a mime
- A glass harmonica player
- A juggler in Seattle
- A hurdy-gurdy player

Radio

I've done radio shows on television and the experience of doing both at the same time is educational, like inviting your parents to meet your friends. Your funny old parents and your flashy new pals and you in the middle.

At a camera rehearsal at Radio City we were standing in place for the Buster the Show Dog radio drama, standing for a half hour so the cameras could figure out how to shoot this strange little show—a drama in which nobody moves, in which actors read off scripts, in which one guy plays the dog and the boy and the priest and another guy does about thirty walk-on characters. A cameraman said to one of the actors, "Move the microphone down, it's obscuring you." She gave him piercing look and said, "It's the camera that obscures. The microphone reveals."

That was our argument all through rehearsal. The TV guys want to impart motion and excitement to something that essentially stands still: a musician playing a guitar, a man telling a story. They rehearse over and over long sweeping shots: the guitarist plays while a Steadicam moves in from the side and across in front and half circles around, a long interesting shot, a view that you'd never get in real life. Listening to someone play a guitar, you'd never have the temerity to walk around inspecting him from three angles like a side of beef, it'd be rude. But here is TV being rude on the viewer's behalf, to what end?

The musician gives us the music and by appearing on TV he also lends his physical image, but to what purpose—other than to publicize himself? Radio has the single purpose of giving you the sound of the instrument as purely as possible, as much as if you were there with your eyes closed (and if the music moved you, you might very well close your eyes).

You don't really want television to show you Leo Kottke playing guitar. Leo's appeal is through his music itself. Television wants a celebrity guitarist who is more interesting for who it is than for what it sounds like: say, for example, if a German shepherd could play the guitar, a simple piece like "Go Tell Aunt Rhody," you wouldn't be satisfied to hear it on the radio and have the announcer say, "That was Rex playing. Good job, Rex." You'd want to see it for yourself, with plenty of camera angles so you know it's the dog picking the strings.

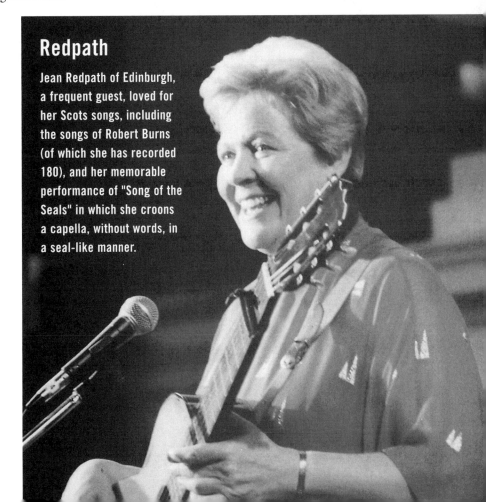

Redpath

Jean Redpath of Edinburgh, a frequent guest, loved for her Scots songs, including the songs of Robert Burns (of which she has recorded 180), and her memorable performance of "Song of the Seals" in which she croons a capella, without words, in a seal-like manner.

Ringsak

Russ Ringsak, truck driver and writer, has been involved with PHC from the beginning, first as a player on the old Jack's Auto Repair softball team, then as a researcher, providing Minnesota notes to GK when the show was based in New York, and as the driver on tours. A blues guitarist and biker and former architect, Russ edits the Greetings segment of the show and decides whose birthday wishes to Mom will be broadcast and which will not.

Rain

Margaret Moos remembers that before the renovation, the World Theater in the summertime was like a swamp. No air conditioning, no windows to open. "It was just awful in there, so we always tried to do the shows in the Sculpture Garden across the street. We'd call the weather service and check and check, and we'd go ahead even if there was a 60–70 percent chance of rain. Sometimes it did rain. We'd make the switch to the World Theater in the middle of the show—Tom Keith running across the street with a microphone, Marge Ostroushko, Buzz Kemper, Mike Moriarity, everyone shlepping microphones. We would move the show over there, turn on the lights, turn on the power, plug in a microphone for GK, and be on the air within ten minutes with him talking while we set up for the band."

Republicans

I took me a trip down to Capitol Hill
I came to the door and I felt the chill
It was changed so much from two months
    before.
They had a liberal detector by the door.
The building was full of wealth and finance,
Men with loud voices and bright-colored pants.

And there was Newt, Newt
A very big suit
With a horn on his belt he can reach down
    and toot
He's going to heaven the Republican route
Big tax breaks for the millionaires
Throw those poor people down the stairs.

Oh, it's Newt, Newt
He's kinda cute.
His hair is shaped like a parachute.
He's got a computer but it doesn't compute,
He learned his math at the deaf institute.

Newt, Newt
A strange young coot
With a gleam in his eye and a smirk on
    his snoot.
And now he's the speaker and Lord he can speak
Like a big balloon with a very slow leak.
What you'd say for a minute, Newt can say for
    a week.
Going to heaven the Republican route
Bought the crackers and threw out the fruit.

Rhubarb

Rhubarb is a beautiful vegetable. It grows wild all over. You just chop it and make pie. You never see it in a supermarket. You only get it for free. This makes it unique. And because it's never advertised or promoted, rhubarb is a private, local phenomenon. Rhubarb was discovered in Minnesota, by two Norwegians, Rudy and Barb Gustafson. They found a patch of it in their backyard in Bemidji in 1933. It had been ignored by the Indians, the French, the Spanish, and the Irish because it is so bitterly sour, but sourness is no hindrance to Norwegians, nor is bitterness. Barb just poured sugar on it and baked it in a pie, as she tended to do with a lot of things she didn't understand; it tasted great, and they named it after themselves, Rubarb. At first it was hyphenated, Ru-barb. Later, an h was added, on the recommendation of a consultant, to give it style. Rudy and Barb made a lot of money off rhubarb, selling cookbooks and demonstrating the use of it, and the money led to problems. Rudy's eye wandered and he met a girl named Wanda, and he tried to rename the vegetable RuWanda, and Barb brought a lawsuit, which lasted years and led to the other meaning of the word rhubarb, meaning: a squabble. But that's all over now, and what's left is this amazing plant, good only for desserts. You pour sugar on but enough of the sourness comes through for flavor.

Rivard

Scott Rivard grew up on a farm near Taylors Falls MN, where as a boy he took parts of an old telephone and wired them so his mother could turn a crank in the kitchen and ring the bell in his bedroom and wake him up for school in the morning. He went to work as a studio technician (at the studio in Minneapolis where "Surfin' Bird" was

Russell

Tim Russell first appeared on PHC from Portland May 5, 1994. He has played many characters in PHC scripts since becoming one of the regular cast. Tim also does voiceovers for regional and national radio and television commercials. He did voices in three recordings of *Star Wars* stories including *Star Wars Dark Forces: Soldier for the Empire,* and he hosts a weekday radio show on WCCO in Minneapolis.

recorded) and, then with several others, formed a new studio, Sound 80, a new audio recording facility. He designed and built the original mixing and recording consoles used at Sound 80, designed a disc-cutting system for "Direct to Disc" mastering, and much more. His recording work includes Leo Kottke's classic *6 & 12 String Guitar* album (with the armadillo cover), the Fisher Nut jingle "We Take a Nut Very Seriously," the St. Paul Chamber Orchestra, and hundreds of other projects. He has been technical director of PHC since 1985.

Romance

Once there was a boy who was the clumsiest boy you ever saw. People said he had two left feet and they were big feet and he tripped over them and he couldn't walk from here to there without bumping into everything. He was hopeless.

Except in winter, when it got cold, and the lake froze, and he put on his skates. He'd go skating off across the ice and it was like flying and it was like dancing. He did beautiful figures. He skated backward. He did sharp turns and he leaped. And all through December and January and February, he was graceful as a bird, he soared, he swooped, he floated.

And then the ice got soft, and he had to hang up his skates, and walk, and trip on steps, and bump into chairs, and step on his shoelaces.

Spring was agony. Summer was miserable. Autumn was heartbreaking; it'd get down to freezing and he'd think maybe tomorrow and then it'd warm up again. And then it got good and cold, and the lakes froze, and then he was released from the prison of shoes and he enjoyed the freedom of skates.

And one winter, skating across the lake, a girl saw him from the shore and she fell in love with that beautiful man, and she waved to him, and he skated over to her and took her by the hand, and they skated together. She was afraid of falling but he held her up and she felt clumsy but she watched him and forgot about herself and soon they danced together almost perfectly. They danced for miles and miles along the shore, past the beautiful birch trees and pines, and when they came back, he had asked her to marry him and she had said yes.

Unfortunately, the wedding was in the spring.

And it was in her hometown, Memphis.

"I know you're going to love Memphis," she cried. "And I know you'll love my family. They're all just as nice as me."

He started out for Memphis in February. The Mississippi had frozen over pretty well, and he skated south, past the high bluffs of Minnesota and Wisconsin and into Iowa, and the ice was still good, and down near Dubuque he saw some open water, but he skated on. Down near Hannibal, he saw a barge coming up river, breaking a channel through the ice, but he stayed near the shore, and he was almost down to Cairo when he heard a loud cracking sound, and he looked around and there was water all around him. He was floating on a chunk of ice about the size of a boat. He floated along awhile and it was the size of a dining room table. And pretty soon it was the size of a bathtub. By the time he got to Memphis, he had learned how to swim.

He made it to the church with one minute to spare, and the organ was playing, and there was his bride at the door.

"I'm not the man you thought I was," he said. "I'm not graceful. Only sometimes. Not now. I don't know if I can walk down that aisle or not." But she took him by the hand and they walked together. He was afraid of falling but she held him up and he felt clumsy but he watched her and forgot about himself and they were married. That night they danced their wedding dance together almost perfectly, around and around the room, past the aunts and uncles, and when the dance was over, it was hardly begun. They had years and years left in which to dance, sometimes on the floor, sometimes on ice, and sometimes they were so in love they forgot which was which.

Rundown

Rundowns for three PHC shows are reproduced here. The first, below, in Margaret Moos' handwriting, is for the show done January 27, 1979, at the Park Square Court Theater in St. Paul. The show ran ninety minutes. The numbers on the left indicate how many songs the regulars were to perform. John refers to John Bergquist, from Eveleth MN and Soupy to Soupy Schindler, who played harmonica and did wild man vocals on 1950s rock and roll songs. The Powdermilk Biscuit Band at this time consisted of Adam Granger, Bob Douglas, Mary DuShane, and Molly Mason. Bill Hinkley, Judy Larson, and Butch Thompson were regular performers also, and when Soupy joined Bill and Judy for the Beach Boys and Beatles songs, they called themselves the Nassoons. Notice that there is not yet a monologue.

The second rundown: "as-done" from the Farewell Show June 13, 1987, indicates the length of time for each segment. The last, for February 13, 1999, displays producer Chris Tschida's notes (made during the last hours of the Saturday rehearsal) on the length of each segment. Chris tells everyone to watch the order of the thirty-one poems and song fragments in the twelve-minute medley. She can't anticipate the length of audience laughter and applause, and the introductions of the guests, thus the provision of "wild cards."

FINAL

A PRAIRIE HOME COMPANION RUNDOWN 2/13/99

2:10	TISHOMINGO WITH OPENING CREDITS
3:00	GK TALK
2:10	THEY CAN'T TAKE THAT AWAY FROM ME
2:35	ROCK THIS HOUSE - PD VOCAL AND BAND
4:45	CELEBRITIES-VALENTINE'S DAY
3:05	HIGH SOCIETY-BUTCH THOMPSON AND JAZZ ORIGINALS
3:05	WILD MAN BLUES-BUTCH THOMPSON AND JAZZ ORIGINALS
2:55	ST. PAUL SATURDAY SHUFFLE-AS FRONTLINE
11:30	GUY NOIR
2:45	YOU CAN LOVE YOURSELF - KEB' MO'
2:45	LOVE IN VAIN - KEB' MO'
3:00	GK TO COVER GUITAR CHANGE
	THE ACTION - KEB' MO'
12:00	VALENTINE'S DAY MEDLEY OF POETRY AND MUSIC
3:35	INTERMISSION - MUSKRAT RAMBLE
3:00	GREETINGS -
3:10	ARE YOU TIRED OF ME MY DARLING? SBECK AUTOHARP
6:30	RHUBARB
3:00	HENRY - KEB' MO'
20:00	MONOLOGUE
1:40	BUTCH THOMPSON - YANCEY ON MY MIND (3 X)
3:10	MANDY, MAKE UP YOUR MIND-BUTCH AND JAZZ ORIGINALS
2:30	KETCHUP
1:00	CREDITS
1:40	CLOSER-BY AND BY (:20 PER CHORUS)

52:45

Add Note order

49:15

***************WILD CARDS **

3:10	KISS ME SWEET (w/ Mazzy voc.)
1:25	SUMMER CAMP FOR LIBERALS —GK REPLACES TR EXCEPT GOV
LINES 3:35	BRAIN SURGERY

5:30PM
WARM-UP

Biscuits
John
Soupy

6:00PM

Hello Love: GK with Biscuits
1 BISCUIT Tune
SPOT & Theme
1 Biel & Judy
1 Bonkch & Judy
2 John   Biscuit Tag

6:30PM
2: Nassoons
2: Soupy, Biel & John
1: Biel & Judy
1: BISCUIT   Biscuit Tag

7:00PM
2: Nassoons
1: Soupy & Biel
1: Bonkch
1: John
1: BISCUIT
Biscuit Close

A Prairie Home Companion

June 13, 1987 / *3:30 EDITION*

Pre-Show: Magnetic Rag: PB w/Strings

5PM Live Broadcast

1	1:30	Hello Love: GK, Strings, Chet, RD, piano, drums
2	1:40	Love's Old Sweet Song: GK, Strings w/audience
		GK talk
3	2:00	Tell Me Why: GK, Strings w/audience
4	2:35	Jitterbug Waltz: Chet w/strings into
5	2:30	Storms are on the Ocean: GK, Chet, Strings
6	4:00	Biscuit Spot & Theme: GK, Strings: Chet, SB
7	2:00	SB Aharp solo
8	3:15	How Can I Keep From Singing: JR w/Strings
9	6:35	Handel Suite 26:00

10	1:30	Greetings w/credit, RD
11	2:00	Roy Blount in balcony
12	3:00	GK w/Chet, Leo, Km: Brownie & Pete
13	4:00	GK w/Leo poem into waltz
14	11:00	Buster, the Show Dog
15	2:00	RD piano solo 27:00
16	4:00	Kamehameha Choir
17	4:00	Intermission: PB organ

18	2:15	Stars & Stripes: VS/TK/organ
19	2:30	Sons of Knute
20	25:00	LW Monologue

21	2:30	Leo & Chet: Sleepwalk
22	4:00	GK, Chet, RD Til Then into GK, KM, SB, Chet Minstrel Show other
23	2:30	JR solo
24	2:30	Hawaii Aloha: Kamehameha Choir
25	2:30	GK Fool Such As I w/Chet 49:00
26	Encore:	One More Spring w/RD piano
		`You're the Top

Saddletop Computer

Got sixteen megabytes of RAM, Barndoors 96, a map program with every gully and butte, livestock prices, rodeo schedule, CD-ROM with Merle Haggard and Bob Wills, the Bull-Riding Game. Got Bronc Buster, Calf Roper, shows ya how to make over a hundred different trick shots. Got the location of every silver and gold strike, and every brand ever branded, every lie ever told, and the closing time of every bar west of the Mississippi. This computer tracks deer. Got every major deer trail mapped out, plus the phone number of every dance hall girl in Montana. Runs on gunpowder and whiskey.

Saxophones

The Great American Sax-Off, broadcast from Pittsburgh, featured two competing bass saxophonists. Those bass saxes are about five feet tall with a bell about eighteen inches across. Vince Giordano, a great-looking six-foot Italian guy in his thirties from Brooklyn, faced John Campo, a five-foot-two, bald Italian in his fifties from Queens. Arnie Kinsella was Vince's second and John Frosk was Campo's. Frosk said, on the air, "Campo, just 'cause Vince is tall, dark, and handsome, and you're short, fat, and bald, don't worry, because they can't see that on the radio. Get out there and kick some butt." Campo had gotten Russell Warner to write a polka for the occasion, "The Slap Tongue Polka." A polka was a sure hit in Pittsburgh, and to write one that good wasn't fair. And the audience wasn't fair. There were twice as many short, fat, bald guys as tall, dark, handsome guys and so Campo got the big ovation and won. The audience was not about to give the prize to someone as good-looking as Vince.

Vince Giordano, bandleader, saxophonist, matinee idol.

Scenery

Scenery tends to put me right out on my feet. In fact, it's how I put myself to sleep at night: I imagine I'm driving my car through *National Geographic* and long before I come to the article on Yosemite, I'm out like a light. One problem with scenery is that there's always someone pointing at it and telling you that it's beautiful. Another is that it takes so long to get there. Scenery is almost never right in the neighborhood. It's always at least a six-hour drive. By that time, your senses are dulled to where nothing looks good. The mountains could fall into the sea, the sea be parted, and you'd just shoot a roll of film and look for a place to eat lunch.

Scott

Sue Scott has been on PHC since 1992. She also performs as a stage actress in Minneapolis at the Guthrie, Illusion, and Cricket theaters and at Brave New Workshop. She is heard in many radio and television commercials.

Sex

Dude: More coffee, honey?
Lady: Half a cup.
Dude: Can I toast you another muffin?
Lady: No, got to run. Got to get to the airport in half an hour.
Dude: They're not store muffins, I baked these yesterday.
Lady: They're good.
Dude: You want another one?
Lady: No thanks.
Dude: Did you read about this new sex survey they did at the University of Chicago? It's in the paper this morning.
Lady: No, I'm reading *The Wall Street Journal*.
Dude: A new survey called "Sex in America." You didn't read about that?
Lady: No, I saw the headline, but it didn't look that interesting.
Dude: It was interesting. They say that people don't have sex as often as they used to think that people do. Or did.
Lady: Huh. Well, I guess I knew that.

Sue Scott using a drinking glass to create the effect of talking on the telephone.

Dude: Yeah, it was interesting. They say that about a third of adults have sex two or three times a week, and about a third have it two or three times a month, and about a third have it once or twice a year or never.
Lady: Oh, really.
Dude: And they say it's about the same for everybody. Right-wingers or liberals, gay people, black people, Hispanic—it's interesting. Right across the board.
Lady: Uh huh.
Dude: You want to read the article? I clipped it out for you.
Lady: Okay Thanks.
Dude: What time're you getting home tonight? You going to Chicago?
Lady: Uh huh. Not that late. Seven-thirty, eight.
Dude: I remember when you used to get home at six. What happened?

Lady: I became president of the company, that's what happened. I'm in Chicago all day on meetings and I get back in the office at four, and I got five more meetings after that.

Dude: It just seems like we used to have more time together.

Lady: Well, let's have dinner tonight.

Dude: Okay. This survey says that almost half of all the people are extremely satisfied, including those people who hardly ever have sex.

Lady: Yeah. That seems about right. You think it should be more?

Dude: Well, I don't know, I was just thinking that—that—(DOOR OPENS)

Kid: Hi, Mom. Hi, Dad.

Dude: I thought you left for school.

Kid: No, I was just going to leave, and I came in to say goodbye.

Dude: Why don't you go?

Kid: I'm going to.

Dude: So do it.

Kid: I said, I'm going to go, but I—

Dude: So get out of here, would you?

Kid: I came in to say goodbye.

Dude: Good. So you said it. Go. The door's over there.

Kid: What's wrong?

Dude: Nothing. Go.

Kid: I just wanted to say goodbye.

Dude: So say it.

Kid: I'm trying to.

Dude: It's simple. Goodbye. Okay?

Kid: You're so angry.

Dude: I wouldn't be if you'd beat it. Goodbye.

Kid: Why are you like this?

Dude: None of your business!

Kid: That's what I thought. Goodbye. (DOOR SLAM)

Dude: SIGH.

Lady: I wish you could be a little patient with him.

Dude: Well, I can't. I'm sorry. What do you want for dinner tonight?

Lady: I don't care. Whatever.

Dude: You want fish? How about haddock? I was thinking about poaching a haddock with a little tarragon sauce, some boiled potatoes, a green salad, a nice white wine, a little candlelit dinner, maybe serve it on trays up in our bedroom.

Lady: I don't know. It just seems like we have fish all the time. But I don't care. Whatever you want.

Dude: Did I say something wrong?

Lady: No.

Dude: Why are you so angry? All I said was how would you like some haddock and wine and we could eat upstairs in the bedroom. That's all.

Lady: Why don't we go out to La Casa Cuisine?

Dude: Why can't we eat at home?

Lady: I'm having Elaine and Dominique for dinner tonight.

Dude: Tonight?

Lady: I told you about this two weeks ago. They're coming for dinner tonight. What are you looking at me like that for? Oh my gosh. I gotta run. See you tonight. (KISS) (KISS)

Shoelaces

The Shoelace Warehouse held more than two acres of shoelaces under one roof. Every kind of shoelace—cotton, decorator laces, leather laces, and bronze laces for babyshoes.

Smells

It was a cold night, cold enough to wake a person up and send you off to find a quilt. I got up and got mine, which my grandma gave to me twenty years ago. This is a quilt my grandma made from scraps of old clothes that my aunts and uncles wore as kids on the farm. They were a big family and didn't have much money, so they tended to wear their clothes right up to the end and so the material in this quilt is very thin and soft and delicate and when I lie under it I think of them because it smells like us.

Each family has a particular smell which we know each other by, the characteristic odor of those who are like us, our kind, the family, us—the smell that says, "You don't have to try too hard to be smart around these guys, they like you okay as you are." When we get up in the morning, we have to take showers and wash it off so we can get nervous and go to work, and then our sweet old smell comes back to us during the day and our mind turns toward home.

Sound

Sam Hudson, PHC staff engineer, doing sound reinforcement for the theater audience. The audience in the Fitzgerald hears Sam's mixture, which reinforces and balances the quieter and louder sounds from the stage.

Scott Rivard, technical director, in the control room at the back of the auditorium in the Fitzgerald Theater, listening on speakers to the rehearsal. During the performance, he will listen by headphones to mix the sound for the broadcast.

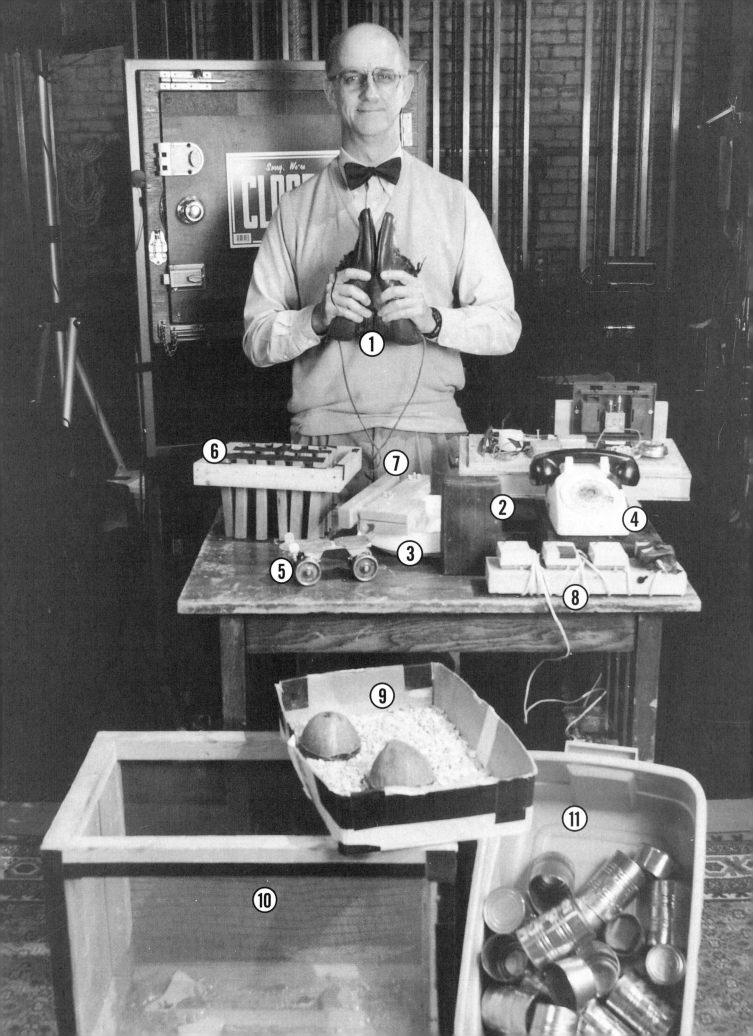

Sound Effects

Tom Keith makes sound effects with a collection of homemade props.

1. Wingtips picked up at Salvation Army for footsteps by pressing the heels of the shoes together and rolling toward the toes.

2. Taped box of cornstarch when squeezed sounds like someone walking through squeaky fresh snow.

3. Styrofoam picnic plates snapped in half sound like breaking wood. Replaces the now-rare balsa wood crates broken by old-time sound-effects men.

4. Telephone for dialing and ringing, used often in Guy Noir sketches.

5. Roller skate makes the sound of an elevator door opening when rolled across the rugged keys of an old typewriter.

6. Wooden legs sound like a battalion of soldiers marching in step.

7. Wood squeaker like someone easing into an antique chair.

8. Doorbells buzz or chime.

9. Coconut shells in box of small gravel, one in each hand, crunched against the gravel, sound like horses' hooves.

10. Glass-breaking box. Toss a wine glass at the angle iron on the bottom. Keith keeps shards of extra glass on the bottom for days when his aim is off.

11. Crash box adds drama to a fall. Matched with car horns and breaking glass for a great car accident.

Social Science

A scientific study of 247 Thanksgiving dinners
   has given us data
Showing that most included roast turkey,
Cranberries, gravy, and mashed potata,
Except for single men, 25-40,
Who didn't eat dinner with their families:
About 48% sent out for pizza,
Of whom two-thirds ordered extra cheese.
Scientific research at 247 Thanksgiving dinners
   has made it clear:
That 45% of the dinners were served
A little bit later than they were last year.
Due to the increased use of appetizers,
Particularly in the south and east,
55% percent of the men over thirty
Were 90% full before the Thanksgiving feast.

Behavior studies at Thanksgiving dinners
Show that 64% of women and men
Intended to take just one small helping
And to say "No thanks" when it came back
   again.
About 46% said, "Oh, just a little."
And the others said, "No thanks—well,
   all right."
Some changed their minds because it looked
   so delicious,
Two-thirds did just to be polite.

Psychological profiles at Thanksgiving dinners
Show that people who had pie made up their
   minds
At the very last minute what kind they
   would have.
Mincemeat and apple showed an 8% decrease;
Pumpkin experienced 10% growth;
But in the nine out of ten homes where two
   kinds were offered,
75% had a little bit of both.

Trained observers at Thanksgiving dinners
Say that 66% of the dishes were stacked,
Washed and dried and put away in cupboards
By women over fifteen, and that's a fact.
Men over thirty showed an average weight gain
Of 2.8 by late afternoon.
Most sat around and talked about exercise,
22% said they're gonna real soon. ➜

Opinion polls at Thanksgiving dinners
Show that thankfulness stands at 38%,
26 satisfied, 16 about the same,
13 can't complain, 7 are content.
Of the thankful ones, 65 are moderately,
Slightly 32, extremely 23.
So, judging from the figures, I'd say
    Thanksgiving
Turned out about what we expected it to be.

Spanish

The train over to Brooklyn was so packed, the people in the middle didn't even need to hang on. It gave new meaning to the word "solidarity." At the next stop, more people got on. I squeezed in and stood, studying the Spanish, a lot of which isn't going to be particularly helpful to me, like the ad for Tide detergent, the phrase "*blanco tan blanco*" (whiter than white). I can't imagine going around New York getting a lot of mileage out of "*blanco tan blanco*," but I just like the words: inscriptions like "*No se apoye contra la puerta*" (Don't lean against the door). Where I come from they just spoke English; they said, "Don't lean against that door," but how much more civil if they'd said: "*No se apoye contra la puerta.*" Life would not have been so harsh. Spanish is the loving tongue, like the song says. My folks used to say to me, "Get a job!" In Spanish, that's "*Aprenda una vocación.*" They said, "Listen to what I'm telling you!" In Spanish: "*Este atento a los instrucciónes.*" And this is just subway Spanish.

Sponsors

There was Clara Harris Air Express Asparagus that shipped Polaris Brand hairless asparagus from the Ontario prairie in sanitary, air-lock asparagus carriers. And Lac Qui Parle County Farmers Co-op Optometrists. SunBrite Drive-Through Counseling. You drive up to the window and describe your problem to the counterperson, and she asks, "Do you want plain counseling or do you want drugs with that?"

Trailblazer Table Napkins ("Use 'em as napkins, or hankies, or use 'em to tie up guys' wrists and gag 'em").

Keepsake Mortuary ("When a loved one is taken from us, there are many options for a memorial and one is taxidermy. For many people, it can be comforting to have our loved one's earthly form beautifully restored and mounted in an easy chair, smiling in perpetuity").

The Lundberg Counseling Agency where counselors don't just listen to you, they tell you stuff ("Listen to me, you pathetic little snot, time to wake up and smell the coffee. Grow up"). In the Yellow Pages under "Discipline."

The National Rifle Association, which presented a testimonial from a Unitarian minister: "I stand up every Sunday morning at a pulpit that offers very little protection—and then I found this .30 millimeter Magnum repeater that mounts to the lectern. I keep it covered with a lightweight green linen altar cloth. The scope is a Red-Dot sight that lets me find targets with amazing quickness, down below or up in the choir loft, and the 26-inch barrel gives me pinpoint accuracy anywhere in the sanctuary. For the fellowship hour, I like this underarm holster that holds a Smith & Wesson 11-shot single-action pistol. It weighs only twenty-four ounces. The church attracts troubled people, and that's fine. That's our mission. But I want to be ready."

Spring

When in Minnesota we arrive at the vernal equinox,
We know that grass and flowers are not quite here,
That more snow will fall on our driveway and sidewalks,
And that spring, as always, will be late this year.

I am not complaining, though if I did, I could go on
    all day,
I am tired, I am deeply depressed,
But I won't talk about it because I am basically okay.
We have always been basically okay in the Midwest.

If it snows in April, we don't curse, except to say, "Uffda."
If it snows in May, we say, "Oh, for pity's sake.
God in your mercy, please do not allow the ice on
    our roofta
Crush us in our sleep. Anything short of that, we
    can take."

And when the crocuses do come up, and tulips,
    and the purple gentian,
We feel joyful, though it is not anything we would
    ever mention.

Andy Stein and Pat Donohue.

Staff

**FORMER STAFF
AND SOME VOLUNTEERS:**

Chris Bannon
Paul Baron
Cliff Bentley
Joyce Besch
Phil Byrd
Christopher Cardoza
Rachel Crane
Lynne Cruise
Randall Davidson
Sara DeBoer
Michele Eaton
Helen Edinger
Scott Edwards
Dave Felland
Robert Fisher
Roseann Fitzgerald
Liz Fleischman
Dorothy Handford
Dennison Hansen
Chris Harwood
Jennifer Howe
Joe Joncas
Janis Kaiser
Mary Keillor
Buzz Kemper
Brian Kilian
Mark Killian
Michelle Kinney
Rob Knowles

Steve Koeln
Ken LaZebnik
Cameron Lidestri
Ray Marklund
Tim Metzger
Rosalie Miller
Margaret Moos
Michael Moriarty
Elizabeth Murray
Christine Nelson
Bill Nicholson
Linda O'Brien
Linda Olle
Marge Ostroushko
Richard Pfleuger
Katy Reckdahl
Ernie Retzel
Dan Rowles
Stephen Schlow
Heidi Schultz
Janet Shapiro
Michael Shields
Preston Smith
Ann Stonehill
Nina Thorsen
Karen Tofte
Brian Tonneson
Dan Tucker
Sue Unkenholz
Fred Wasser
Shane Wethers
Peggy White
Ilene Zatal

Stein

Andy Stein plays violin and saxophone in Guy's All-Star Shoe Band. He started his career as a musician playing with Bill Hinkley at the Ark in Ann Arbor in 1967. He has performed with many groups (including Asleep at the Wheel and Commander Cody and His Lost Planet Airmen) and orchestras. His orchestration for Schubert's *Death and the Maiden* was premiered by the St. Paul Chamber Orchestra in 1998. On Fridays, Andy flies to wherever PHC broadcasts from. The rest of the week he does studio work in New York or plays in Broadway shows.

Andy recalls the first American Radio Company season in Brooklyn. He would take the subway over, get scrambled eggs with lox and onions at Junior's Delicatessen on Flatbush Avenue, and go to the theater for a harrowing rehearsal with the Coffee Club Orchestra and Rob Fisher. "We did underscoring that was written by Russell Warner sitting in the wings, scoring a Lonesome Radio Theater script Garrison had finished late the night before, and we did band features ranging from ragtime and Charles Mingus to Beach Boys and Puccini, and we'd back up guests from Marilyn Horne to Big Joe Williams to Chet Atkins and Johnny Gimble to Bill Hinkley and Judy Larson. And then during the broadcast they'd hand me a note saying GK is going to read something and he wants four or five minutes of fiddle behind it."

Stoicism in Mist County

It was beautiful summer weather all week and a good week for fishing—the week when the farmers had a lull in their fieldwork and could go out and fish—sit and rock in a boat and work on your sunburn. Rollie Hochstetter pulled in a stringerful of sunnies, fishing in Sunfish Bay about a hundred yards off the end of the Kruegers' dock, not far from the weeds, fishing with worms, about two feet off the bottom using a three-fourths-inch red plastic bobber. Clint Bunsen wasn't far away, in his boat, contemplating the mysteries of life—the sun on the cool water at 7:30, hot coffee, the peacefulness of the rod and reel in his hand. His serenity was disturbed by all the activity at Rollie's boat, so Clint said, "You going to keep those puny little things? I'm going for the big ones. I'm not sure those are legal size, are they?"

Stage

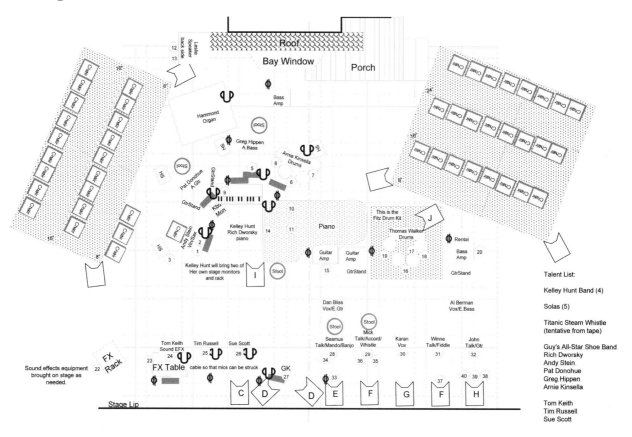

Stage plan by Scott Rivard, customized for each show, allows fast changeovers during the performance.

Rollie says, "You know, to tell you the truth, I don't go for those big ones, they're too damn bony. These medium size are the good eaters, you know that."

Clint sat and studied his line for a long time and contemplated the wisdom of Rollie: if you can't have something, find a reason why you wouldn't want it. Big fish are too bony, small ones taste better. You don't want to be rich and famous because just look at those people, do they look happy? No sir, I was reading in the paper this morning—Norwegian bachelor farmer talk, looking at a picture in a magazine—"I wouldn't have a woman like that if one of them was to come up and beg me." Old man with brown teeth and runny eyes, looking at a New York model—no sir, she could offer him money, desperate for his love, but he would stand on principle and by God turn the hussy from his door.

He imagined Rollie as a monk in a boat, praying, "Lord, do not send me any of those big ones as they are too bony, Lord, as thou surely dost know. Grant thy servant a little fish, one of the good eaters."

Supreme Court

There is a seat open on the U.S. Supreme Court and evidently the President is still thinking over the nomination. It's a seat that Justice Harry Blackmun of St. Paul occupied for twenty-four years and so we in Minnesota think of it as the Minnesota seat. I'm not promoting myself for the Supreme Court, but if your country needs you, you naturally want to respond, even if the need may not be evident to others immediately.

I happened to glance at the Constitution the other day, the way a person so often does, and I

Stage manager Jason Keillor and a local stagehand in Austin TX, studying the stage plan in spring 1998.

noticed that the Constitution doesn't require that a Justice be a lawyer or have any legal education. It only says that judges "shall hold their offices during good behavior." I think I could do that. I think they could use a writer on the Court.

There's a hundred candidates for the Court the President could choose from and everyone would think it was a great choice. I'm not one of those people. But then those great choices—you start cross-examining them and you find one little tiny flaw, the one really bonehead thing they said twenty years ago to somebody once, and everyone is shocked by it. Then they find out that the nominee also has two unpaid parking tickets from 1979, and that's it, they have to withdraw and the President winds up looking bad. But you appoint someone like me, the shock is all going to be at the beginning. Gradually, people will be amazed there isn't more dirt than there is. I'll come up for confirmation hearings before the Judiciary Committee and afterward, people will say, "You know, he said a couple of things that made sense."

Surgery

Often sketches on PHC involve surgery, which is graphic on the radio—the clink of tools, the suction, the hushed voices, the snips of the scissors. Actor Dan Rowles remembers the mad doctor who operated on Buster the Show Dog and tried attaching his tail to his forehead because "people would pay a lot of money for a dog like that," and the times GK went to the dentist and Tom Keith made a low, grinding drill sound that made you grab the arm rests of your chair. Once GK had a vasectomy on the radio and the doctor poured a bucket of ice in his lap as he started the procedure. And there was the eye operation where the surgeon had to pop the guy's eye out of the socket to fix it, and a surgeon doing tongue transplants to make Minnesotans more articulate. Dan was listening in the hall, and every time GK snipped out a tongue, the nearest usher groaned and had to lean on the wall.

Sutton

Vern Sutton sang on the first PHC broadcast in 1974 and on scores of broadcasts since. He is a music professor at the University of Minnesota and later director of the music school there who has an nonacademic love of performance. Hits included "Old Shep," "Begin the Beguine," "Stars and Stripes Forever," "The Teddy Bears' Picnic," and for years he (with Philip Brunelle) improvised a Thanksgiving Cantata from a long list of items submitted by the audience, organized into sections, each in a different style. He also played speaking roles, usually weaselly characters like IRS agents, brothers-in-law, and petty bureaucrats.

Sweden

GK: 1999 is going to be impeachment year in America, during which Congress will plow slowly through the same material we've been reading about all of 1998, so maybe it's time to consider moving to Sweden.

Sven: Okay, then. Passport? *Tak sa mykka. Har du lingonberries?*

GK: . . . asks the friendly border patrolman, as he waves you through customs at Stockholm International Airport. Soon the comfortable blue-and-yellow bus brings you into the heart of Stockholm, where at 3 P.M., the sun has set and the cocktail hour has begun. Too often stereotyped as grim stoics and obsessively hard workers and people who jump in front of trains and portrayed in Bergman movies as haunted men and women who

Vern celebrating on the June 13, 1987, Farewell show at the World Theater.

sit for long hours staring out a window and then say something bitter and cosmic—to the contrary, Swedes are a fun-loving people who enjoy cross-country skiing and spend their long winter nights drinking mulled wine, and telling folk tales about trolls and elves and feasting at the legendary smorgasbord, heaping up their plates with pickled eel and rancid fish and a cheese so strong it actually has little wiggly lines coming up from it—but, for the "Amerikaner," bologna and Velveeta and Spam are also provided. Sweden is a relaxed culture, where many people (Lapps) remain seated for most of the year, and why not? The generous welfare system provides a large monthly stipend to anyone who wishes it.

Q: Will I receive free medical care and an excellent education as well?

A: Yes.

Q: What about the impeachment hearings?

A: In the past six months, Swedish television has devoted two minutes and fourteen seconds to the entire story. Swedes think it has to do with taking a harmonica on a ski trip with someone named Linda. You'll hear more about gravlax than you'll hear about impeachment.

Q: Are taxes high?

A: No impeachment hearings all year. Guaranteed.

Q: What can I do for a living?

A: You'll teach English. Swedes are anxious to learn American slang so they can be hip. Words like "kul." "Totally awesome." "Like, chill, dud."

Q: What about income tax?

A: December is magnificent in Sweden. Christmas (or "Jul") lasts for three weeks, endless feasting, mulled wine, folk tales, dancing.

Q: I don't know.

A: Swedes love Americans, the streets are safe, generous welfare benefits, and no impeachment hearings. Isn't it time you made the switch to Sweden?

Sweet Corn

Over the years, sweet corn has changed from the Iowa Chief, the epitome of sweet corn art in my youth, to the Illini Super Sweet, which is considered superior, and now a new strain, called Sweetheart, which I think is salacious. You can't improve on perfection, which the Iowa Chief was. This new strain crosses the line that separates good

family eating pleasure from illicit sweet corn sensuality that, frankly, makes a man uncomfortable to sit down to Sunday dinner.

Not that Iowa Chief wasn't sensual; it was. We'd have it on Sunday and then I'd walk with Donna Macauley over to young people's Bible reading and in four blocks I thought awfully hard. We fundamentalist boys couldn't dance, so we learned the pleasure of walking with girls. I put my arm around her waist and hooked my little finger into the belt loop on her skirt and she did the same to me, and we walked, arms around back of each other, hooked on, arms riding across each other's butts, feeling our hips move, synchronizing your steps, which, because she was shorter, came out in 9/7 time, or 15/8—I heard a Ukrainian step dance once that reminded me of us. We walked toward our rendezvous with the epistle of Paul to Timothy, with powerful urges to stop short of that, to find a dark place and to remove each other's husks—it was the effect of the sweet corn.

Sweet Mystery of Life

Since 1971, the Sweet Mystery of Life Center has been a central clearinghouse for answers to some of life's many questions. Oftentimes, these answers come to us suddenly, driving to dinner at a friend's house, suddenly you think, "We're all one, and we're all interconnected," or you think, "The end is the beginning. It's all continual," but when you get to your friend's house, they're talking about the weather or plumbing or about great deals on charter flights to Jamaica, and there's no way to slip "We're all one, we're all interconnected" into the conversation. Driving home later, you can't remember whether it was "We're all one" or "All for one and one for all" or "A stitch in time saves nine" or what. That's why you should have called it in to the Sweet Mystery of Life Center. Your answer will be used to help other people and it'll also be kept on file under your name so that years from now you can find out what the answers were back when you had them.

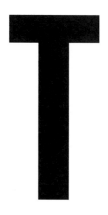

Talent

Thirty acts, mostly amateurs, have appeared on the Talent from Towns Under Two Thousand (TUTT) contests 1995–1999. Janet Sorenson of Fisher MN won the first contest by singing "He Taught Me to Yodel" (with yodeling). Ten-year old Emily Shackelton from Biwabik MN was chosen from the PHC TUTT audition answering machine, and won the hearts of the audience in 1996 by singing "Colors of the Wind." The 1999 contest winner was also a youngster, Jason Moody, a seventeen-year old violinist from Dover ID. Groups won in 1997 and 1998: Kirkmount, teenagers Simeon, Sam, and Alex Bigney from Woodland Hills UT, and Virtual Consort, a trio of arch guitar, trumpet, and bass, from small towns in VT and MA. The smallest towns sent Jake Krack, a thirteen-year-old fiddler from Freeman IN (population twenty); Uncle Henry's Favorites, a string band from White Hall VA (population fifty), and singers Al Malone and the Melody Men from Lebanon AL (one hundred).

Tap Dancing

I'm singin' in the snow just singin' in the snow
What a wonderful feeling it's forty below.
I'm laughing at frost. And at people who drive.
I look at my breath and I know I'm alive.
Let the icy winds beat, and the hail and the sleet
I just have to dance when there's ice 'neath
   my feet.
My heart seems to glow. I'm romantic, I know.
But I'm singin' just singin' in the snow.

Tennessee Valley Authority

(SFX: PHONE RING)
Tom Keith: Hello, TVA.
GK: Hello. Which came first—the chicken or the egg?
Tom: The chicken.
(SFX: PHONE RING)
Tom: TVA.
GK: Can I wear a teal shirt and lemon slacks with white shoes?
Tom: Only after Memorial Day.
(SFX: PHONE RING)
Tom: TVA.
GK: Who was better—Herman's Hermits or the Dave Clark Five?
Tom: DC Five, no contest.
GK: You sure?
Tom: I'm the Tennessee Valley Authority.

Thanksgiving

(to the tune of "The Sloop John B.")

We drove up to Whitefish Bay,
Two hours drive each way
To spend Thanksgiving Day with my brother
  Jerome,
His second wife Sue,
Their three children too,
I thought on the way up: I'd rather stay home.

We got there at quarter to noon,
About two hours too soon,
A terrible marital silence hung in the air,
The turkey was raw,
It hadn't started to thaw,
Sue was weeping, Jerome had gone off
    somewhere.

The house and the kids were a mess,
Sue had been sick, I guess,
And her aunt was there and an uncle who may
    have been dead.
We dined about nine,
On wieners and wine,
In a cold bitter silence until Jerome stood up
    and said:

Call up the lawyer today.
Send the children away.
Family is nice sometimes but it's too darn hard.
We'll split up and run,
Go off one by one,
And live in a shack in the woods with weeds
    in the yard.

Call up an airline today.
You and me we'll go away.
Family is nice sometimes but not all at once.
We'll have a nice Christmas
On a tropical isthmus.
And we'll have you over for dinner in a couple
    of months.

Emily Shackelton, 10, of Biwabik.
GK: "I didn't understand show business
until I stood on stage and introduced Emily
to come out and sing. The moment she
walked out, the audience melted like cheese.
A blond girl with glasses and a ribbon in
her hair and an angelic face and a great
sense of pitch, and when she nailed
'Somewhere Over the Rainbow,' all the
mommies and daddies and grandfolks
and little kids in the audience, everyone
other than the actual atheistic communists,
went to pieces. People dabbed at their eyes.
It was a living Norman Rockwell cover.
If the hostship had been put to a vote,
I wouldn't have stood a chance."

Theme Songs

"Oh hear that old piano / From down the avenue. / I smell the roses, I look around for you. / My sweet old someone, coming through the door, / It's Saturday and the band is playing— / Honey, could we ask for more?"

"Hello Love"

Well, look who's coming through
    that door
I think we've met somewhere
    before
Hello love, Hello love
Where in the world have you been
    so long?
I've missed you so since you've
    been gone
Hello love, Hello love

Make yourself feel right at home
Hope you plan on staying long
Come in love, Come in love
I must say I was sure surprised
You're the last thing I expected
    to find
Hello love, Hello love

I've heard it said time and again
You often go back where you've
    been
I never really believed it was true
But I left the door unlocked for you

And it's wonderful now, you're back
    with me
And things are like they used to be
Remember love, Remember love
You're back with me, my world's
    complete
So don't mind me if I repeat
Hello love, Hello love

Thompson

Butch Thompson first appeared on A Prairie Home Companion on July 13, 1974, the second live broadcast. Butch remembers: "It was pretty casual back then. Margaret or somebody would call me and ask if I was busy on Saturday. More than once I remember saying I couldn't get there by showtime, and being told to show up as soon as I could. Sometimes I'd go onstage without remembering what key something was in. If Garrison was going to sing, I usually couldn't go wrong with E major." Butch's interest in jazz began in his childhood in Marine on St. Croix MN a after his mother went to St. Paul and bought him some boogie-woogie records. He studied both piano and clarinet, and at nineteen began his professional career with the Hall Brothers New Orleans Jazz Band of Minneapolis. Butch specializes in classic jazz from 1895 to 1940, including the music of Scott Joplin, Fats Waller, Eubie Blake, James P. Johnson, Willie "The Lion" Smith, and Jelly Roll Morton. Butch regularly tours Europe, Japan, and Australia, and can be heard on more than one hundred recordings including his latest solo series on Daring Records of Boston.

Toast

Toast and Jelly Days was a big success—I say "was" because it was just one day, last Sunday, but it seemed longer than that to the Toast and Jelly Days Committee. They had begged and borrowed every toaster in town for the toast booths on Main Street, only to have the power go off when they plugged them in. It was an hour without power and a delay in the festivities, which always bothers the organizers more than the rank and file. Most of the fun at these events is not in the plan, don't you know, and frankly, it was fun to see the Committee running around in circles, trying to hook toasters up to car batteries, trying to rig up solar toasters, trying to find briquettes.

The winner of the Toast Toss was Carl Krebsbach, who tossed his toast twenty times over his shoulder, and had it land jelly side up thirteen. The winner of the Toast Eating Contest was Duane Bunsen, who put away eleven slices in two minutes, and who, a few minutes later, tossed his toast too. There was a Toast Tasting and it was decided that the best toast belonged to Dorothy of the Chatterbox—it's actually a bread-baking contest, because the toast must be homemade—and she got the Toast of the Town award.

The Toaster Race—which is run by teams of ten in relays, each team member having his or her own toaster, and each team having one 150-yard extension cord—was won by the Lutheran Youth Team, which was first with the darkest. The Toaster Toss was won by Ernie Mueller, whose toaster threw two slices of whole wheat twelve feet, ten inches into the air. He'd been working on it down at the garage, one of those old four-slice models that he modified into a two-cylinder with California springs. That was an event that used to be held indoors but no more.

Tongue Tone

Tonga! The top name in tongue tones—tasteless, nontoxic Tonga Tongue Tone gives you an attractive tinted tongue without tarnishing teeth. Coloring your tongue used to be kid stuff, but now, not only teenagers but teachers, technicians, top executives use tongue tone for that bright elegant today look—in tan, topaz, turquoise, tortoiseshell, tutti-frutti, or any of twenty-two different tongue hues and tints. Tonga Tongue Tone—tasteless, nontoxic Tonga comes in twist-top tube or tablet. It's the tried and tested method of tinting the tongue without tarnishing teeth. And now try tongue tattoos too. Faces of famous stars—keep them on the tip of your tongue! Tom T. Hall, Ted Turner, Terry-Thomas, Twyla Tharp, Toni Tennille, Tut Taylor, T. Texas Tyler, Tiny Tim, Mister T., Tina Turner, and Tommy Thompson.

Tongue Twisters

On "Guy Noir, Private Eye," Pete was once in love with Bebe Babalu, a bubble dancer at the Bebopareebop Club, who bathed in bubbles to the tune of "Bibbidi-Bobbidi-Boo," and made his heart go boom-boom-boom.

Later, Bebe lowered the boom and matriculated at Bathsheba Bible College in Babylon NY, giving up bubbles for Bibles to be a missionary and go to Addis Ababa. Pete also loved Gigi Jensen, a Norwegian on Fiji, on a voyage with the legendary Major Agee. Pete was the ship's engineer, trying to dislodge a chunk of sludge from the starboard scuppers with a six-foot squeegee when Gigi Jensen approached wearing a pair of wedgies.

Another Guy Noir episode involved a sea trip by supporters of the San Diego Snake Sanctuary, including Sandy and Sidney Deco of Cincinnati, who at a trendy Hindu disco in Rawalpindi, the Rama Lama A Go-Go, met Judy Toledo and her brother Bingo.

And Sammy Marconi driving a semi load of organic salami from Miami. His dad was a famous swami named Rama Lama Ronnie and his mom, Naomi, won an Emmy for *Salome* in which she danced the shimmy in her jammies. Later she was chummy with an anonymous economist from Menomonie WI.

And Erica Rhodes once played the part of Kathy Kirkpatrick selling Girl Scout cookies (available by the bag, sack, box, cask, keg, bucket, crock, crate, or gherkin) from a Girl Scout troop in Piscacadawada-quaddymoggin, a name used often in PHC scripts—Bob Elliott wrestled with it, as did Sarah Jessica Parker, Diana Krall, Allison Janney, and many other guests.

Junior Woodchuck Tour, 1976: Sean Blackburn with GK.

Tours

The show has toured to forty-four states, beginning with a trip to Fargo ND in 1974. Some notable tours include:

JUNIOR WOODCHUCK TOUR: May 1976, twelve shows tenting through twelve towns in two weeks in MN, IA, WI. For two weeks the band practiced a five-voice arrangement of "Blue Shadows on the Trail," to sing the last night at Moorhead. Someone hit a bad note in the first bar and Rudy Darling laughed so hard he fell on the floor.

DEATH MARCH TO THE PRAIRIE TOUR: April 1977, sixteen shows in sixteen towns in sixteen days. In Rochester MN, GK leaped onto the stage, hit his head on a low ceiling, and fell to his knees.

SPAGHETTI TRANSMISSION TOUR: April 1978. The rented motorhome lost its transmission in Eau Claire WI. After it was repaired, Tom Keith was sent back to fetch it and on his way to Rochester, on a left turn, a large pot of spaghetti fell out of the refrigerator.

THANKS ANYWAY TOUR: October 1980 to southern MN and Ames IA. The tour was going well, the musicians and crew relaxed, and they stopped at a farm in southern Minnesota whose owners had invited them for lunch. During the convivial conversation at the meal, they heard a commotion in the barnyard and discovered that Robin and Linda Williams's dog, Jake, had gotten out of their motor home and was heading toward the sheep pen. Dog, sheep, and farmer recovered, but Robin is still embarrassed.

UNLIKELY TOUR: June 1982 to Los Angeles and Ashland OR, where the live broadcast was transmitted by a complicated combination of land lines, microwave, and satellite.

DEFINITELY LAST MOTOR HOME TOUR: October 1982 to MN, WI, IL, MI in a moody GMC vehicle.

TOUR DE FORCE TOUR: May 1983, twelve shows, three broadcasts in Middlebury VT, Manhattan, and Boston. In VT the satellite truck went on the fritz and technician Tim Metzger had a tiny part flown in from DC to save the show. In NYC an exciting relationship with the telephone company resulted in

Second Annual Farewell Tour finale at Radio City Music Hall, June 4, 1988.

a local phone exec installing the broadcast lines hours before the show.

SECOND ANNUAL FAREWELL TOUR: May 1988, Middlebury VT, Worcester MA, and June 4, Radio City Music Hall in NYC. Things were very hectic putting together a program with little time to rehearse. Just minutes before the show, Robin Williams handed Rich Dworsky a rough chart of "Across the Blue Mountains," asking him to play on it. Rich played brilliantly on a song he'd never heard of before, and Robin recalls that performance as one of the musical high points of his life.

THIRD ANNUAL FAREWELL TOUR: May 1989, fourteen cities in SC, OH, IN, WI, IA, MO, OK with Robin and Linda Williams as Marvin and Mavis Smiley.

FOURTH ANNUAL FAREWELL TOUR: June 1990, Iowa City with Jean Redpath, Peter Ostroushko, Greg Brown, Dave Moore, and Kate MacKenzie.

MOONSHINE TOUR: February 1994, with a broadcast from Spartanburg SC, then to Roanoke, Chapel Hill, Greensboro, Myrtle Beach, Charleston, and a broadcast from Orlando. In Roanoke, GK spoke at a Rotary Club luncheon. In his speech he praised Roanoke, the "moonshine capital," for its tradition of breaking the law for something as wonderful as moonshine. After the show the staff returned to the Holiday Inn. As Chris Harwood, the music librarian, and David O'Neill unpacked the bus, a car pulled into the parking lot, shut off its lights, and coasted toward them. A man got out and asked if this was where GK was staying. He said he had something to give him, opened his trunk, and produced a brown paper bag with a mason jar full of clear liquid—moonshine. He was so moved by GK's speech that he had dipped into his private stock. The crew nervously carried that moonshine from one state to another through the whole tour. After the last show GK cracked it open and the guys gathered on his hotel balcony, sipping the moonshine and smoking big cigars. Most of the women stayed clear, although Stevie Beck took a gulp, and then sang a chorus with Russ Ringsak of "White Lightning." The nondrinkers and some women stayed indoors and sang every "girls group song" known to man. The whiskey was harsh and yet somehow smooth after you got over the burning in your throat.

Town Hall

Town Hall, the site of PHC's New York shows, is on West 43rd Street between Sixth and Broadway, near the Tai Chi Chuan Center, the Sam Bok Oriental Market, and a bar called Jimmy's Neutral Corner. At the corner is Times Square, with its five-story billboards of people in their underwear, and along Broadway are stores that sell large vases and porcelain statues and Oriental doodads and, of course, camera and electronics stores that if you stepped in and expressed interest in a particular piece of merchandise, they would probably offer it to you at a special price not available to everyone. East on 43rd, in what used to be the RCA Victor studio, where original-cast Broadway musicals were recorded and Elvis made an early album, the IRS has a storage facility.

A. J. Liebling had his office a block east, at 25 West 43rd, at *The New Yorker* magazine. He could look down the street and see the Hotel Dixie and the Paramount Building, where, as a young reporter, he went to interview the Hollywood femme fatale Pola Negri, whom Liebling had fallen in love with when he'd seen her in a German silent film, *Passion*, in Hanover NH, when he was about to be kicked out of Dartmouth for cutting chapel. At the Paramount, Negri was appearing in a show in which she sat on a swing and sang. Liebling interviewed her as she lay in a white peignoir on a white chaise longue like a crumpled gardenia petal and said, of Rudolph Valentino, "He was the only man I ever loved. But I am fated always to be unhappy in love. Because I expect so much." The Hotel Dixie (now the Hotel Carter) was where Jimmie Rodgers died of TB. It was the home of Liebling's friend, Colonel John R. Stingo, the horseracing columnist for *The National Enquirer*. Colonel Stingo said, "I sit up there in my room at the Dixie, working away on my column. I finish, and it is perhaps one o'clock. Up there in my retreat, I feel the city calling to me. It winks at me with its myriad eyes, and I go out and get stiff as a board. I seek out companionship, and if I do not find friends, I make them. A wonderful, grand old Babylon."

A. J. Liebling wrote about the war, about France, about boxing, about food, about newspapers, and whenever the show comes to Town Hall, GK makes sure to have a plate of oysters in his memory.

Trail Usage

(WESTERN THEME)
Announcer: THE LIVES OF THE COWBOYS: Stories of the men who made the West the West... brought to you by Western Lubrication—and now today's story...
(HORSE HOOVES, CATTLE)
Dusty: Well—I am sure lookin' forward to hittin' Billings on Wednesday.
Lefty: Me too.
Dusty: I wonder if that girl is still dancing at the dance hall, the one with the green eyes—
Lefty: You liked her, didn't you?
Dusty: I did. Except for the fact she was a damn Democrat.
Lefty: Lot of those dance hall floozies are, you know. You come in off the trail and there they are, dancing in their little outfits with the fringe bouncing—
Dusty: You sit there mesmerized by 'em and—
Lefty: And then they start in talking about the environment.
Dusty: The environment! (CLICK OF GUN, GUNSHOT, CREAKING AND FALL OF TIMBER).
Lefty: What you go and shoot that tree for, Dusty?
Dusty: Too damn many trees, Lefty. Sicka trees and sicka politicians. I wouldn't shake hands with one if I was offered a dollar to do it.
Lefty: (WHINNY) Easy. Easy. Look over yonder there—Howdy, ma'am!
Woman: Good afternoon. I'm here taking a survey on trail usage. Would you mind answering a few questions?
Lefty: Nope. Long as they ain't too hard.
Woman: Is the purpose of your trip business or pleasure?
Lefty: We're on a cattle drive to Billings, ma'am. Those are longhorns out there.

Woman: Okay—"business"—are you planning to stop in any towns en route?

Dusty: Nope, we're ridin' straight through to Billings and sell these longhorns.

Woman: Okay—"stopping in Billings." And how much money do you plan to spend in Billings?

Lefty: All of it. Every dime. Gonna just throw it to the wind. Spend it on booze and women and poker.

Dusty: Throw it down any old rat hole we find.

Woman: Okay, "plan to spend total income." Now—I'm going to read off a list of things that might be built in the future along the trail, and I'd like you to tell me if you'd be interested, very interested, or not interested in using them. All right?

Dusty: Okay. Shoot.

Woman: Recreational facilities, such as golf or tennis.

Dusty: Hell, no.

Woman: A health club offering exercise room, aerobics classes, and nutrition counseling.

Dusty: Hell, no.

Woman: A performing arts center offering concerts, plays, and art exhibits.

Dusty: Hell, no.

Woman: An adult education center offering evening classes in things such as weaving, ceramics, and poetry.

Dusty: No way.

Woman: Okay, thank you very much for your time.

Dusty: You're welcome. Come on, Lefty. Giddup. (HORSES RIDING ALONG) Boy, for dumb. Health club! Recreation—

Lefty: I sorta liked that adult education center idea.

Dusty: Ceramics?

Lefty: No, poetry.

Dusty: Poetry! What you need that for?

Lefty: Not everything has to be useful, Dusty.

Dusty: That's the dumbest thing I heard all day!

Lefty: I just like 'em, that's all. Like this one
When in disgrace with fortune and men's eyes,
I all alone beweep my outcast—

Dusty: You all alone what?

Lefty: Beweep.

Dusty: What does that mean?

Lefty: To cry. To grieve.

Dusty: Well, why didn't you say so?

Lefty: When in disgrace with fortune and men's eyes, I all alone beweep my outcast state,
And trouble deaf heaven with my bootless cries
And think upon myself and curse my fate.

Dusty: What does "bootless cries" mean? How can a cry have boots on? You mean he stuck his boot in his mouth while he was crying? But then he ain't bootless—

Lefty: I give up.

Dusty: Let's go find us some conservative dance hall girls.

Lefty: Ha! There ain't no Republican floozies anywhere. You want to have fun, all there is is those dance-and-spend Democrats.

Dusty: Well, okay. It's better than crying over lost boots. C'mon, giddup!

Tschida

Chris Tschida (producer), born and raised in St. Paul, attended Holy Spirit Grade School, where she played the Scarecrow in *The Wizard of Oz*, thus setting her path in life. She majored in theater at Macalester College, spent eight years at the Guthrie Theater as director of outreach programs, managing national tours of *The Rainmaker*, *Talley's Folly*, *Great Expectations*, and other productions. Moved to the American National Theater at the Kennedy Center, a project of Peter Sellars, and then to the Brooklyn Academy of Music for which she managed international tours, including the 1986 tour of *The Cherry Orchard* to the Soviet Union and Japan. Joined PHC as producer in August 1990. Married to the writer Richard Mosher. She loves to travel. Loves to see shows. Has seen five in one weekend.

U,V

Uncle New York

I have a niece two years old who knows me better than people who've known me all my life. She first met me when I lived in New York and she brought her parents and visited me there. It made a big impression on her, so that a couple weeks ago when she was coming to visit me again and her parents said, "Whose house are we going to?" the child looked up at them and smiled and said, "We're going to Uncle New York's."

Uncle New York. That's me. To be an uncle is pure luxury. An uncle is lavish and funny and at the end of the evening, the uncle gets to say goodbye. An uncle doesn't make you go to bed. Uncle New York is the one who keeps you up late. I bring gifts, like this box of Italian chocolates, don't show it to your parents, they'll think it's too expensive, and here is a book, don't show it to your parents, they'll think it's too advanced for you, but I think you'll like it, a child of your obvious intelligence.

Frankly, your parents are a little dense, don't you think? When they get to talking, suddenly I find myself yawning—oh! excuse me! How about you leave them home, and let's have lunch sometime, you and me, and I will tell you stories about Manhattan, that glittering jewel. Your poor old parents could never appreciate it but you'll.

'Cause I'm your Uncle New York—
I make orchestras play and the stage light up
  wherever I go.
And anything you say, I'll never say no.
We'll go to La Côte Basque, we'll ask for
  a corner booth,
We'll sit on display, objets d' beauty and youth.
Blue point oysters and steak tartare,
You and me, how cool we are.
We'll go to SoHo, impress Yoko Ono and
  Yo-Yo Ma
And no one will guess we're bozos from
  Minnesota.
'Cause we're cool and rude and our attitude is
  drop dead east,
Uncle New York and his favorite midwestern niece.

GK and daughter Maia Grace, at a rehearsal at Fitzgerald Theater, February 1999. She was the subject of many songs, starting with "Baby Blues" a few months after her birth: "I was awfully hungry / The diaper was bad news / Couldn't reach my pacifier / That's why I've got these baby blues / The lowdown, left alone, lying in the bedroom baby blues."

Unforgettable

GK almost missed a show in Stillwater when he went home to take a nap and took the phone off the hook.

Tom Keith remembers when the show was in Mantorville MN in the 1970s and the local police radios came through on the house sound speakers. PHC staff asked the police to hold off communicating on their radios for ninety minutes and they did.

GK dropped the microphone once, just after a script about cannons.

A waitress came from Mickey's Diner to gather orders for take-out food from the performers and the audience seated on the Fitzgerald stage. Potatoes O'Brien was the favorite.

Studs Terkel, May 16, 1998, celebrated his 86th birthday and a scantily clad woman presented a three-tiered birthday cake on stage. The candles took so long to blow out that their heat melted the frosting.

When the van didn't show up, Chris Tschida "borrowed" a car without the owner's knowledge to get performers to the airport in Baton Rouge LA.

In Durango CO, 1998, bad weather caused flights to be canceled, so the crew hired a driver and vehicle to drive them eight hours through the mountains. The driver had just come off a full day shift so one of the crew drove while the driver slept in the back.

U.S. History

"THERE . . . THEY . . . WERE" from February 1990 to April 1992, re-enacted "Great Moments in History." GK, Bob Elliott, Tom Keith, and others, as the American Historical Radio Repertory Company of the Air, brought "to life once again those moments when the moving finger wrote and the tide of history rose and THERE . . . THEY . . . WERE." Columbus didn't get around to naming everything—just a few places—capital of South Carolina, a couple of college towns in Ohio and Missouri, and a circle up in New York. Old Wrong-Way Paul Revere rode south and warned everyone on Cape Cod to close up their summer houses. George Washington was coached to bring his arm more overhand across the body with a little more wrist to throw the silver dollar across the Rappahannock. Lindbergh settled on a plain cheese sandwich for his flight across the Atlantic. The National Association of Federations sponsored the series.

Varieties of Religious Experience

Many Minnesotans traveled out to California. They came here to join the Lutheran Church, the Macramé Synod of the Lutheran Church, where the sign in front of the church doesn't say anything about repentance, it says, "Mistakes inspire the artists to make richer patterns in the tapestry of our lives." Or they wander into the jazz church, the Episcopal Church, St. Pheloneous where they sing, "The theology's cool, the liturgy too, just kneel down and stand up and do what the others do. Episcopalian, saving my love for you. Ooh, ooh. We've got white folks and black, gay and morose, some white Anglo-Saxon men but we watch them pretty close. Episcopalian, saving my love for you." When the organist plays the offertory and the usher comes around to take up the collections, sometimes people forget where they are and say, "I'll have a Manhattan and a Gibson for my wife and keep the change."

Various Acts

Animals often appear on the show as sound effects, but live animals occasionally have been on the show too, beginning with animals from St. Paul's Como Zoo in August 1976. Once a chicken was hypnotized by a guest. Tom Keith barked on the air to get listeners' dogs to bark back, and one did. Murray, the sea lion from the Nautilus Amphitheater in San Diego, barked his sea lion sound on the show in February 1991, and in July 1997, a buffalo parked itself next to the satellite at the Yellowstone show, alarming the sound crew.

Many dancers have performed on the broadcast, among them tap dancer Beth Obermeyer; Mike Seeger, playing the fiddle and flatfoot dancing; John Hartford, fiddle and flatfoot; Natalie McMaster, fiddle and fancy footwork; and Sandy Silva, step dancing. An Egyptian belly dancer in 1975, the Night O' Rest Motel Dancers in 1984, a Hawaiian dancer in 1987, polka dancers in 1997, and the Arthur Murray Dancers in 1999, have graced the stage. ➡

Very Enduring

Studs Terkel, the Grand Old Man of radio, on PHC,
October 1998. He grew up in Chicago, heard
President Harding's funeral on the radio and the 1924
Democratic convention. An actor, he made his radio
debut as the gangster Butch Malone on *Ma Perkins*,
the one who said, "Up against the wall, youse guys,"
but went on to do forty-five years on station WFMT,
interviewing authors and musicians and creating doc-
umentaries about uncelebrated people, many of which
wound up as books: *Division Street: America*, *Hard
Times*, *Working*, *The Good War*, and *Coming of Age*.
Describes himself as looking like "a minor mob figure
the day after he died." On PHC, he did a stream-of-
consciousness cooking segment, "Cooking with
Studs," played an old con man, and read some thun-
dering 19th-century narrative poems.

High schoolers sometimes appear as guests. Early ones were the cheerleaders from St. Paul Central in May 1976. The Rocori Spartan High School Drum Line, the Anoka High School Marching Band (who marched on the stage through the back door), the Harding High School Marching Band of St. Paul, the Beloit Memorial High School Choir, and the Kamehameha Schools Concert Glee Club have also been on the show.

Veteran

From a show in Austin TX, June 5, 1998:

> I've been so long in the music biz
> I don't know what town this is,
> I've been on the road since Willie Nelson
>   was young.
> From the Catskills to the Cascades
> From Canada to the Everglades
> There isn't a low-down dive where
>   I haven't sung.
>
> I was a friend of Johnny Cash
> Back when he wore a thin moustache
> And leopardskin briefs to show off his body.
> I was a friend of Willie and Waylon
> When they were into tennis and sailin'
> And sang in the Kingston Trio with Pavarotti.
>
> I knew Molly Ivins when she used to live
> In North Dallas and was a conservative
> (That was before she ran off with Lyle Lovett).
> I knew George Bush when he was poor
> And worked as a clerk in a liquor store
> And lived in a two-room apartment right up
>   above it.
>
> I started young and ever since,
> In bars and joints and Holiday Inns,
> I've stood up and sung for people the songs
>   I wrote.
> I go back before there were amps,
> Just megaphones and kerosene lamps,
> And you'd get paid in chickens, sometimes
>   a sheep or a goat.

Violas and Violins

Violists are good people who have no ego, because there is so little solo music written for them and so many jokes told about them. When there is a long viola passage, the rest of the orchestra stares at them in astonishment as if watching blind people shooting baskets. Violists come to feel moody about this, and late at night they like to build a fire in a Dumpster and drink red wine from a carton and roast a chicken on a clothes hanger and talk about going to Mexico with someone named Rita.

The first violins are proud people. During breaks in rehearsal they like to sit and go over the hard parts so everyone knows it wasn't them who screwed up. The first violins hardly ever look at the conductor. They know that he takes his tempo from watching their bows go up and down, so what's to look at? It's the winds he's conducting, it has nothing to do with them. The violin is not for Lutherans, it's for people who express themselves. It has soul, it weeps, it cries out, it argues—face it: it's a Jewish instrument. There is no Itzhak Peterson or Pinchas Soderberg or Jascha Hansen. If you're Jewish, go, play already. Lutherans? I don't think so. But maybe second violin.

The second violins sit with percussionists right behind them, it's like having a gun to the back of your head. You feel like a thoroughbred hitched up to a beer wagon. The music is beneath you, but somebody has to do it, and there you are, sawing away, sacrificing your bright future to provide accompaniment for others.

Violence

PHC sound effects man Tom Keith is a leader in the campaign to crack down on violence on radio and served on the Radio Sound Effects Council that drew up guidelines on what should and should not be broadcast. For example, throwing guys in suits off cliffs (a Tom Keith specialty, one that has drawn reams of angry letters from suits) is okay so long as the sharks waiting at the foot of the cliff and whipping the water to a white froth in their feeding frenzy are not portrayed in a sympathetic manner, e.g., given hats to wear or given names like Sylvester or Stacy.

We oppose unnecessary violence, which desensitizes children to the pain that is caused by, for example, throwing a guy off a cliff into shark-

GK rehearsing onstage in Austin TX, spring 1998. The house, in background, has traveled with PHC since the Radio City shows of 1988. A bane of stagehands, it nevertheless shows up very handsomely against a well-lit sky.

infested waters. Necessary violence is another matter.

For example, the giant condor with its wingspan of eight feet and its cry that sounds like a knife on a blackboard, which we often use in sketches in which a naked guy is tied to a rock and the condor pecks out his liver. It's pretty terrible.

Many listeners seek out public radio, believing it is gentler than Howard Stern, and then they hear a man getting eviscerated by a giant bird—Howard has never gone that far on his show, he only interviews naked flatulent lesbians—and of course they're shocked. Studies show that exposure to violence on radio is ten times worse for children than violence on TV because violence on radio is so much more real.

Unfortunately, there are people in the world who cannot be dealt with in any other way than by getting a liverectomy from an immense bird while naked on a rock. Howard Stern may be one of those people.

Many listeners have complained about the vivid scenes of brain surgery on the show, saying that they had to pull the car to the side of the road and put their head between their knees.

Others disliked the sketch about the thunder-storm touching off an avalanche that rumbled down the mountain toward eleven-year-old Timmy and his kitty cat as the anthropologist Dr. Jenkins chugged along in the Jeep with his chimp Bobo, who spotted the kid and carried him and Mr. Kitty to safety as the avalanche hit the natural gas tanks and set off the blaze that warmed the earth's crust to where the dinosaur eggs hatched and the creatures terrorized the village so that cruise missiles had to be launched but the dinosaurs caught the missiles in their big mitts and hurled them into the sea where they exploded and a school of dolphins underwent a big mood swing and commandeered a submarine and raised the periscope and saw the meteoroid zooming toward Earth and launched nuclear warheads that deflected the meteor away from Los Angeles and toward the dinosaurs but also touched off a rockslide heading straight toward Timmy looking for his cat whose ankle was caught in the railroad tie and Ranger Buck brought the chopper in and rescued the boy and Bobo found Mr. Kitty and released his ankle seconds before the Starlight Express thundered by.

We welcome their concern.

War

Gulf War. 1991.

It was a wonderful war,
With the rockets flying up from the ships
    off-shore
And it was on TV
And we lay on the couch and watched it,
  Lucy and me.
And she said, "It's so awful.
America at war again."
But actually it didn't look that bad on CNN.
It was a war movie war.
And everybody knew what they were
    fighting for
And not many people died,
And almost all of them were on the other side.
And the weapons worked great.
And we demonstrated commitment and
    strength,
And it lasted a month, which was exactly the
    right length.

Water

A tip from the American Six-A-Day Institute:
almost everything you need to know, you can find
out by remembering what you told your children.
You told them: drink liquids. Six big glasses every
day. You assume people know these things and often

they don't. People, you don't drink enough water.
You get sick, wonder why, buy vitamins, join groups,
read books, get weird ideas about wellness. Folks,
the well you need is in the ground, water comes out
of it, drink it, you'll feel better. You really will.

All day I face the database without the taste of water,
    Cool water.
    I watch the green computer screen and wish I'd
seen some water,
    Cool clear water.
    I've been walkin' miles down corridors and
aisles past the dusty office files and I'm hoping now
that I'll find water.
    It's here somewhere just downstairs, there's a
water cooler there, and it's bubbling for you
and me—
    Water.
    Cool clear water.

Who's Whom

The best thing about public radio is meeting the
people who listen to it, and now you can, with a
copy of Who's Whom: The Directory of Public
Radio Listeners in the United States. Take it with
you when you travel, knock on any door and—
    "Hi! I'm Curt Ecklund. Mind if I come in
and listen?"
    "Honey? It's another public radio listener!"

Oct 3 Fitz — ANN HAMPTON CALLAHAN / MONO — / AUTUMN

Oct 10 Fitz — Lots of positive response - esp / Hopefuls / R-L tune / Boll...

Oct 17 Fitz — Trio Voronezh

Oct 24 Fitz — Joyce Sutton + choir / MONO—

Oct 31 Fitz — Chenille Sisters / Mono + ...

Nov 7 Fitz — Guy Noir v. Jesse / Mono ...

Nov 21 Atlanta — John Twomey

Nov 28 New York — ERNEST STEIN

Feb 13 Fitz — LOVE POEMS SONGS / STEVIE BECK

Feb 20 Fitz — KELLEY HUNT

March 27 Fitz 981 — Boys of the Lough (5) / Hopefuls: R+L Williams / Leo Kottke

April 3 Fitz 983 — Easter / Battlefield Band (4) Leo Kottke / Battlefield Concert 782

April 10 Fitz 979 — JOKE SHOW / Robin + Linda Williams / Paula Poundstone

April 17 Peoria — Previews of ...: Virtual Consort + New Contestants

April 24 Northrop Aud — SPRING / 940 / ¡Cubanismo!

May 1 Fitz 897 — Dave Van Ronk / Butch Thompson / Plymouth Sax Singers of Philip Brunelle

What's Goin' On: Schedule for the 1998-1999 season, in the PHC offices in St. Paul.

When you're in the public radio audience, it's like being in the Masons except not as big. You get to know everybody, and you know you can trust them.

"So what do you do?"
"I sell life insurance."
"Great! I'll take some."

Who's on the Show?

Who else is on our show today, Tim Russell?
Tim: Peter Lorre, Piper Laurie, Lorrie Morgan, Morgan Stanley, Stan and Ollie, Good Golly Miss Molly, Molly Ivins, Ivan the Terrible, Evel Knievel, Ish Ka Bibble, Bo Belinsky, Lickety Split, Click and Clack, Clint Black, Black Sabbath, Sabbathani Baptist Church Choir, Dire Straits, Twisted Sister, the Hills Brothers, the Mills Brothers, the Mothers of Invention, the Father of Waters, Muddy Waters, Huddie Ledbetter, Buddy Guy, Sleeping Beauty, Judy Tenuta, Rudy Giuliani, Julia Roberts, Robert Lowell, Lowell George, George & Tammy, Tammy Faye, Fay Wray, Ray Floyd, Floyd Little, Little Feat, Little Richard, Richard Nixon, Willie Dixon, Chicken Little, Wilt the Stilt, Milton Berle, Earl the Pearl, Pearl Bailey, Beetle Bailey, the Beatles, Ma Barker, Yo-Yo Ma, So's Your Mama, Mama Mia, Mia Farrow, Clarence Darrow, Daryl Strawberry, Sister Carrie, Harry Carey, Ben & Jerry, Jerry Rubin, Rueben James, James Earl Jones, Jon Bon Jovi, Moby Dick, Dick & Jane, Jane Fonda, Rhonda Fleming, Flem Snopes, Snoopy, Sneezy, Sleepy, Dopey, Dewey, Huey, Louie, 2 Live Crew, Rod Carew, Wally Ballou, Lou Rawls, Rollie Fingers, Debra Winger, Singin' Sam, Waltzing Matilda, the Tennessee Waltz, the Tennessee Two, the Three Musketeers, the Four Tops, the Dave Clark Five, the Six Fat Dutchmen, the Chicago Seven, George Ade, Lady Madonna, Donnie Osmond, Ozzie & Harriet, Harry James, James Beard, Weird Al Yankovic, Frankie Yankovic, Vic Tanny, Al Franken, Frankenstein, Andy Stein, Tyne Daly, Ponce de León, Leon Russell, Russell Means, and me, Tim Russell.

GK's desk at Minnesota Public Radio, looking out on 7th Street. GK: "I don't write here, that's why it's this neat. I write on my kitchen table. This is the desk I sit at and write thank-you notes and choose poems for *Writer's Almanac* and autograph books."

Williams

Robin and Linda Williams first appeared on the show in 1976, first as a duo, then with their band, and now as half of the Hopeful Gospel Quartet. They have spent the better part of the last quarter century on the road, and when they're not criss-crossing the country in their big motor home, they live in the sunny Shenandoah Valley of Virginia.

Winter

It's January in Minnesota, cold, windy, snowy, the time of year when true Minnesotans feel more alert, more alive, and somehow filled with a sense of the beautiful possibilities of the moment.

Winter does shine in Minnesota, even in the darkest night, the snowbanks glow—the light from stars a million years away reflected from trillions of crystals, each one unique—so that as you walk on a starry night (DOG BARKS)—through the fields of snow and (DOG BARKS, GROWLS)— what is it, Rex?

Rex: (DOG, COLLAR JINGLE): Easy for you to get all rapturous about winter. You don't have to go outdoors to pee like I do. Got to go out in the yard, find my spot. (SHIVERS) Ohhhh, that's cold when you lift your leg. Brrrr. I'd a lot rather squat but you never know who might be looking. And you scout around for a spot and you smell where other dogs have been and it's like reading their résumé and their medical file—whole life story, right there in a patch of yellow snow—it's damn depressing, let me tell you.

(MUSIC)
Winter is what makes people behave right. I learned that as a child growing up in a sod hut out on the prairie. My father was a woodcutter, so we didn't have much money, but he taught me to act right and have high standards anyway. All Papa knew about America, he learned from watching Fred Astaire movies. To him, Americans were people who danced at the drop of a hat.

Tom Keith

(TAP DANCING)
I'm puttin' on my long johns
Puttin' on my Gore-tex
And my woolen socks.
I'm getting out my parka
Starting up the Chevy
Shoveling the walks.
I'm steppin' out, my dear, to breathe an atmosphere
that's seventeen below.
It's like jazz that easy feeling as across the ice I go.
For I'll be there...
Skating in my top hat,
Skiing in my white tie,
Dancing in my tails.

Wife: Honey, would you mind if we didn't go out
to a movie tonight—it's so cold out—
Guy: That's fine.
Wife: Are you sure? If you really want to go, I
mean, I'll put on a down coat and go—
Guy: It's fine to stay home.
Wife: I know you're crazy about English costume

dramas, so—maybe I oughta go. You'll be so disap-
pointed.
Guy: Me? English costume dramas?
Wife: You love them. All the Jane Austen–type
movies with tall women in long dresses named
Cecilie—you're always after me to go.
Guy: I thought you liked them.
Wife: Me! Ha! I love film noir. Slasher movies.
Guy: I thought you loved Merchant-Ivory films.
Wife: I hate Merchant-Ivory films. I went to films
for your sake. I despise films. It's movies I love.
Guy: Why didn't you say so before?
Wife: Because it wasn't this cold before. It's too
cold for dishonesty, darling. Look at me. I despise
films and I also despise northern Italian cuisine. I
hate fresh ground pepper. I despise cilantro. And I
hate wine. It gives me gas. It's fifteen below zero.
It's truth time. I want a pizza and a six-pack of beer.
And I want to stay home and take you to bed and
rip your clothes off and afterward watch *Psycho*.
Guy: Okay. I think that can be arranged.

Woe Be Gone

Written by John McCusker of the Battlefield Band after his first appearance April 6, 1996, on PHC.

World Theater

The Fitzgerald Theater opened August 10, 1910, as the Sam S. Shubert Theater, one of the Shubert chain, the first theater west of Chicago needing no pillars to support the balconies. No seat was farther than eighty-seven feet from the stage. An entrance on Exchange Street allowed people arriving in horseless carriages to avoid traffic with horses.

The Shubert was built for vaudeville and plays, but eventually live theater couldn't compete with twenty-cent talking pictures, and in 1933 a silver screen was mounted in the proscenium and the Shubert became the World. It was an art-movie house, then a second-run theater, until 1978, when it closed. Robert Dworsky, the owner, was about to board the place up when PHC, having outgrown the St. Paul-Ramsey Arts & Science Center auditorium, decided to move into the World on March 4, 1978. The opening show included Mayor George Latimer singing, and Butch Thompson playing piano. MPR bought the World from the Dworsky family in 1980. With 960 seats, the World housed PHC until January 20, 1984, when plaster began to fall. MPR staff hauled a ton of gear, cleaned the vacant Orpheum Theater three blocks away and fixed its plumbing, in time for the show the next day. A "Save the World" committee raised three and a half million

dollars to renovate the World. Restored to its former glory, it opened again with 996 seats in 1986. On September 24, 1994, to celebrate St. Paul's F. Scott Fitzgerald, the World was renamed the Fitzgerald.

Writing

Writing is a blessed life, no matter how hard it gets at times, which it does. It tests your integrity severely, especially writing simple descriptive narrative, telling what happened and who said what and who is telling us about it, which is the hardest writing there is. To bring your mother onto the page and let her speak and have her rightful presence might take a gifted person two weeks of hard work, whereas to agonize over your mortality and the wrongs done to you by a bad daddy can be accomplished by anyone in fifteen minutes. You write for the listener, to lead people out of the barns of boredom and toward the green hillside of romantic comedy. You don't have any right to bore people who don't have the opportunity to bore you right back. A writer should entertain people, give them a little more courage, defend the hopeless, praise what other people can't see is beautiful, find humor in dreadful circumstances, satirize pretense and cruelty, and love this world. It's not satisfying to write to express yourself, you can do that so much better by splitting firewood.

X

Even the Scrabble-playing cowboy who insulted Dusty in the saloon couldn't think of one:

Dusty: Ya big dope!
Cowboy: Ha! Dope! Why not dodo, dingbat, yahoo? Huh? Why not airhead, buffoon, crumb-bum, dork, eunuch, feeb, guttersnipe, has-been, imbecile, jackal, kretin, lunkhead, meathead, numbskull, oaf, peabrain, quack, rascal, stoopnagel, turkey, upchuck, vulture, weasel, yahoo, or zero?

Years Ago

GK had an early-morning radio show beginning in 1969 called *The Morning Program*, *A Prairie Home Companion*, and *The Prairie Home Morning Show*. From Jul 1976 until November 1982 with his engineer, Tom Keith, GK did the three-hour weekday program of recorded music as well as the Saturday evening broadcast. The Saturday evening radio show, the subject of this book, began in April 1974, with three ninety-minute shows taped at the Walker Art Center with Vern Sutton, Philip Brunelle, the Wolverines Classic Jazz Orchestra, Judy Larson and Bill Hinkley, and others. One show included the slide lecture on the penis, "very short, and needing the cooperation of every member of the audience."

July 6, 1974, was the first live broadcast, from the Janet Wallace Auditorium at Macalester College, St. Paul, 4:30 P.M. Sutton, Brunelle, Hinkley and Larson, Bob DeHaven, a longtime familiar radio voice of the upper Midwest from WCCO radio, accordionist Ernie Garven, and the Brescian String Quartet performed before an audience of twelve in a four-hundred-seat hall. Margaret Moos sold tickets ($1.00, fifty cents for children).

The year 1974 saw the first appearances of Butch Thompson, the Hall Brothers Jazz Band, Peter Ostroushko (as a teenager), and Charlie Maguire, singer-songwriter. In October the show moved to Variety Hall Theater, eighty-two seats in Park Square Court across the hall from KSJN, where the newsroom served as the backstage. October also saw the first road trip, to Fargo ND and to Moorhead MN with Hinkley and Larson, Dakota Dave Hull, and poet Mark Vinz.

1975

Butch Thompson, Vern Sutton, and Sean Blackburn played often this year. First live broadcast road show, from St. John's University, Collegeville MN. The National Endowment for the Arts began to support PHC, which moved to St. Paul-Ramsey Arts & Science Center auditorium, 220 seats. To celebrate the move, they opened a bottle of champagne. The radio audience heard the cork pop, and seconds later, when that cork hit a six-year-old kid in the head, a cry of pain. The kid, Ben Ellingson, didn't hold a grudge, though, for he returned to the PHC's 20th anniversary show, where he was introduced to the audience. This year saw the first appearance of Robin and Linda Williams. The December 20 show featured classical guitarist Jeffrey Van plus Thelma Buckner and the Minnesota Gospel Twins.

1976

PHC broadcast from all over St. Paul and Minneapolis: the St. Paul-Ramsey Arts & Science Center Sculpture Garden, Nicollet Island, the roof of the Walker Art Center, Lake Harriet, and the College of Art and Design. Steve Gammel, Becky Riemer Thompson, Janis Hardy, and Philip Brunelle performed often. This year saw the first and second Mouth-Offs.

1976

1977

PHC did a benefit for and with the St. Paul Chamber Orchestra with William McGlaughlin conducting his arrangement of the "Help Me Rhonda" Suite. Summer outdoor broadcasts came from the St. Paul-Ramsey Arts & Science Center Sculpture Garden, continuing through the summer of 1982. Vern Sutton, Philip Brunelle, Dakota Dave Hull, and Sean Blackburn appeared frequently. The show came in September from the Guthrie Theater, Minneapolis, with the Red Clay Ramblers and in November it moved to St.Thomas College, St. Paul, a six-hundred-seat auditorium.

1978

More collaboration with the St. Paul Chamber Orchestra, including the PHC-commissioned "Weaver's Song and Jig" by Libby Larsen for the Powdermilk Biscuit Band and Orchestra. In March, PHC moved to the World Theater on Exchange and Wabasha, St. Paul. Butch Thompson was

joined often by Claudia Schmidt, Papa John Kolstad, the Chenilles, Bill Staines, Jerry Rau, and the Middle Spunk Creek Boys.

1979

February 17: First national live broadcast, from 4,700-seat Northrop Auditorium at the University of Minnesota. Carried on National Public Radio's "Folk Festival USA" series, with a cast of more than a hundred. SRO. August 4: Outdoor live broadcast from the Lake Harriet Bandshell, Minneapolis. Audience of ten thousand saw Vern Sutton, Butch Thompson, Biscuit Band, Chatfield Brass Band, and Jack Curtis and Whitey Evans and the Westerners. In December, Rich Dworsky made his first appearance.

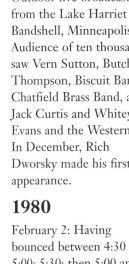

1980

February 2: Having bounced between 4:30 P.M., 5:00; 5:30; then 5:00 and then 5:30 again, then 7:00, 5:30, 6:30, and 6:00 P.M., the PHC broadcast time settled at 5:00 P.M. CST Bill Hinkley, Judy Larson, Adam Granger, and the Butch Thompson Trio were regular guests during the year. In March came the first live satellite broadcast, from Crown Center, Kansas City, at a public radio conference, with Butch Thompson, New Prairie Ramblers, Ken Bloom, and Pop Wagner. In May, the national weekly broadcast began from the World Theater, with the Red Clay Ramblers, New Prairie Ramblers, Randy Sabien and Larry Baione, Spider John Koerner, and Butch Thompson. This year saw the first appearance of Greg Brown, the release of the PHC fifth anniversary album (a year late), and the October broadcast from Ames IA before an SRO crowd of 2,500 that won the Peabody Award. MPR bought the World Theater.

Judy Larson, Bill Hinkley, GK, Bob Douglas, Rudy Darling, Worthington MN.

1981

Stoney Lonesome (with Kate MacKenzie), Jean Redpath, and Roy Blount Jr. made their first appearances, and become frequent guests. Other guests this year included Bessie Jones and the Georgia Sea Island Singers, Jimmy Driftwood, the Persuasions, and the Red Clay Ramblers. The first live road show broadcast from outside the Midwest came from the Boston Conservatory of Music.

1982

Chet Atkins and Jethro Burns made their first appearances. Humorist Howard Mohr began a stint of several years as a regular guest. Other guests this year were Odetta, Queen Ida, Sharon Isbin, and frequently, Pop Wagner. *The Family Radio* album was released. The eleven-minute "Thanksgiving Cantata" by Vern Sutton and Philip Brunelle, was composed from notes of thanks written by members of the audience. A fourteen-year-old kid sneaked every Saturday into the World Theater to watch rehearsals. After a few weeks, Ray Marklund handed him a camera, saying he should make himself useful.

He continued hanging around, later became an usher, and even later helped package Powdermilk Biscuit posters for mailing. He stayed around through college, and now David O'Neill works as a PHC production assistant and MPR's special projects manager and archivist.

1983

Peter Ostroushko and Greg Brown became weekly regulars. In August the "Dept. of Folk Song" began as regular feature. The *Tourists* album and the *News from Lake Wobegon* four-cassette "butter box" were released. During the year the Butch Thompson Trio, Claudia Schmidt, Stoney Lonesome, Charlie Maguire, and Jean Redpath played often.

1984

On January 20, plaster fell from the ceiling of the World, necessitating a swift move to 1,650-seat Orpheum in St. Paul. "Dept. of Folk Song" Clearance Show, fifty-one songs received from folks, including "Great Green Gobs," "Junior Birdmen," "Amphioxus," "Calorie, Calorah," and "Joe's Got a Head Like a Ping-Pong Ball." July 6–7, observance

GK with the Biscuit Band, St. Paul-Ramsey Arts & Science Center Sculpture Garden, 1977. A few people got a kick out of driving by and honking so they could hear themselves on their car radios.

of tenth anniversary of PHC, including a live broadcast with both the mayor of St. Paul, George Latimer, and the Governor of Minnesota, Rudy Perpich, in the theater. This year saw the Yale Russian Chorus, BeauSoleil, the Canadian Brass, the Tannahill Weavers, Claudia Schmidt, the Boys of the Lough, Peter Schickele, Bobby McFerrin, Manhattan Transfer, and Doc Watson among others. Tapes of older shows were broadcast in Australia and Sweden.

1985

Time magazine discovered PHC and put GK on its cover. In the summer the show moved to Red Wing MN, and in the fall broadcast from Atlanta, Baton Rouge, Laramie, Seattle, Claremont CA, and Hawaii. They returned to Cottonwood MN to a blizzard. Johnny Gimble and Chet Atkins played this year, and often afterward. The Barrett Sisters, the Paul Winter Ensemble, and Emmylou Harris performed. Howard Mohr appeared often with his "Raw Bits" and "Minnesota Language Systems" spots.

1986

Rich Dworsky had replaced Butch Thompson as the "house pianist." PHC moved back to the World Theater in March, and had a grand reopening there in April. The show traveled to Alaska and Hawaii in July. The July 12 broadcast from Juneau is remembered as the "Just Say Goodnight" show. GK got caught up in his monologue and almost ran out of time. Stagehand Steve Koeln came on stage with a note, "Three minutes to end of show," and then another, "90 Seconds," and finally he handed GK a slip of paper that said, "Say Goodnight." PHC broadcast from the Grandstand at the Minnesota State Fair in August, where engineer Scott Rivard enjoyed using the sound system of the band Alabama.

1987

On February 14, GK announced that PHC would cease in June. The last eighteen shows from February 14 to June 13 ran in an edited, time-delay version on television on the Disney channel. The Farewell broadcast was the first and last broadcast

Second Annual Farewell finale, 1988, New York.

Taj Mahal in Red Wing MN, August 1985.

to run over its time, by forty minutes. Bob and Ray (Elliott and Goulding), Bobby McFerrin, and cowboy singer Glen Ohrlin (who'd been a guest in 1976), the St. Paul Chamber Orchestra, New Grass Revival, Doyle Lawson and Quicksilver, the Yale Russian Chorus, Pat Donohue, and Yo-Yo Ma performed this year.

1988

Reruns were broadcast during most of the year. The Farewell had been so fun GK decided to do a Second Annual Farewell, a tour culminating in a show from New York's Radio City Music Hall in June. In November the "Prairie Home Folk Song Show" with Ray Stevens and the Judds broadcast from Vanderbilt University in Nashville; in December, "An American's Christmas in Copenhagen" was broadcast, complete with the Cathedral Choir of Copenhagen, a visit to other English-speaking residents, and a cookie-baking episode.

1989

More old shows were rebroadcast in February. "A Pretty Good Night at Carnegie Hall" aired on radio and on the Disney channel. In May and June, the "Third Annual Farewell Tour" took shows to eleven states. In November the show resumed as the "American Radio Company of the Air" with broadcasts from the Brooklyn Academy of Music (BAM). Rather than broadcast fifty shows a year, the season ran for twenty-five shows, and in subsequent years, ranged from thirty-four to thirty-two shows. The Broadway Local Theater Company began its run (to continue through June 1994) with actors Ivy Austin, Pamela McLernon, William Parry, Richard Muenz, Walter Bobbie, Lynne Thigpen, Paul Binotto, Tom Keith, and also Alice Playten, Sue Scott, and John McDonough.

1990

The American Radio Company broadcast from BAM and from Lamb's Theater in New York City.

GK, Emmylou Harris, and Ralph Stanley 1986.

Regulars included the Broadway Local Theater Company and Rob Fisher and the Coffee Club Orchestra. Other guests this year included Maureen McGovern, Tito Puente, Pete Seeger, and Flaco Jimenez. The Mark Twain show came from Mark Twain's house in Hartford CT on December 1.

1991

Shows came from Seattle, San Diego, the Bronco Bowl in Dallas (where people had to go through the bowling alley), Chicago, Lexington KY, Memphis, Nashville, Milwaukee, and London. In New York, PHC broadcast from Lamb's Theater, Symphony Space, and the New York Public Library. The show also went to Willa Cather's hometown, Red Cloud NE, and then to Burlington VT for three weeks. Among this year's guests were Carl Perkins and the Appalachian Association of Sacred Harp Singers. A live broadcast from London in March 1991 began at 11:00 P.M. After the show the cast and crew, hungry at 2:00 A.M., could not find an open restaurant.

Jethro Burns, 1986.

Desperate, Chris Tschida liberated the morning buns set out in their hotel's breakfast room. Someone had pretzels, and someone else had a bottle of wine, so they all sat in the dark hotel lobby and had an ad hoc dinner.

1992

In March, GK announced a return to Minnesota. Broadcasts came from the World Theater (six), and eighteen other locations, including a "PHC Hymn Sing" from Concordia College in Moorhead, a Buddy Holly show from Clear Lake IA, and a Walt Whitman show from Brooklyn. Mr. (Fred) Rogers appeared this year, as did Robert Bly and Allen Ginsberg.

1993

Shows broadcast from the World Theater, Birmingham in a blizzard, St. Louis, Tulsa, Fort Worth, Lincoln NE, Seattle, San Jose, Madison, Chicago, Cincinnati, and Town Hall in New York. In October the show resumed the Prairie Home

Companion name. Rich Dworsky played piano, and guests this year included the Turtle Island String Quartet, Toby Twining Music, Marilyn Horne, and Lyle Lovett.

1994

Tim Russell made his first appearance. Other guests in the year included Cokie Roberts, Vince Gill, Iris DeMent, and, on the 20th anniversary show, Ernie Garven, who had appeared on the first broadcast. One of the audience for the first show, Anne Ulmer, came back to attend the 20th anniversary show. In October, the World Theater became the Fitzgerald. The show toured in February, May, June, July, and November. The year ended with two New Year's Eve shows from St. Paul.

1995

The year opened with six shows at the Fitzgerald, and then February, March, and April broadcasts came from Baton Rouge, Amherst, Nashville, and St. Paul. May, June, and July broadcasts came from Hartford, San Diego, Concord CA, Salt Lake City, Jackson MS, Chautauqua NY, and Interlochen. Summer vacation extended from July through September. Fall season guests included Janis Hardy,

GK swingin' in Moorhead MN, 1992.

Seattle in 1991.

Maria Jette, Jearlyn Steele Battle, Elizabeth Comeaux, James Galway, and Joel Grey, the latter singing a Yiddish parody of "Home on the Range." Other guests this year were the Mormon Tabernacle Choir, John Prine, Gil Shaham, R. Crumb and the Cheap Suit Serenaders, Eric Bogle, and Jack Lemmon playing the piano.

1996

PHC broadcast from St. Paul, Vancouver BC (with a translator turning English into French), Anchorage, Chapel Hill, Columbus OH, Billings, San Antonio, Savannah, Interlochen, Town Hall in New York, Ann Arbor, and Memphis. "Where Do Jokes Come From, and Where Do They Go?" in April was the first of the annual joke shows. James Earl Jones made his second appearance, and September 28 was the F. Scott Fitzgerald show.

1997

Broadcasts from the Fitzgerald, from Dallas, Muncie IN, Norfolk VA, Columbia MO, Ithaca NY, Akron, Miami Beach, Oklahoma City, Seattle, Yellowstone Park, Chicago, and New York City. The Polka Show came from the ballroom in Gibbon MN. At a show in June, in Woodville WA, a Seattle suburb, the GAS band had been on a break, and were called back for additional rehearsal. Greg Hippen leaped onto the stage, not seeing the business end of a large boom stand in his landing path. His forehead struck the counterweight of the boom stand, putting a deep gash just above his left eye, about two hours before show time. The paramedics cleaned him up and took him to the hospital, three miles away. The emergency room had a long waiting list, as this was a Saturday. The nurse on duty said Greg had eight hours before his injury would heal too much for them to stitch it. The driver took

Greg back to the stage and he performed with a large bandage on his forehead, and returned to the hospital after the show to have the injury cleaned and stitched.

1998

Shows from St. Paul, San Francisco, Portland OR, New York, Canton NY, Austin, Durango, Portland ME, Spokane, Kansas City MO, and Atlanta. The year's guests included writers Ian Frazier, Billy Collins, and Rita Dove; Frederica Von Stade, Dave Frishberg, Tish Hinojosa, and Iris DeMent.

1999

Shows from St. Paul, Peoria IL, Minneapolis, and in the summer, Butte MT, Greeley CO, Reno, Knoxville, and Wolf Trap in VA. The Tannahill Weavers, the Boys of the Lough, Gillian Welch, Geoff Muldaur, Keb' Mo', Garrick Ohlsson, Al Franken, and Robert Bly appeared. PHC celebrates its 25th anniversary.

Yelling

Holistic Yelling is the vocal exercise that helps you center and release anger. So often, the expression of anger seems to trigger even more anger, but Holistic Yelling releases anger in one clean burst. Bottled-up anger causes cancer, strokes, heart attacks, bad skin, bad hair, and headaches. You can spare yourself a lifetime of misery by learning the simple technique of Holistic Yelling. Just one yell every day could add years to your life. Gather all of your anger together—your anger at your good-for-nothing family, your lousy job, being overworked and underpaid, and your ungrateful friends, they just take and take and take and take and never give back—and yell! Feels good, doesn't it? One good clean yell. No wailing, no screaming and shrieking, no hollering, just the Holistic Yell. Send for the video "Yelling Your Way to Mental and Physical Health" or join us for our cable show on Saturday mornings at 8 titled *Holistic Yelling* or drop in at your local bookstore and ask for a copy of a *Guide to Wellness through Yelling*.

Za Zu

The chorus in "Let's Have A Party," performed on the 20th anniversary show by the Biscuits and the Shoe Band:

> Za zu, za zu
> Za zu, zu zu zu
> I can't dance, 'Fraid to take a chance
> I can't dance, I got ants in my pants.

Zenith

Sinclair Lewis's name for St. Paul, but for us it's a dark night in Zenith, a city that knows how to keep its secrets, but high above the empty streets, on the 12th floor of the Acme Building, one man is still trying to find the answers to life's persistent questions—Guy Noir, Private Eye. "He's smooth, he's cool, he's quick with a gun, a master in the boudoir, a guy in a trenchcoat who gets the job done, that's me, Guy Noir."

Zero

GK has a digital countdown timer which counts backward onstage at his feet, and Rich Dworsky has one at his piano. At fifteen minutes before the start of the broadcast, stage manager Jason Keillor signals Rich to begin the preshow music for the audience in the theater. When the countdown timer reaches zero, technical director Scott Rivard cues Jason that the show is on the air, and Jason cues Rich to begin the "Tishomingo Blues" theme. Near the end of the show, Scott sets the countdown timers again, to display the minutes and seconds remaining in the broadcast. GK and Rich each keep an eye on the countdown so they can finish the closing musical piece, the credits, and GK's last words, allowing a few seconds of applause before the end of the broadcast and Scott begins the crossfade to the Public Radio International logo. When the countdown timers read 00:00:00, the broadcast is over.

At the Opry

(GK began publishing in The New Yorker *in May 1970, with "Local Family Keeps Son Happy," and over the years wrote scores of casuals, Talk of the Town pieces, Notes and Comment, and two long non-fiction pieces, of which "At the Opry" was the first. It was edited by William Whitworth, now editor of* The Atlantic Monthly, *and fact-checked by Katherine Bouton, now an editor of the* New York Times Book Review, *and appeared in the issue of May 6, 1974, in the department "Onward and Upward with the Arts." GK's trip to the West Coast, paid for by this piece, on which he lost a story about Lake Wobegon in the Portland train depot, is alluded to in the preface to* Lake Wobegon Days.*)*

THE MONDAY-MORNING TRAIN rolled south through the hills of Tennessee, the sun rose in little towns along the line, and in the first coach I woke up to the voices of two women in the seat behind mine.

"When I point, you look and you'll see the house where that freight train went through."

"Did anybody get killed?"

"No, it was a freight train. He and his wife were out late at a dance and it went right through their bedroom."

"It's a wonder nobody was killed."

"But there was nobody there."

The women, whose names were Margaret and Lottie, had boarded in Louisville and were going on to Birmingham to visit Margaret's daughter and her

four children. They had packed a box of ham and meat-loaf sandwiches, fruit, pickles, crackers, and pecan pie, which they now opened for some breakfast. They asked me where I was going. I said, To Nashville to see the Grand Ole Opry. Friday is the last show in the old Ryman Auditorium before the Opry moves out to Opryland U.S.A. I'll be there a week and maybe write about it. I am a writer.

"Well, it must be hard on your family," said Margaret, after asking if I had one. "I sure do hate to leave my little ole Bob," she remarked to her friend.

"Does Bob cook pretty well?" asked Lottie.

"I fixed him quite a bit before I left," Margaret said. "He told me last night, he said 'Hon, you stop worrying about me and go have yourself a good time.' "

"That's what you ought to do, all right."

"But, I can't!"

"No," Lottie admitted. "It's hard, that's for sure."

It is hard. I had got to feeling good and lonesome already, sleeping upright with my legs stuck out in the aisle, and no sooner did I hit Nashville and set foot on Broadway toward the Opry than I wanted to catch the next train back home where I belonged. From Union Station, Broadway rises to the United States Courthouse and then falls into a valley of bars, pawnshops, peep shows, souvenir shops, and massage parlors that lie behind the warehouses on the Cumberland shore. Rising above it all like a mammoth brick tent is the old Ryman, and not a hundred feet from its fabled back door a woman lurking in a purple-painted doorway greeted me and stuck out a lurid green brochure offering a relaxing massage for twenty-one dollars, by one of twenty-two topless and bottomless women.

"No thanks," I said. I am a family man myself, and what I require is not paid pleasures of the flesh but a good breakfast in my *own* kitchen *every* morning, and seeing the elm tree still standing, and conversing with ones I love. This dusty street with garbage bags piled on the curb and the 1952 Cadillac Hank Williams died in displayed in a showroom and loudspeakers at the Gray Line tour terminal offering a look at Johnny Cash's house I did not need.

What decided me on staying was a good lunch at Linebaugh's Restaurant, across the street, a song I heard on the jukebox there, and what happened right before lunch. I walked into a new-and-used-instruments store on my list of sights to see. A young clerk was showing a customer a box of guitar picks. I looked

Ryman Auditorium, Sam Jones' gospel tabernacle that housed the 1897 reunion of Confederate soldiers and, from 1941 to 1974, WSM's Grand Ole Opry.

over the guitars hanging on the wall, at a dobro (which is a cousin to the Hawaiian guitar), and at a mandolin. Behind the counter, looking out the front window, an old man in a black beret scratched away at a fiddle. I thought I knew him, but I didn't recognize the tune. "You don't happen to need a fiddler?" he said.

The clerk said, "Well, I'd say you're as good as Roy Acuff anyway, but we don't have need for one today. Try us tomorrow."

"Yes, that is about as good as I am, and I'm getting sorrier and sorrier." The old man laid the fiddle away and left the store.

I asked the clerk if Mr. Acuff came in there often. "Every day," he said.

Mr. Roy Acuff is the King of Country Music. Born 1903, Maynardsville, Tennessee. Once a ballplayer, like many country stars. Tried out for the Yankees but suffered a sunstroke. He is a wealthy

man, a partner in Acuff-Rose Publications, and a lifelong Republican who ran for governor in 1948. Scheduled to introduce President Nixon at the dedication of the new Grand Ole Opry House at Opryland U.S.A. on Saturday evening. He has the gift of a truly distinctive voice, and if you've heard "Wreck on the Highway" sung right, or "The Great Speckled Bird," or "Precious Jewel," you've heard Mr. Acuff or somebody who learned it from him. He is one of my favorite singers. However, he didn't know this, and when I caught up with him half a block away and asked if he was sad to be leaving Ryman, he shot me a look that would have made a lesser man run for the train.

"Ryman should've been torn down long ago," he said. "The real Opry fan won't be sad to leave Ryman. He'll be a lot more comfortable out at Opryland."

RYMAN AUDITORIUM, the Mother Church of Country Music, was built in 1891 as the Union Gospel Tabernacle and later renamed to honor Captain Tom Ryman. According to the popular legend, Ryman was the owner of a Cumberland riverboat fleet notorious for liquor and prostitution, was converted through the Reverend Sam Jones' preaching of a sermon entitled "Motherhood," and subsequently gave a lot of money to build the tabernacle. Even with the stage, added later, Ryman looks and feels like a gospel hall, where the Word was shouted and the old revival hymns were rocked out on those long hot Sunday summer afternoons and nights. In its oaken pews, the buttocks slide into a slight hollow worn there by bodies that have gone before. Relatively few of those bodies sat under conviction of sin, though; after the balcony was built for the 1897 Confederate reunion, Ryman could seat thirty-three hundred, more than would come to revivals every week, and it soon became a concert hall and theatre. Caruso sang in it, and John McCormack

and Galli-Curci; Will Rogers ("The Poet Lariat")
spoke; W. C. Fields appeared in 1928, with "Mirth
Provoking Lampoons on the Popular Games of
Gold and Pocket Billiards." The Earl Carroll
Vanities ("60 Scenes of Lavish Splendor, 56 of The
Most Beautiful Girls in The World, 1000 Laughs")
and Paul Whiteman (Himself) and His Orchestra
appeared. Aimee Semple McPherson took Ryman
for five nights in 1934. Tallulah Bankhead played in
The Little Foxes. Eleanor Roosevelt spoke on "The
Relationship of the Individual to the Community" in
1938. The Opry came to Ryman in 1941. In 1963,
the National Life and Accident Insurance Company,
the owner of the Opry, bought Ryman and changed
its name to the Grand Ole Opry House, but it was
still called Ryman, even in Opry literature.

The Grand Ole Opry is the oldest continous
radio show in America today. It was originally called
the "WSM Barn Dance." Its founder—George D.
Hay (born 1895, died 1968), a former Memphis
newspaper columnist who was known as the Solemn
Old Judge, hired by WLS in Chicago in 1924,
voted most popular radio announcer in America by
readers of *Radio Digest*—was also the founder of
the "WLS Barn Dance." The twenties were a good
time for fathering institutions. Hay was hired early
in November of 1925 by National Life to run its
new station, WSM ("We Shield Millions"), in
Nashville, and at 8 P.M. sharp on Saturday,
November 28th, he stood before a new carbon
microphone in Studio A and announced the "WSM
Barn Dance" and its first performer—Uncle Jimmy
Thompson, an eighty-year-old fiddler who claimed
to know a thousand tunes by heart and who would,
Judge Hay said, honor any requests. A few tunes
later, the telegrams began to arrive.

In a matter of weeks, the program became a
show. Fans came to look through the studio glass
and watch Uncle Jimmy and the new string bands
that soon overshadowed him, such as Dr. Hum-
phrey Bate and the Possum Hunters, Sam and Kirk
McGee and Fiddling Arthur Smith (the Dixie-
liners), the Gully Jumpers, the Fruit Jar drinkers,
and the Crook Brothers. (In a booklet that the
Judge wrote about the Opry in 1953, he said of the
early musicians, "They are down-to-earth men.
Most of them have large families.") After the show
moved to a larger studio, a policy decision was
made at the highest level of National Life to let

fans come in and watch. Later, to accommodate the
crowds, the show moved to the Hillsboro Theatre,
then to the Dixie Tabernacle, in East Nashville,
then back downtown to the War Memorial
Auditorium (where the Opry started charging
admission), then to Ryman.

"The Grand Ole Opry is as simple as sunshine,"
the Judge wrote in later years, explaining its success. "It has a universal appeal because it is based
upon good will and with folk music expresses the
heartbeat of a large percentage of Americans who
labor for a living." By 1927, the show had grown to
three hours of folk music and good will (the Judge
liked to read letters on the air and send out birthday greetings). It followed "The R.C.A. Hour," with
Dr. Walter Damrosch conducting the New York
Symphony Orchestra. It was still called the "WSM
Barn Dance." The new name came to the Judge in
a flash of inspiration. "For the last hour, we have
been listening to music taken largely from grand
opera," he exclaimed on December 10, 1927, after
Dr. Damrosch had concluded his program with a
remark about the inappropriateness of realism in
the classics, "but from now on we will present the
Grand Ole Opry!" He was some namer, the Judge.
Other country music shows remained Barn Dances
or Jamborees, but with one majestic stroke the
Judge put his on a mountain. Neither grand nor
old, it suddenly became the Opry. The stars joined
so that when they toured they could come "Direct
from the Grand Ole Opry," directly out of the
radios all over half of the U.S. that tuned to 650—
clear-channel WSM, "The Air Castle of the
South"—on Saturday nights. And National Life,
too, found out how useful it was to be from the
Opry; so many more doors opened when the insurance agent said, "Hello, I'm from the Grand Ole
Opry, and Roy Acuff asked me to give you this
brochure personally."

AS I WAS WAITING for lunch in Linebaugh's on
Monday, a song title on the jukebox caught my eye
and I played it, and played it again, and again.
"Precious Memories (Of the Grand Ole Opry)," by
Tommy Howard. It reminded me of that beautiful
old hymn: "Precious mem'ries / How they linger,"
How they ever flood my soul; / In the stillness of
the midnight, / Precious sacred scenes unfold."
Tuesday, I took a long walk up past the train station

and across the Interstate to Music Row, the neighborhood of recording studios and old houses made over into music-publishing companies, to find Tommy Howard, only to be told that Mr. Howard was a cook at Linebaugh's and that Toward Records, which released his song, was his own label. At Linebaugh's, the word was that Tommy Howard *had* been a cook there for quite a while but now he cooked at another restaurant. A waiter told me that Howard came by Linebaugh's every afternoon, though, so I waited, and while I did I listened to "Precious Memories (Of the Grand Ole Opry)." Voices sing, "Precious mem'ries, / Oh, how they linger, / That portray the past to me / With that soulful country music / From the Grand Old Opry stage." Then a man's voice full of age and Texas and memories steps into the music to recite a poem about the last night in Ryman Auditorium—how it brings back a vision of "Uncle John some forty years ago; / Yes, it was on Uncle John's radio that I heard the *first* Grand Ole Opry show:

> No he wasn't really kin, but he
>   done his neighbors right,
> And we all went to see him every
>   Grand Ole Opry night,
> And by that old R.C.A. battery set,
>   the gooseneck speaker type,
> Everybody was all ears in a kero-
>   sene lamp light."

It seemed such a truthful song that when a man sat down beside me and introduced himself as the author, I was glad to see he was old enough to have heard that first show. He was dressed up in a black coat and bow tie and had a black bowler in his hand; his face was well weathered, wrinkled and tanned, though very boyish in expression.

"When I wrote 'Precious Memories,' they were talking about tearing down the old Ryman," he told me. "But you notice I didn't mention that in the song, and I'm glad now I didn't, because it looks like they might not. I recorded it last February up here at L.S.I. Studio. George Lewis—he owns the studio—produced it, and he got somebody to write down the music. I don't remember who, but I paid him seven dollars and fifty cents per song. We did four songs in three hours. There was a man and a woman sang harmony—I don't sing myself—and a blind man

played the piano, and there was a lead guitar, a bass guitar, drums, and a fiddle. It cost me a hundred and two dollars per man, and twice that for the leader. I just told them to make the fiddle sound like Bob Wills and the guitar like Ernest Tubb and the piano like Del Wood. You see, I was in a hurry, of course, and we had to get it done in three hours or pay extra.

"I had a thousand copies pressed in five days—they worked overtime to do it—and I paid two hundred and sixty-one dollars for the pressing. I mailed out about sixty records to radio stations—that's about thirty-five cents a copy for *that*—and altogether I figure 'Precious Memories' cost me a thousand dollars. But I wanted to do it right. So far, I've heard it's being played on a station in Fort Worth, but that's just hearsay. And that's all I've heard. I'm *hoping* to sell some myself this week."

He had to go, he said, to see about the posters he was having printed up to publicize "Precious Memories" (and "The Conversion of Tom Ryman," which is on the flip side of the record), but he left me sheet music for four of his songs, a mimeographed booklet of selected lyrics, and a photograph of himself as Professor Odie Thinkendore—a comic but philosophical character he hopes to take on the road as soon as "Precious Memories" sells a lot of copies or he otherwise comes into demand as a performer. He promised to meet me again on Thursday.

THE FIRST STAR of the Opry was Uncle Dave Macon (the Dixie Dewdrop), born 1870, a longtime farmer and drover (the Macon Midway Mule and Wagon Transportation Company) turned comedian and banjo picker, and everybody's favorite for twenty-six years after he came on the show, in 1926. The Opry's move to Ryman put Uncle Dave back into the neighborhood of his youth. Uncle Dave grew up on Broad Street (now Broadway), where his parents operated a small hotel. ("Two doors up from here," Mr. George P. Linebaugh told me. "They catered to show folk. Circus people and the like.") Uncle Dave attended Fogg High School, at Seventh and Broadway, two blocks up from Ryman, and it was at a circus on a vacant lot where the Courthouse now stands, at Eighth, that the young man viewed Joel Davidson, the celebrated comic banjoist, and was inspired to try his hand at picking.

Uncle Dave played the Opry until a few weeks before his death, in 1952, played the Loews vaudeville circuit in the South, played for his neighbors at parties, and toured in tent shows. His records are out of print, all but a few songs. Photographs show a portly gentleman decked out in black suit and vest, a plug hat, and high-top shoes, flashing a golden smile as he leans dangerously far back in his chair, kicks up a leg, and flies off into a choice selection from his large and varied repertoire, anything but his show-stopper. The stopper was a standup number. He called it "Uncle Dave Handles a Banjo Like a Monkey Handles a Peanut." Those who attempt a description of it today say that mere words cannot do it justice. The banjo was passed behind the back, between the legs, and over the head, swung out to the side, fanned with the hat, and set upright on the floor and danced around—and not a beat was missed, not even when the old man was old.

When he was in town for the Opry, the Dixie Dewdrop always used to stop in at Linebaugh's to enjoy the plate lunch. Bill Monroe, who is the Father of Bluegrass, still does, and so does the King of Country Music, and so does Ernest Tubb, the Texas Troubadour. "On nights he played the Opry, Uncle Dave would stay at the Merchant's Hotel next door," Mr. Linebaugh told me. Mr. Linebaugh is seventy-four. He runs a plain restaurant, and he speaks one sentence at a time between slow drags on his cigar. "Uncle Dave would have his dinner with us every night he was in town. He wore his red bandanna, and of course everybody recognized him. He loved people and he loved to tell stories. He was quite a character, Uncle Dave, and he was a good man."

Linebaugh's is famous for the young songwriters who are supposed to have written big hits on its napkins, but Mr. Linebaugh's own friends are the older musicians, like Beecher Kirby (Bashful Brother Oswald), who is the dobro player and comic in Roy Acuff's band, and Sam and Kirk McGee. Sam McGee is eighty, lives on his farm near Franklin, and picks guitar on the Opry. He first saw Uncle Dave perform more than sixty years ago. Sam and his brother, who plays fiddle and banjo and guitar, recorded with the old man in New York in 1925, and they joined the Opry the same year. "I am the oldest man living still playing on the Grand Ole Opry in service and age," Sam McGee writes in the Opry souvenir picture book, "and unless I'm out of town, making a personal appearance, I'm going to be there for our 11:00 P.M. show with my brother, Kirk."

IN 1968, National Life and WSM decided that the Opry needed a new auditorium. "When they began thinking in terms of space for parking and other considerations," an Opry brochure reads, "the plan for a park was conceived." The park opened in 1972. "Opryland U.S.A., a 369-acre complex, is designed to be 'the home of American music,'" the brochure continues. "The park is divided into entertainment areas that combine live musical shows, natural animal habitat areas, restaurants, gift shops, and sensational thrill rides." In 1971, National Life announced that it intended to tear down Ryman; in December of 1972, the company reaffirmed its decision and said it planned to "enshrine some of [Ryman's] materials" in a chapel to be built at Opryland. Meanwhile, some people, including members of the Tennessee Historical Sites Foundation (now called Historic Nashville, Inc.) and the Historical Preservation Committee of the Nashville city council, had taken an interest in saving Ryman, and the company took note of their views in its 1972 statement. "In the past couple of years, of course, there have been a few individuals who have undertaken to promote interest in preserving the Ryman," the company statement said. "Some of this promotion has even assumed the proportions of agitation." The agitators suggested that the federal government might be pleased to acquire Ryman as a historic site. In response, the company brought in a New York consultant, who concluded that Ryman was not worth saving as a theatre. The agitators considered his report inconclusive. The Historical Preservation Committee called a public hearing on the matter. The company reconsidered and said it had not yet made plans to tear Ryman down. The hearing was postponed until the various proposals could be studied by National Life.

That was last spring. Since then, the *New York Times* has come out for preservation, as has Dinah Shore, who is from Nashville and taped part of a television show in Ryman in February, as well as an architecture historian for the National Trust for Historic Preservation, who said, "There is so much heritage connected with the Ryman that, in my opinion, it could easily qualify as a national landmark." Its hand strengthened, the committee called a new public hearing for the Tuesday night before the last show. The hearing was held in the Metropolitan Court-house. A National Life spokesman, a vice president, spoke first. "I want to put at ease the rumor that National Life intends to tear the Ryman down," he said. He said the company had not reached a decision and would keep an open mind, welcoming the viewpoints of all concerned. It was left to the agitators to commend the company's forbearance, while simultaneously urging that Ryman *not* be torn down but be preserved by all means at anyone's disposal. Ryman's "intimacy of scale" was attested to by an architect, its acoustical qualities by a local music critic, and its safety by the city fire marshal; its heritage was warmly spoken of by everyone.

The heritage that got mentioned that night was more of the Caruso variety than of the Acuff, and I got the distinct impression that preservationists are not, by and large, real country-music fans. This impression was strengthened by the testimony of a spokesman for Historic Nashville, Inc., a private group of wealthy citizens interested, he said, in buying old buildings and finding new uses for them. The spokesman said that Ryman might be used as a conference center or dinner theatre, or perhaps as an intimate theatre-conference center with offices and small shops built in under the Confederate balcony. The word "boutiques" was used. *Scented candles where once we sat and looked on Ernest Tubb? Kahlil Gibran greeting cards in the Stationer Shoppe, and a Red Lion Publick Alehouse to greet the visitor seeking the spot where Hank Williams stood?* I thought of a newspaper clipping I'd read that afternoon at the library in the Country Music Hall of Fame. An Opry publicist, the story said, had delivered a speech to a local women's club, defending the Opry as a "cultural institution." He cited a number of Opry performers who had attended or graduated from college, and he mentioned two opera singers who had recently attended Opry shows. It made me want to weep.

"THE OPRY is a warmhearted show—we have always looked after our people," Grant Turner, who has been an Opry announcer for thirty years, told me Wednesday afternoon. "My only worry is that we keep the people in our imagination and not build the Opry too big." Mr. Turner had come into Tootsie's Orchid Lounge to reassure Tootsie that the Opry people wouldn't forget her after Friday night. Tootsie's is the most famous tavern on Broadway; its back door is across the alley from the back door of Ryman. This week, the hit song on Tootsie's jukebox was "What's Tootsie Gonna Do (When They Tear the Ryman Down)?" by Bill Sterling and John E. Denny. ("Tootsie has fostered more hillbillies than anyone I know," Mr. Denny, whose father, the late Jim Denny, managed the Opry in Hank Williams' day told me later. "Roger Miller, Hank Cochran, Wayne Walker, Mel Tillis, and hundreds of others ate on the cuff in Tootsie's before their royalties came in, and a lot of them, their royalties never did come.") Photographs and album jackets cover the wall over the bar, and patrons have autographed almost every square inch of the tabletops and the other walls. "Professional radio people who visit the Opry are amazed at the confusion—the musicians are milling around the stage, and so on—but that's part of its appeal," Mr. Turner told me. "You know, the Opry is like an old department store with stuff stacked in the aisles. You can move it to a nice new *building*, but will the people still come? Nobody goes to a building, you know. But the new Opry House is really quite beautiful. It makes me think of a castle. 'The Air Castle of the South,' as we used to say. You must come and see us out there."

TO SAVE MONEY for his recording ventures, Tommy Howard lives in a seventy-dollar-a-month three-room apartment a few blocks from the Opry. I visited him Thursday evening in his living room, which is also his office. Dozens of tapes and boxes of unsold records were stacked on a desk in the middle of the room and on a metal bookcase behind it, and a microphone on a floor stand was plugged into a tape recorder set into the top of a table beside the desk. "*Sometimes* I wonder if I'll ever make it," he said. "I get discouraged now and then, sure, but it's just one of those things. You got to believe in yourself."

Tommy Howard was born in Haskell County, Texas, north of Abilene, during the winter of 1912, he told me. Uncle John in "Precious Memories" was a friend of the family, name of John Lackey, who farmed nearby. "He was the same as us. Sharecroppers, I guess you might say. We farmed on thirds-and-a-fourth; a third of the feed and a fourth of the cotton went to the landlord. Uncle John lived in a little four-room house, same as ours, with his wife and four children. Weekends, his family'd go visiting, but he wasn't much for that, so he'd stay to home and have me down Saturday night, and we'd fix pancakes and listen to the Opry.

It was a battery radio, like I wrote in the song, with the gooseneck speaker you'd set up on top. Sid Harkreader, Sam McGee, Uncle Dave—we heard all of them, but I guess my favorite was Roy Acuff. We'd listen to the whole show—sit there all evening, never say much—and then I'd walk home. Uncle John's oldest daughter, Opal, married one of my cousins, and just to mail them a copy of the record made it worth it for me. The family thought enough of me that they had me say a few words at Uncle John's funeral. I just made mention that he wasn't a churchgoing man, but he loved the Lord. That was around 1938, 1940."

By then, Mr. Howard was a preacher in the Assembly of God. He was married, and he and his wife adopted a son. He told me he couldn't talk about those years, because it would make him too sad. In 1958, his wife divorced him. "I went thirty days without sleep and I thought I was losing my mind after she left. Went to a doctor, he said I was just shook up and would get over it. But I seemed to stay tore up all the time. So I quit the ministry. Seeing people happy together, I'd think of what happened to me. I guess I just loved her too much. I started writing songs after that—heartbreak songs mostly, to get my mind off it. Nowadays, I write mostly gospel. In September, 1963, I came to Nashville with a songwriter named Aubrey Gass. He'd written 'Dear John,' that Hank Williams recorded. We got in backstage at the Opry and I met Ernest Tubb, but we got to talking and I never got around to showing him my songs. I spent all my money on that trip. In fact, had to write a hot check to get out of the hotel, and went back to Dallas and sold my pickup to cover it. I came back for good in June, 1965. Paid a week's rent, had three-eighty in my pocket, and went to work at Linebaugh's as a cook on the night shift, six to six. We called it the can-to-can't shift—you work as much as you can until you can't.''

Mr. Howard made the rounds of music publishers, and when none of them bought his songs he started a series of desk-drawer publishing companies of his own—Tommyjard Music, Drawot Music, and his current company, Thinkendore—and began recording on his own. His first record, "Mom's Menu," came out in 1966 on the Rose label, he told me, and earned him $5.28 in royalties. "It was about a rooming house and café that Mom and Pop

Freeman used to run up here on Fifth and Broad, across from the Opry." He said that his second, "Talk about Me," was released in 1967, on the Snap label. "I paid for a thousand copies," he said, "and I've still got a lot of them." "Mom's Menu" is one of Mr. Howard's many Broadway songs, which deal with Linebaugh's ("The tables there at Linebaugh's have stories of their own"), the songwriters who hung around Broadway and the Opry, the conversion of Captain Ryman, and the street in general ("Folks talk about their boulevards, avenues, and streets, / But have you heard of Broadway in Nashville, Tennessee?"). And Ryman Auditorium.

It was one of those songs, "Goodbye, Dear Ole Ryman," that got Tommy Howard his first break. "First somebody recorded it with a seventeen-piece band, but it never came out, which was too bad. He had nine violins and three cellos on that session; it must've cost plenty. Then I brought it out myself in April of 1972 on the Delta label. I paid for two thousand copies, but it didn't get anywhere. Then I got a call down at Linebaugh's to go see somebody at R.C.A. Victor. It turned out Hank Locklin had liked it and wanted to record it." Hank Locklin is a regular on the Opry, an older star whose big hit, after two decades, is still "Send Me the Pillow You Dream On." On "Goodbye," which is still on Linebaugh's jukebox, he sounds like a young man as he sings, in a clear tenor voice, "Goodbye, goodbye, dear ole Ryman, / The home of the Grand Ole Op-e-ry, / As long as my mind will let me, / Forever you'll be in my memory." Nonetheless, the record didn't sell well, and it wasn't included on the next Hank Locklin album. "Goodbye" earned Tommy Howard, as writer and publisher, a little over eight hundred dollars. The money was invested in "Precious Memories."

ON FRIDAY, the day of the last show in Ryman, Tommy Howard was busy putting his posters in the windows of music and record stores along Broadway. Backstage at Ryman that afternoon, Opry manager Hal Durham was working in his office, finishing up preparations for that show and the Saturday-night show at Opryland. He told me he'd started lining up acts for the show three weeks before, calling the agents of the sixty Opry regulars to see who would be available for this weekend. Opry regulars, he said, are committed to at least twenty-one appearances on the show per year, for which they are paid musicians' union scale—thirty-one dollars for each fifteen-minute segment in which they perform. Bill Monroe and Lester Flatt were on the road this weekend, he said, and so was Loretta Lynn, but he expected to have thirty-three acts Friday night and fifty or more on the Saturday show. The President's scheduled visit to the Saturday-night show and the opening of the new Opry House had brought to Nashville scores of writers and photographers, most of whom had asked to attend the Friday show as well, and Mr. Durham said he was trying to figure out what to do with them all. "They'll all want to be backstage," he said, "but you can see for yourself there *isn't* much backstage. And the fact is, you can't hear the show back here."

From the manager's desk, it is about six strides through his secretary's office to the Ryman green-room. Illuminated photos of Opry stars look down on a small, narrow area furnished with canvas chairs and patio tables, a Coke machine, a table with a coffee-maker on it, a pay telephone, and signs reading "No Smoking on Stage" and "No Admittance to Stage Except Entertainers & Announcers." A door opens onto a circular stone stairway that leads down to the alley. A cast-iron stairway leads up to the radio control booth in the balcony. A ramp dips down and up onto the stage.

At the Hall of Fame, I'd seen an old photograph of Uncle Dave leaning against what looked like a log hitching rail with big wooden pegs stuck through it and rope lashed to the pegs, and, walking across the stage, I saw the rail, looking exactly as it did when it was photographed. The rope leads up to the flies and backdrops hanging high over the stage; looking up, I could make out a Martha White Flour backdrop and one for Beech-Nut Chewing Tobacco, and the Opry backdrop, a painted canvas barn almost the width of the stage. After examining the hitching rail, the backdrops, the oak floor, the piles of equipment—poles, risers, microphone cable—at the back of the stage, the old upright pianos (two), the stage clock with the jump second hand, the microphone stands (enclosed in white box sleeves with "WSM Grand Ole Opry" painted on vertically), and many other things that I would have liked to look at longer, I approached, indirectly, the front of the stage and stood, hat in hand, at center stage before the very footlights. In the late-afternoon light, I could just make out the inscription on

the face of the balcony ("1897, Confederate Gallery"), the refreshment stands at either corner to the rear of the balcony, and the two great half circles of pews. I stood there for some minutes, thinking thoughts that shall remain solely my own, until somebody sitting in a rear pew on the main floor shot off a flash camera, and I walked quickly offstage, as if I had someplace to go.

I walked down the curving stone stairway and stood in the alley beside the stage door to get some fresh air. I was dressed in a white linen suit, brown cowboy hat, and brown boots. Across the alley stood a family—a man and a woman, two girls, and a boy—who suddenly took an interest in me. The children stared and tried not to stare, the woman nudged the man, and finally, with great effort, the man managed to come over and stand by me. He looked beyond me up the stairs to the door for a few seconds, and then, still looking up there, said, "I hate to bother you, sir"—I flinched; he was old enough to be my own dad—"but we came down from Indiana this morning, and I was wondering if you might know where we could get tickets."

No, I was sorry, I didn't. Had they signed up at the ticket office? The ticket office would put them on a waiting list, and if there were any cancellations—No, he said, the waiting list was full, you couldn't even get your name on it. If there were just one or two of you, I said, you could try sneaking in, but—Well, tell you what, I said, go around to the back door and ask for Sy Gordon and ask him if he won't just show you around, not to see the show but at least to give you a look inside.

I'd met Mr. Gordon a few minutes before. He's a captain (retired) in the Nashville Fire Department, who has been a guard at the Ryman since 1944. The family headed for the back door, and I cut up the stairs and onto the stage to tell him they were friends of mine. By the time I got to the back door, he had already let them in. He led them backstage, through the greenroom, and out onto the stage. He was explaining something to the man, pointing up at the flies, when suddenly the woman realized she was onstage. "My Lord," she said, and she put her fist over her mouth. "Children," she said. The boy and the two girls walked right up to the footlights and looked out into the auditorium, but their mother stood fixed in one spot until her husband took her arm and they walked slowly up the ramp offstage and past the pews and out the door they had come in.

What inspires such awe in us—her and me, too—I don't claim to know, but radio is mysterious in its ways. You listen to the Opry and pretty soon you have a place in mind—a stage where Uncle Dave sang and told jokes and swung the banjo, where the Great Acuff wept and sang "The Great Speckled Bird," where Hank Williams made his Opry début with "Lovesick Blues" (offstage, Uncle Dave turned to Cousin Minnie Pearl and said, "Who *is* that boy?") and the crowd wouldn't let him go, where Elvis sang (and Bill Monroe sings) "Blue Moon of Kentucky," where Cousin Minnie calls out "How-*dee*! I'm just so proud to be here"—and eventually you have got to go (average distance travelled, four hundred and seventy miles, according to an Opry survey) and be there, too.

I remember my first trip to the Opry, driving a night and a day from Minnesota with a friend, listening to the Friday-night show coming down through Kentucky, getting into Nashville Saturday morning and finding that the Saturday-night show was sold out. I watched my first Opry from the Allright parking lot beside Ryman. It was a hot July night, and Ryman is not air-conditioned; the windows on the Allright side were open. Leaning over the stone wall of the parking lot and looking through a window of the auditorium, which was about ten feet away, I could see the lower two-thirds of Lester Flatt as he sang "Is Anybody Going North to Cincinnati?" Even from outside, the Opry had much to recommend it. The music drifted out—high lonesome voices, sweetened with steel guitars, singing about being left behind, walked out on, dropped, shunned, shut out, abandoned, and otherwise mistreated, which a fellow who's driven eight hundred and sixty-one miles to crouch in a parking lot can really get into. Scores of others crouched, too, or listened to transistor radios. A man, sunburned neck and Braves cap, sat in a camper parked against the wall I was looking over and listened to the camper radio, his two boys sitting and lying on the hood. When Stonewall Jackson came on, the man climbed out and crouched beside me to see Stonewall for a minute, and then brought his boys up for a look. "That's Stonewall," he said. "You see him? Now let Curtis have a turn." Then standing in the alley on the other side of Ryman with a hundred others, waiting for Loretta Lynn to come out of her blue touring bus out front and walk down the alley and in the stage door. When finally she came out, it had started raining a little. She wore a long white gown, and the crowd whispered when they saw her, she was so lovely. Flashbulbs, a few, and some women called out "Hi," or "Good to see you," and she smiled a magnificent shy smile. Then we ran around to the parking lot to see her sing "Coal Miner's Daughter":

> Well, I was born a coal miner's daughter.
> In a cabin on a hill in Butcher Holler.
> We were poor but we had love; that's the one
>   thing that Daddy made sure of.
> He shovelled coal to make a poor man's dollar.

THE FIRST MUSICIAN to arrive for the last show at Ryman was Harold Weakley, drummer in the WSM staff band, which backs up singers who don't bring their own. He walked onstage an hour before show time while two stagehands were still setting up: three floor microphones (with guitar mikes attached) up front, and microphones for the piano, the snare drum, the guitar amplifiers, the announcer's podium, and the Four Guys, the staff vocal backup group. While they worked, the guards opened the front doors, and in filed the people who had been waiting for more than an hour already, lined up on the sidewalk in both directions from the entrance. A family took seats in the front row and opened a brown sack full of sandwiches. We all watched the stagehands. And then the backstage crowd arrived and spilled out onto the stage: musicians and their families, people who looked like musicians but wore street clothes, people who looked like newspaper or magazine writers or public-relations men or Opryland executives, and one man in a plaid sports jacket who, even from the balcony, where I was sitting, looked to be the definite Roy Acuff.

The writers and photographers took up positions at both ends of the stage, behind iron railings that had been erected to keep them from wandering into the middle of the show. A stagehand untied a rope at the hitching rail and lowered the red barn. A man carrying a large suitcase walked through the barn door leading a little girl by the hand. He knelt at the front of the stage, opened the case, and assembled the legs and pedals of his pedal steel guitar. He was joined by a fiddler and a piano player. From the stage and backstage came the sounds of the first tentative chords and runs, the fiddler tuning to the

piano, and the steel man tuning to himself.

Even before the curtain closed and opened and the last show began, the attention that the audience directed at the stage was intense. By the time Bill Anderson and the Po' Boys came on and the first notes came out and Grant Turner raised his arms for applause, it seemed as if the show, which looked small compared with what you'd imagined at home as you listened to the radio, couldn't bear up under this scrutiny, would sink from view under all the passengers onstage. Photographers worked the show from four sides: they squeezed under the railings to get in among the musicians, they came in through the barn door, they crept along the footlights. Television news cameras worked the audience as well, switching on brilliant floodlights to sweep a section of crowd (filming the reaction of the crowd, which was stunned by the light); and, crowded up to the railings, the stage audience of reporters and important people (who, I found out later, couldn't hear the show very well) peered at the outer audience, which looked at them. Young children had been brought to see this and were told to remember it; all of us knew it was something we'd always remember, yet the harder we looked, the more it slipped away.

I will always remember: a father patiently explaining to a boy about five why the stage was so crowded, why this show was different; Brother Oswald coming up to the balcony to see the show (people reached for his hand and brought children over to meet him), then going back down to put on bib overalls and play dobro on "Wabash Cannonball," sung by Roy Acuff; musicians coming and going between songs, checking the lineup sheet tacked to the back of the piano, talking and tuning up off-mike, then, when the moment was nigh, getting right in place and playing instantly; Joe Edwards, fiddler and sometimes lead guitarist on the staff band, jumping in on a moment's notice and playing as cleanly as if he'd been rehearsing all afternoon; the Four Guys, huddled around a floor mike behind the piano, improvising vocal harmony; Hank Locklin singing "Goodbye, Good-*bye*, dear ole *Ry*-man." But every time the floodlights came on, every time a photographer angled right up to a scene and stuck his camera into it, I felt the show receding from memory even as I watched it; and I got up and went downstairs, backstage.

I was walking across the stage, behind the barn, heading for the control booth, when I spotted an old man standing alone at the back wall, out of the traffic. He smiled, and suddenly I knew him from a picture in a country-music history book which had showed the same lopsided smile on the face of a young man with a fiddle in 1926. It was Fiddling Sid Harkreader, who had played with Uncle Dave. Mr. Harkreader was glad to talk with me, because he was eager to clear up a point of history to anyone who would listen. "It has been reported in the newspapers," he said dryly, "that I claim to be the first fiddler who ever played on the Grand Ole Opry. That is not true. Uncle Jimmy Thompson was. What I said was—and you take this down—I *said* that I was the first fiddler to play on *WSM*. That was shortly before Judge Hay started the Opry, on November 28, 1925." He looked to make sure I had it right so far. "I was also the first country musician from Tennessee to make a commercial recording in New York. Along with Uncle Dave Macon. That was on July 12, 1924. We made eighteen sides for Vocalion. Uncle Dave and me were also the first country musicians to play here in the Ryman Auditorium. We played here on December 19, 1925."

I asked Mr. Harkreader if it had been fun playing with Uncle Dave.

"Uncle Dave was always fun," he said. "We had a *lot* of fun. I remember him singing, 'When my sugar walks down the street, / All the little birdies go tweet, tweet, tweet.' "

"The music is a lot louder now than it used to be, isn't it," I remarked, apropos of nothing in particular.

"Sometimes it is *too* loud," Mr. Harkreader said. He was looking for a reporter who had misquoted him on Monday, he told me. "He was standing just as close to me as you are now," he said, "and he goes and writes I was the first fiddler on the Opry. Well, I'm going to put him *straight*."

Take care of yourself, Mr. Harkreader, it was good talking with you.

Before the show, Gordon Evans, a WSM engineer, had invited me to visit the control booth. When I got there, after talking with Mr. Harkreader, Jim Hall, Evans' co-engineer, had just finished a half-hour shift at the controls; Evans sat in a close space between high equipment racks, adjusting volume levels on a desk-sized control board in front of him and watching the stage through a double-pane window to see which musicians would be playing on the next song. I counted thirty sliding volume knobs (called "pots," or potentiometers) that appeared to be in use. For each song, Evans adjusted at least six or seven of them, conferring occasionally with the announcer, Grant Turner or Hairl Hensley, over an intercom, talking over a telephone to an engineer in a sound truck in the alley who was recording the show for Opryland

Records, or talking over a second telephone to an engineer at the WSM studios. Out of the monitor above his head came Jim and Jesse McReynolds singing, in high bluegrass harmony, John Prine's song "Paradise" ("When I was a *child*, my *fam*ily would travel / Down to *west*ern Kentucky, where my *par*ents were born"). With his right hand, Evans brought up the volume on the fiddle and bass, turned down the drummer, faded the applause mike, and picked up the telephone to the sound truck; his left hand had already adjusted two dials on the equipment rack, and now, as he told the recording engineer to expect a steel guitar on the next song, it was waving in time to the music; when the chorus came ("And Daddy won't you *take* me back to *Muhl*enburg County, / Down *by* the Green River where *Par*adise lay"), he was in it, humming bass.

The best place to see the Opry that night, I decided, was in the booth with my eyes shut, leaning against the back wall, the music coming out of the speaker just like radio, that good old AM mono sound. The room smelled of hot radio tubes, and, closing my eyes, I could see the stage as clearly as when I was a kid lying in front of our giant Zenith console. I'd seen a photograph of the Opry stage in a magazine back then, and, believe me, one is all you need. So it was good to let the Opry go out the same way it had first come to me, through the air in the dark. After the show, it was raining hard, and the last Opry crowd to leave Ryman ran.

THE FIRST PRESIDENT to visit the Grand Ole Opry, Mr. Richard Nixon, was scheduled to touch down at 6 P.M. Saturday, ride to Opryland, watch a little bit of the first show in the new Opry House, unveil a plaque, speak, play the piano, ride to the airport, and take off shortly after 8. (He kept close to schedule.)

As I awoke, slowly, Saturday morning, it dawned on me that I didn't know where Opryland was, or how to get there, or whether I wanted to go. By midafternoon, I knew that Opryland was eight miles from the hotel by freeway and six by river, either way as practical as the other. There was no bus to Opryland; a rented car could be returned on a Sunday only at the airport, and I was leaving on the Sunday train; the route by road was not direct, one would have to hitch two or three rides to get there; and my boots weren't made for walking. My dad's cousin Harold, the only Nashvillian I knew well enough to ask if I could borrow a car, was out of town for the weekend. So it was more than prudishness that kept me from Opryland, but I was relieved not to be able to go and not to have to see the President introduced by Roy Acuff, or to sit in the "specially designed contoured pew-type benches covered in burnt orange colored carpeting" or to lay eyes on this "vibrant and viable" building that "conveys a feeling of intimacy, informality, warmth and charm . . . yet contains the ultimate in modern electronics, acoustics, lighting, and audio-visual equipment," all described in an Opry brochure. This was nothing but plain prudery, and priggishness, and ordinary low-grade snobbishness on my part; I was ashamed of it, and I intend to correct it, but I hadn't time to correct it right then, and I left the hotel lest somebody call and offer me a ride.

I bought a green transistor radio for $6.95 in a pawnshop across the street from Linebaugh's. After dinner, I walked around looking at the old warehouses on Second Avenue North, also on my list of sights, got back to the hotel around five-thirty, took a long bath, and climbed into bed and turned on my radio. The Saturday-night Opry had just begun, with Roy Acuff singing "Wabash Cannonball," and he followed it with "You Are My Sunshine." Wilma Lee and Stoney Cooper did "Midnight Special." There was a minute of dead air, then long, long applause for the Nixons as they entered and took their seats. The President's appearance at the Opry didn't sit quite right with me, but Roy Drusky, who was the next performer in this alphabetical show, put it right with a heartfelt rendition of "Satisfied Mind":

How many times have you heard someone say
"If I had his money I'd do things my way."
But little do they know that it's so hard to find
One rich man in ten with a satisfied mind.

The Crook Brothers, Herman and Lewis, played a dance tune for the President, and Billy Grammer (who had sung at rallies for Wallace for President) and Stonewall Jackson sang. Then the President. Another standing ovation. (The President is considered a patron of country music, because he has invited Merle Haggard, Johnny Cash, and Roy Acuff to perform at White House functions, and earlier in the week I had been surprised to find, in

a morning of research, no country songs about him. I found two about Watergate—"At the Watergate the Truth Come Pourin' Out," by Joan Wile and Alan Thomas, and "Senator Sam," by C. Hicks and C. Burt—and several about Governor Wallace, including "Man from Alabam," by Ray King and W. Morris, and "The Solid Man," by Tommy Howard. But "Man from San Clemente" and "President Dick" remain unwritten.) The WSM staff band brought Mr. Nixon onstage with a lilting "Hail to the Chief," played like an Irish fiddle tune, which it probably is. The President's selections on the piano were "Happy Birthday" (for his wife on her birthday), "My Wild Irish Rose," and "God Bless America." "He is a real trouper, as well as one of our greatest Presidents," Mr. Acuff said. Mr. Nixon spoke. He said country music comes from the heart of America, it speaks of family and religion, and it radiates a love of country that is much needed today.

Most of this was done in the name of Mrs. Grissom's salads and Rudy's Farm Country Sausage. After the President left, on the Goo Goo Cluster candy portion of the Opry, Jim and Jesse McReynolds sang "Freight Train" and Hank Locklin "Danny Boy." Hank Snow gave us "I'm Moving On," his all-time great hit, and Ernest Tubb did his, "Walking the Floor Over You." Dottie West sang "Country Sunshine" for Stephens Workwear, Western Jeans and Slacks, and the Wilburn Brothers did "Arkansas." And then— then—the moment I'd been waiting for. Sam and Kirk McGee from sunny Tennessee played "San Antonio Rose." It was the acoustic moment of the show, when the skies cleared and the weeping steels were silent and out of the clear blue came a little ole guitar duet. Stunning and simple, and so good after all the *sound* I'd heard that week—the sweetest "Rose" this side of Texas. I turned out the light, turned off the radio, and went to sleep on it.

In the morning, the radio was on the floor, its plastic cover cracked. I believe it would still work, but I will never play it again. It is my only Opry souvenir. Inside it, the McGee brothers are still picking and will forever, Minnie Pearl cackles, the Crooks are dancing, Jim and Jesse ascend into heavenly harmony, and the Great Acuff rides the Wabash Cannonball to the lakes of Minnesota, where the rippling waters fall.   □

Full Circle: on PHC broadcast from Ryman Auditorium, June 4, 1994, GK remembers his trip to Nashville twenty years before to see the Opry do its last Ryman show.

Sue Scott, Russ Ringsak, Jason Keillor, Tiffany Hanssen, Tom Keith, and Mike Danforth watch from the wings.

Photography Credits

BACK COVER: PAPERBACK
(top row) Reynold Marklund, Rob Levine, Fredric Petters; (bottom row) left and right photographs by Rob Levine